Divided We Stand

6-29-07

Matt,

I hope this book
encourages you to continue
to work for change in our
culture;"

God bless
Love
Dad

Divided We Stand

The Rejection of American Culture since the 1960s

John Harmon McElroy

ROWMAN & LITTLEFIELD PUBLISHERS, INC.
Lanham • Boulder • New York • Toronto • Oxford

ROWMAN & LITTLEFIELD PUBLISHERS, INC.

Published in the United States of America
by Rowman & Littlefield Publishers, Inc.
A wholly owned subsidiary of The Rowman & Littlefield Publishing Group, Inc.
4501 Forbes Boulevard, Suite 200, Lanham, Maryland 20706
www.rowmanlittlefield.com

PO Box 317, Oxford, OX2 9RU, UK

Distributed by National Book Network

British Library Cataloguing in Publication Information Available

Library of Congress Cataloging-in-Publication Data

McElroy, John Harmon.
   Divided we stand : the rejection of American culture since the 1960s / John Harmon
McElroy.
      p.   cm.
   Includes bibliographical references and index.
   ISBN-13: 978-0-7425-5081-0 (cloth: alk. paper)
   ISBN-10: 0-7425-5081-8 (cloth : alk. paper)
   1. United States—Civilization—1945-   2. National characteristics, American.
3. Values—United States.   4. Counterculture—United States—History—20th
century.   5. Anti-Americanism—History—20th century.   6. Social conflict—
United States—History—20th century.   7. United States—Social conditions—
1945–I. Title.
   E169.12.M258   2006
   306'.0973—dc22   2005021866

Printed in the United States of America

∞ ™ The paper used in this publication meets the minimum requirements of American
National Standard for Information Sciences—Permanence of Paper for Printed Library
Materials, ANSI/NISO Z39.48-1992.

For Ony
whose love is described in
1 Corinthians 13:4–8,
and in memory of
George Thomas, Norman Olsen,
James Tuttleton, and Avelino Hernandez

Contents

Preface

This discussion of the rejection of American culture by many Americans in the second half of the twentieth century focuses on the antagonism between the historical beliefs of the American people and the ideas of a movement that began in the United States in the 1960s by proclaiming itself an alternative or "counter" culture.

Calls for a new culture to replace the culture Americans have acted on historically as a people were sometimes made before the protests and demonstrations in the 1960s that launched this movement that called itself a counter-culture. In the 1930s, for instance, the leading liberal philosopher of the United States in the early twentieth century, John Dewey, urged "the construction of a new social order" through "collective social planning" and through deliberate, active application of the "social sciences" in "education and the formation of social policies" (see chap. 2 of Dewey's *Liberalism and Social Action*). Prior to the last four decades of the twentieth century, radical proposals for the sort of thing Dewey called "social engineering" came mainly from academics like him and were seldom taken seriously. Since the 1960s, however, sweeping changes to America's way of life have actually been effected through legislative acts, judicial decisions, and educational policies.

This study of the rejection of America's historical culture over the last forty years completes my examination of American culture undertaken in *Finding Freedom: America's Distinctive Cultural Formation* (1989) and continued in *American Beliefs: What Keeps a Big Country and a Diverse People United* (1999). Those works respectively describe the combination of demographic and geographic conditions that led to the formation of a national culture in the United States and the historical beliefs that comprise that culture. My intention in the present work is to address the rise of widespread anti-Americanism in the United States over the last four decades, this anti-American-ism being the chief sign of the counter-culture movement's considerable success. Whereas before the 1960s Americans were all but unanimous in regarding their homeland as the most dynamic model of freedom in the history of the world, since then many influential Americans have come to think of the United States as the fount of the world's evil. Or, if they are not actively hostile toward America, they are indifferent toward and have no positive feeling about their country. By identifying the nature and origin of the counter-culture movement's antagonism toward American culture, this book calls attention to the most serious internal threat to America since the divisive conflicts of the 1840s and 1850s that preceded the Civil War.

My understanding of the meaning of culture (a term applied far too loosely in too many commentaries on contemporary America) is an essential component of this attempt to understand what has happened in America since the 1960s. Generally speaking, what has happened is that a new view of American life as oppressive has been advanced, which is sapping confidence in the beliefs that have historically guided the behavior of the American people and defined their sense of right conduct—in other words, their culture. Also threatening American beliefs are two trends predating the 1960s: the doctrine of strict materialism and the practice of instrumental government. These two threats are discussed in chapters 8 and 9.

The clash in the last forty years (which is still going on) between the ideas of the counter-culture movement and the historically established beliefs of American culture has been rightly designated a culture war. The outcome of this culture war is yet to be determined. But the gains of the counter-culture (sometimes referred to as "political correctness") have been substantial. This is a movement whose demands go far beyond any normal call for specific reforms. It aims at nothing less than the substitution of the counter-culture's ideas of correct behavior for the belief-behavior of American culture.

Acknowledgments

I owe special thanks to Prof. Nina Rukas and the late Prof. Jerrold E. Levy for urging me to expand the final chapter of my *American Beliefs* into a book on American culture in the post–World War II period. For their generous investment of time and care in reading my first draft, I am particularly grateful to Mr. and Mrs. Alfred Litwak, Prof. Charles Moskos, and Prof. Daniel O'Neil; I am likewise grateful to Mr. Ivan Dee for reading and suggesting further improvements to subsequent drafts. For calling my attention to helpful materials and for their encouraging interest in my work, I wish to thank Dr. Joseph Brewer, Dr. Francisco De La Moneda, Prof. Lawrence Evans, Prof. Louis Fanning, Prof. Frank Gado, Prof. Robert George, Col. Russell Heller, Prof. Lyell Henry, Prof. Frederick Kiefer, Mr. Robert McCartney, Mr. John Mosher, Dr. Edward Nigh, Dr. Gabriel Sanchez, Col. Sam Sharp, Prof. Peter Wild, and Prof. Edward Zajac. For giving me much needed computer assistance, I am indebted to my daughter Lisa and her husband, Kevin Button, and my wife, Onyria McElroy; and for help with the proofreading, I thank my granddaughter Sara Button. The attentive, professional aid that I have received at Rowman & Littlefield from Laura Roberts Gottlieb, Andrew Boney, John Shanabrook, Jen Link, and Jenni Brewer has also been much appreciated. I am solely responsible for any deficiencies or errors that may remain in the work.

JHM

CHAPTER ONE

The Culture War in America in the Late Twentieth Century

The United States of America emerged from World War II in 1945 the most powerful nation ever seen in history, as measured in terms of military might and capacity to produce goods and services. This is a remarkable fact because just two hundred years earlier, in 1745, America had been a collection of thirteen dependent and sparsely populated colonies strung out along the edge of a Stone Age wilderness of continental extent.

During the Second World War, under the urgent necessity to create, equip, deploy, and maintain tremendous armies, air forces, and fleets in far-away places, and under the equally urgent necessity of supplying America's beleaguered overseas allies, the production in the United States of food, minerals, and military supplies, especially airplanes and ships, reached levels previously thought to be impossible. The capacity of the American people to organize and accomplish such immense feats made the United States of America a superpower. In the years immediately after the war, America, which had remained unscathed while the homelands of her allies and foes in Europe and Asia were being devastated, had the only intact economy capable of aiding the shattered economies of the postwar world on a large scale. The government of the United States considered such foreign aid to be in America's best interest, as well as in keeping with American ideals.

As the sole military power occupying postwar Japan and overseeing its reconstruction, the United States had a profound effect on Asia by assisting in rebuilding Japan as a democracy dedicated to peaceful enterprise. In Europe, however, a united German people could not be helped in that way because of the Soviet occupation of eastern Germany. After the war the

Soviet Union would not permit East Germany, or any other area in its "sphere of influence" (i.e., the area under its control), to accept the Marshall Plan aid that the United States offered to every war-torn country of Europe, including the Soviet Union. And the Soviets controlled much of the continent. The only nations free of Soviet occupation at the war's end were the island-nations of Iceland, Ireland, and Britain; the countries on the peninsulas fringing Europe (Greece, Italy, Spain and Portugal, Denmark, Norway, and Sweden); and on the main part of the continent half of Germany, western Austria, France, Finland, the Low Countries (Belgium, Luxembourg, the Netherlands), Switzerland, and Yugoslavia (which had an independent communist government). In short, the sphere of influence that the communist dictator of the Soviet Union, Joseph Stalin, claimed in 1945 was nothing less than half of Europe.

The Soviet Union entered World War II in September 1939 in collaboration with Nazi Germany. By prearrangement with the Nazis, the Soviets invaded and occupied eastern Poland while German armies seized western Poland. The Soviets also invaded and took the neighboring Baltic countries of Lithuania, Latvia, and Estonia, and large districts of Finland, while the Nazis sent their forces to occupy countries to the west and north of Germany. Only when Nazi armies swept through Soviet-occupied eastern Poland and the Baltic countries in June of 1941 and invaded the Soviet Union itself did the Union of Soviet Socialist Republics (USSR) become an ally of Britain and (after America's entry into the war) the United States. Before America entered the war as a belligerent in December 1941, shipments of military supplies from the United States to the Soviet Union through the Arctic Ocean were crucial to Soviet resistance of the German onslaught, which came within sight of Moscow before being stopped. By the war's end, the Soviet counterattack against Germany had reached Central Europe. The nations the Soviet Union then occupied and controlled in Central and Eastern Europe, in combination with its own prewar territories (the easternmost parts of Europe and Asia's northern half all the way to the Pacific), comprised an extent of land larger than the British Empire at its height. It was an empire of contiguous rather than overseas colonies stretching across eleven of the thirteen time zones of Eurasia, Earth's largest landmass. The Soviet Union became a superpower after its spies in the United States acquired the technology for building an atomic bomb.

In conjunction with its traditional allies, the United States instituted democratic government and free enterprise in West Germany while the Soviets installed in East Germany a communist government and economy.

The difference was soon apparent: democratic West Germany's "miracle" of postwar recovery and prosperity far surpassed the lackluster economic performance of communist East Germany. The takeover of China by communist revolutionaries in 1949, however, encouraged Soviet leaders to believe that the ideology of communism would eventually triumph throughout the world, with Soviet leadership at the head of the movement. (As it turned out, China, unlike the puppet communist regimes the Soviet Union installed in the nations it held captive in Europe, proved unwilling to take orders from Moscow.)

The Soviet Union employed its superpower status in the postwar period to instigate "liberation movements" to communize nations throughout the world. The United States met that challenge with a policy of containing communist expansion through steadfast use of America's economic and military power in alliance with other Western democracies. In 1949, the year that China fell to communist revolutionaries and the Soviet Union tested its first atomic bomb, America formed with Canada and ten still-free nations of Europe the North Atlantic Treaty Organization (NATO) to restrict the Soviet empire to the half of Europe already under Soviet domination.

World War II thus set the stage for the forty-year conflict between the United States and the Soviet Union that came to be known as the Cold War. This was a struggle between the existing culture of the United States and the Soviet aspiration to create a worldwide culture in the mold of "scientific communism."[1] It was a conflict between a culture based on freedom and a totalitarian ideology that wanted to become a culture.

American culture arose in the seventeenth and eighteenth centuries from the self-determining behavior of hundreds of thousands of self-selected immigrants from many countries of Europe and eight generations of their American-born descendants. These men and women shared a common commitment to making a better life for themselves by civilizing the North American wilderness. At the core of their beliefs was their conviction that freedom and the other rights of man come from God. The ideology on which the Soviet Union was founded maintained that the rights of man come from the state. The Soviet Union wanted to use its power to force into being, through a worldwide coalition of revolutionary "cadres" directed by the "vanguard" of the Communist Party of the Soviet Union, a culture in which all men would, according to the Marxist theory of history, eventually live in an equality of condition. Communist ideology promised a planned way of life based on the philosophy of materialistic determinism and an allegedly scientific understanding of man's history as expounded in the writings of Karl

Marx. Once a communist culture had been created through the use of enlightened state power, which would establish the rights of man and institute a classless society of social justice, there would (theoretically) be no further need for the state, which would then "wither away." American culture was based on a belief in societies in which men freely joined together to pursue their own interests (not the systematic salvation of mankind) under minimal governments whose powers would be limited by constitutions formed through free consent. Faith in God—as the creator of mankind, man's birthright to equal freedom, and the "natural law" by which men and women should be guided—was the cornerstone of this existing culture.

The culture war between the United States and the Soviet Union came to an abrupt end in 1991 when the USSR imploded and vanished from the political map of the world, sixty-nine years after its founding in 1922. But the ideology that produced the Soviet Union has not vanished. The ideas that man is an object for scientific manipulation and that the state should be the instrument by which human beings can obtain a good life persist.

The Cold War was a culture war over whether communist ideas or the beliefs of American culture would triumph in Western civilization. And there was a home front in this struggle: a culture war in the United States that was part of the Cold War. In the second half of the twentieth century, Americans who passionately shared the Soviet idea of human beings as the products of their political, social, and economic environments rejected American culture and worked unceasingly within the United States to subvert and replace American culture with a politically correct culture. In its struggle with the Soviet Union on the international scene, the United States was finally spectacularly triumphant. But the culture war on the home front continues. Whether domestic opposition to American culture will be triumphant or whether it will be rolled back is still an open question. Certainly the success of the counter-culture movement in enacting and institutionalizing its ideas has not been trivial. The ideology of the counter-culture, an ideology that runs counter to American culture, presently dominates major aspects of life in the United States.

The doctrine of strict materialism, on which the government of the Soviet Union in the 1920s and the Nazi regime in the 1930s in Germany were founded, would have human beings believe that their lives are, like those of every animal, determined by their environment and their genes. This strictly material view of man has been of growing influence in Western civilization ever since the publication of Charles Darwin's *The Origin of Species by Means of Natural Selection* (1859) and *The Descent of Man and Selection in Relation to*

Sex (1871). Yet the histories of the USSR under communist rule (1922–1991) and of Germany under Nazi rule (1933–1945) conclusively demonstrate that a strictly material concept of man does not furnish a good basis for human life. The policies of both of these now defunct totalitarian states emphasized certain aspects of Darwinian thought: the idea of genetic superiority in the case of Nazi Germany and the idea of a "class struggle" for survival in the case of the Soviet Union.

American culture believes there is more to human beings than the doctrine of strict materialism can account for.

Too many Americans do not take seriously the consequences of believing in a strictly material view of man and are too easily turned away from the view of human beings as the creation of a transcendent Being who has given them souls. Yet human life can have no defining sacredness apart from belief in God. The twentieth-century histories of fascist rule in Germany and communist rule in Russia make that conclusion quite clear, for both of those states were based on the doctrine of strict materialism that sees man as merely an animal, and both murdered tens of millions of human beings in their attempts to achieve their political goals.

Twentieth-century fascism and communism, whether found in Europe or Asia, treated human beings as material to be used by the state to fulfill grandiose political plans. Neither of those movements was restrained by a belief in the sacred character of human life. Men and women had value to them only insofar as they had utility for the state and its purposes. In the twentieth century, under communist governments in Europe and Asia, between 85 and 100 million human beings have been killed for political purposes through execution, deliberate starvation, and forced labor. (Some 20 million of these political murders, including a deliberate, state-ordered famine in the Ukraine, took place in the Soviet Union.) In European countries governed by the German national socialist party (the Nazis), 25 million human beings were killed for political purposes.[2]

Is man just another kind of animal species? That question demands an answer because Western civilization is on the brink of yielding to the idea that man is entirely and only a material entity whose salvation lies in a total application of science to every human problem. But yielding to the doctrine of strict materialism ignores the glaring, just-mentioned fact that more than 100 million human beings have been killed in the twentieth century by political parties that were based on that doctrine. This evidence of the consequences of the philosophy of twentieth-century fascism and communism could not be more convincing. Yet, many Westerners still seem to think that it does not matter whether one believes human life has a sacredness conferred by God, and they persist in supposing that science, improved material conditions, eugenics, or government can provide a sufficient, dependable foundation for human dignity.

Cultural belief in freedom, practical improvements, and a God-ordained equality of birthrights produced the United States. An exclusively materialistic concept of man produced the Soviet Union and Nazi Germany. Both of these failed social experiments believed in the instrumentality of governments systematically improving human life. The United States—history's greatest democratic society—is a successful experiment in self-government under God by self-determining individuals. The historic beliefs that the American people have acted on now for two centuries constitute principles of responsible individualism, equal freedom, and practical improvement. These cultural principles have unified a continent-sized country (the area of the United States is 3,787,000 square miles; Europe's, 3,800,000)[3] and a people made up of individuals from highly diverse immigrant backgrounds.

Culture is conformity. It is conformity to a set of simple beliefs that have been expressed through behavior for many generations and that are being expressed in the behavior of generations presently alive. Cultural beliefs structure the social relations that men and women participate in. They form a vital human bond, not in terms of blood kinship but in terms of *a shared sense of the right way to live*. Conformity to the belief-behaviors of one's native culture is natural, because human beings require the moral stability and justification and the social unity that a culture provides. Cultural conformity is healthy, necessary, and normal. What is called today in the United States political correctness is the set of ideas that the counter-culture movement would have Americans conform to as their culture.

Individuals modify their opinions and judgments as they mature; new technologies replace old ones; styles of clothing and grooming change from one generation to the next; tastes in food, manners, and music come and go. But cultural beliefs abide from generation to generation. They are not the beliefs of one, two, or even three generations of a people. They are the set of simple beliefs that many generations no longer alive have validated by acting on them and that continue to be validated by the behavior of living generations. Only the most extraordinary circumstances can make a people want to change the living heritage of cultural beliefs that their ancestors have established and that they themselves are perpetuating through their behavior in the present.

Human beings are normally unconscious of their cultural beliefs. Yet they are as essential to our well-being as the bones inside our bodies, of which we are also normally unconscious. A culture is a society's durable, inner structure of beliefs about right behavior that allows the members of that society to function as human beings. Cultural beliefs give human beings their day in and day out moral justification and social identity, which are two of the necessities of human life wherever it exists. Cultures are the historical habits of belief that determine the thinking of a society about what matters most to human beings: right behavior. The function of a culture is to provide unity and stability. No culture fosters diversity and change. Furthermore, a culture is never the product of a revolution (though the political movements called revolutions can incapacitate or greatly impair a culture). A culture is a set of convictions about right behavior that accumulates over a period of more than three generations of a people.

American culture, for instance, formed because of hundreds of thousands of individual "revolutions" in the lives of middle-class and lower-class Europeans during the eight generations from 1610 to 1770. That is to say, American culture was the cumulative effect of the decisions of many persons from those classes of European society to leave their native cultures for the sake of finding freedom in the new society that was forming on the Atlantic coastal plain of North America. Among the beliefs that the behavior of those eight generations of self-selected immigrants and their descendants enculturated, and which have been passed down to the present by subsequent generations of Americans, are:

Everyone must work.
A written constitution is essential to government.
Helping others helps yourself.
Society is a collection of individuals.
Achievement determines social rank.
Every person's success improves society.
Almost all human beings want to do what is right.
God gave men the same birthrights.
(For a more complete identification of American cultural beliefs, see appendix A.)

Every culture is unique in having a *set* of beliefs that no other culture duplicates in its entirety. A culture's uniqueness, in other words, is comparative rather than absolute. Only the entire set of a culture's beliefs is unique. There will always be some beliefs in the set that can be found in some other culture or cultures.

(A group of cultures sharing many of the same historical belief-behaviors make a civilization, as when we refer to Western civilization or Islamic civilization.)

Cultures are historical in nature, and it takes at least four generations for a sense of history to begin to be present in a society because normally three generations are alive in a society at any given time. It is only when the youngest generation has a sense of participating in a way of life that a deceased generation of ancestors also practiced (a fourth generation that their elders knew but they did not) that a sense of history, or the past, exists in a society. It may be assumed that this sense of history would most likely be fully accomplished only after the three-generation cycle had been repeated at least once, that is after the sixth generation had died. Then there would be no generation alive in that society that could have known any of the three generations that first began to behave according to the set of beliefs that structures the way of life of current generations. Then a complete sense of history and of cultural ancestry would exist.

New cultures apparently arise in this way: when enough persons in enough generations of a society have *consciously* acted on the same set of ideas, those ideas thus acquire a historical validity or authority. The ideas may then be said to be enculturated. Once that happens, once ideas are enculturated by being consciously acted on by enough persons in a society over a long enough period of time (these matters are not susceptible to precise description), then from that point on those ideas are transmitted as *unconscious beliefs*. (That is why we are normally unaware of our cultural beliefs.) Interrupt the transmission of a society's enculturated, unconsciously transmitted beliefs by changing the behaviors that express and perpetuate them from generation to generation and the culture will be deformed. The historically shared sense in that society of right behavior will begin to decay, and the society, if the interruption continues, will lose its unifying sense of a right way to behave. It will become dissolute and decadent; its members will no longer feel that they belong to a coherent society. The situation in America today seems to be one in which we have entered an incipient stage of possible cultural breakdown. This is to say (although the situation is still uncertain) that the beliefs of American culture appear to be losing their unconsciously exerted historical authority because a large segment of influential Americans during the last forty years have rejected them and no longer act on them. Similar signs of incipient cultural decadence seem to be evident in other societies of Western civilization as well.

If the deconstruction of an existing culture was desired in order to put a new culture in its place, an effective way to begin the process would be to persuade as many young people as possible in the culture that conformity per se is wrong. (Anyone who was in college in the United States in the 1950s will probably remember hearing in their classrooms and encountering in the media the idea that conformity was wrong and that their generation was too "silent," too "conformist.") As a counter-culture, the movement would further develop by separating these youths from the beliefs expressed in the behaviors of their parents and grandparents. It would try to persuade as many young people as possible that conformity to those belief-behaviors was unworthy of them and that they should open their minds to new ways of thinking and acting. That would prepare them to accept the possibility of acting on new ideas. And the movement would make the generation coming of age the point of attack on the existing culture because young people represent the part of society that is most vulnerable to having its cultural beliefs changed. They are still in the process of acquiring the beliefs of their culture through unconscious imitation of the behavior of their elders that expresses and transmits the beliefs. If the youngest generation in a society can be separated from and persuaded to reject the cultural behaviors of the older generations among whom they live, the transmission of culture will be interrupted and subverted. Hence, the significance of the seemingly harmless slogans so often heard in America during the 1960s: Don't Trust Anyone Over Thirty, and Question Authority.

The counter-culture movement that swept American campuses in the 1960s and 1970s manifested the processes by which an existing culture can be dismantled in preparation for constructing a new culture. The movement that called itself a counter-culture or alternative culture in the 1960s changed the behavior of many young Americans and did weaken the transmission of America's capitalistic, Christian culture. This movement sowed in the American middle-class a set of "liberated," socialist, secular ideas that, it was hoped, would become a new culture.

The above judgment does not mean, however, that a single organization or some sort of secret cabal directed the counter-culture's assault on American culture. Activists in the counter-culture movement have been quite overt. And they have not belonged to a single organization having a single directorate such as the Communist Party of the Soviet Union (CPSU) had when it existed. What has happened in the United States in the last two generations is that, for various reasons, a significant number of younger Americans in tacit agreement with each other have rejected the culture of their parents, grandparents, and long-dead cultural ancestors. They have done this without necessarily having or uniformly espousing a coherent substitute to replace their native culture. The counter-culture movement has, in other words, been preeminently negative rather than positive, and much more oppositional than constructive. Active participants in the movement have worked tirelessly as individuals and as members of diverse ephemeral groups, on many fronts and in similar ways, to get rid of American culture. *Change* has been the password by which they recognize each other, change in the name of a higher morality and a greater intelligence than American culture allegedly possesses, change as synonymous with being progressive.

A much larger number of Americans have either been sympathetic with this movement or have passively gone along with it (as I myself did briefly) without being aware of the counter-culture's purpose of ultimately replacing American culture. However, the movement to replace American culture could never have succeeded to the extent that it has if a much larger segment of the American public had not been cowed into nonresistance. This has been done by making them afraid of being labeled "racist," "sexist," "insensitive," or "unfair" if they spoke out against the zealous righteousness of the counter-culture minority.

The great majority of Americans in the last forty years have, it seems, either tolerated or ignored the politically correct behavior that has been effected (largely through changes in American law and federal policies) by counter-culture activists. They have as a matter of course quite naturally preferred to attend to their own lives and to go on acting on the cultural beliefs of their forebears without giving much thought to something as seemingly vague and inconsequential as a culture war. This indifference to the culture war on the part of the majority has been of course encouraged by participants in the counter-culture movement, who often claim to represent nothing more than the normal rebelliousness of youth and normal generational changes in styles of clothing, music, and conduct. This is untrue. The counter-culture movement represents the desire to have a new culture, and that is anything but normal. Unless this fact is recognized—the fact that the "change" that has been called for in America in the last forty years is not a normal reform but an attempt to generate a new culture—there is little hope that anything effective can be done about the problem.

The inaction of the majority of Americans in the face of the persistent assaults on the historical beliefs of their culture during the last forty years is mainly what has allowed a set of ideas contrary to the beliefs of American culture to be implanted in the United States. Now, of course, the question is whether the generation presently coming of age in America (the third since the counter-culture movement was launched in the 1960s) will also tolerate the counter-culture movement's assaults on American culture or whether it will rather resist them. It is the behavior of this generation that will, in all likelihood, determine the outcome of the culture war that has been fought in the second half of the twentieth century in the United States and that has greatly damaged American culture.

The next chapter considers the causes and nature of the counter-culture movement; chapters 3, 4, and 5 compare and contrast American cultural beliefs and principles with the ideology of the counter-culture. Chapter 6 looks at what seems to be the counter-culture's principal strategy for subverting American culture, a strategy that I call "bending." Chapter 7 examines the way public education in America has been bent during the past forty years. Chapter 8 continues the discussion with a look at a related long-term trend in government, and chapter 9 addresses the rise and consequences of the doctrine of strict materialism. The book's concluding chapter considers, as its title suggests, the future prospects of American culture, which I think are good in spite of everything that has transpired in the United States in the last forty years. For when it comes to the politics of culture—that is, whether to change or preserve a culture—I believe that most human beings are conservative.

CHAPTER TWO

The Rejection of American Culture

Several historical and psychological factors influenced the rejection of American culture by a considerable number of Americans in the latter half of the twentieth century. At least eight factors or conditions might be said to have contributed to the phenomenon: a minor but persistent tradition of socialism in America; an influx in the 1930s, 1940s, and 1950s of European socialists escaping the war in Europe and its aftermath, a good many of whom obtained influential positions in American society, particularly in academia; a general feeling among American intellectuals that American culture was anti-intellectual in not according them the respect intellectuals enjoyed in Europe, which left some of them in a mood to accept the idea of a deliberately created culture in which intellectuals would play a leading role; a certain feeling of guilt among Americans over their country's flourishing economy in the years following World War II when the economies of so many other countries of the West had been devastated by the war (what might be thought of as "survivor's guilt"); the sense of guilt that many white Americans felt in regard to American Indians, Mexican Americans, and black Americans who in the 1950s were still being excluded from full participation in American society; the strong appeal, especially for academics and the young, of theories that claimed to explain everything; the idealism of young people; and finally, the appeal that some of these young people found in rebelling (with or without a cause) without knowing, or in some instances even caring, whether the proposed new order would be practical or better than the one they were invited to oppose. These eight factors can be called the domestic, or internal, factors that after World War II prepared the way for various degrees of negativity toward, and among some Americans an outright rejection of, American culture.

In and of themselves, however, these domestic factors could not have produced an effective movement to replace American culture. An external catalyst was necessary to coalesce them. That catalyst was America's Cold War with the Soviet Union. In the post–World War II period (as I have noted above), the goal of Soviet foreign policy was to replace capitalism and Christianity with a global culture of communism. (The Constitution of the Soviet Union in effect at the time of the Soviet Union's dissolution declared that "the Soviet people" were "conscious of their internationalist responsibility" and of "the international position of the USSR as part of the world system of socialism."[1]) For members of the Communist Party USA and other Americans who wanted a socialist future for the world, the alleged benefits of the international triumph of communism justified the use of every means of undermining the confidence of capitalist countries in their cultures and systems of free enterprise and government. These means included telling the Western democracies that they were no different morally from the countries that made up the communist Eastern bloc. (Some Americans were inclined to believe that view and to regard communist movements such as those in postwar Greece and later in Cuba, Vietnam, and Central America as authentically democratic in nature.) American communists and their sympathizers tried in every way they could to persuade their fellow Americans to oppose America's postwar policy of containing communism, particularly the U.S. intervention in Vietnam in the 1960s. They infiltrated and tried to take over or influence the leadership of labor unions and other institutions. They also created a swarm of ephemeral, ad hoc alliances, associations, coalitions, committees, leagues, organizations, societies, and unions to influence public opinion and affect public behavior. At the same time, they organized demonstrations to confront civil authorities and to protest the "Establishment" or "System."

Another long-term but broader trend also undermined American culture in the late twentieth century. This was the increasing authority in Western civilization of the doctrine of strict materialism that had accompanied the steady rise of science from the early nineteenth century onward. This influence was especially pronounced in the post–World War II period because science's already great prestige had increased tremendously as the technological application of scientific knowledge produced military equipment like radar and sonar, and weapons like the atom bomb, that were crucial to victory in the war. The additional authority acquired by science created an intellectual climate in the postwar period in which human problems were likely to be regarded exclusively in terms of material cause and effect—

material realities being the proper subject of scientific investigation and technological solution.

For some Westerners, that intellectual climate gave communism, with its alleged scientific understanding of social and economic problems, the aura of being a more up-to-date economic and political system than capitalism and free government. Communism seemed to be more than a messianic hope. It offered a scientific messianic hope, and thus became a kind of political religion for some Americans. In the decades following World War II, there was a flood of explanations that treated human behavior in scientific terms, including many comparisons of human and animal behavior. This deluge of books and articles in anthropology, politics, psychology, and sociology made it no longer respectable in intellectual circles to think of human life in Christian terms, that is, as having a sacred origin, or to think of human beings as having souls. The consequences for American culture of this shift were profound because America's system of government was and is based on a cultural belief in the God-given birthrights referred to in the Declaration of Independence. The strictly material concept of man as nothing more than another species of animal, created through random genetic variation and adaptation to an environment, has considerably diminished the number of Americans who believe in God-given human rights. It perhaps even devitalized the convictions of some of those who have continued to believe in such birthrights.

The world wars of the twentieth century themselves had an incalculably negative effect on the civilization to which American culture belongs. The devastation and slaughter of these wars diminished the sacredness of human life, and the horrific scale and savagery of such violence among the civilized, Christian nations of Europe called into question the teachings of the Judeo-Christian tradition on which Western civilization ultimately depends for moral coherence. The brutality of these wars particularly led Western intellectuals, who were already skeptics in regard to religion, to scorn the Christian view of man and Christian redemption and to embrace the neo-paganism of strict materialism. The American homeland was spared the horrific holocaust that befell Europe in 1914–1918 and 1939–1945, but millions of American soldiers, sailors, and airmen either participated in the slaughter or witnessed its aftermath firsthand. In 1919 and 1945 American veterans returned to "God's country" (as they fondly and significantly called their homeland) shaken by what they had seen and experienced overseas. They came home with an understanding of the world beyond America's isolating, protective oceans, and with an appreciation of their country's culture. The wars strengthened patriotism among those generations but also made those generations wonder whether American beliefs had the universal validity they had thought they had.

Quite apart from the deaths of hundreds of thousands of young Americans in the prime of their most productive years, America's involvement in the two world wars of the twentieth century had a generally disruptive effect on American society and its culture. During World War II, for instance, up to 40 percent of American men between the ages of eighteen and thirty, many of them married, were uprooted from their homes and communities and subjected to experiences they would not have had except for the war. For most of them, the experiences did not include participating in the slaughter of battle, but for millions of them it did. And the American servicemen who survived were changed in ways that made it difficult for them on their return to adjust to normal American life. The families they had left behind had also experienced disruption, most notably the American women during the Second World War who left their homes to work in factories and offices or to serve in their country's uniformed services.

In regard to the desanctification of human life and the cultural damage wrought by the first of the twentieth century's two great wars, Sir Winston Churchill, secretary of state for war in Great Britain during World War I, offered this notable overview:

All the horrors of all the ages were brought together, and not only armies but whole populations were thrust into the midst of them. . . . Every outrage against humanity or international law was repaid by reprisals—often of a greater scale and of longer duration. No truce or parley mitigated the strife of the armies. The wounded died between the lines: the dead mouldered into the soil. Merchant ships and neutral ships and hospital ships were sunk on the seas and all on board left to their fate, or killed as they swam. Every effort was made to starve whole nations into submission without regard to age or sex. Cities and monuments were smashed by artillery. Bombs from the air were cast down indiscriminately. Poisoned gas in many forms stifled or seared the soldiers. Liquid fire was projected upon their bodies. Men fell from the air in flames, or were smothered often slowly in the dark recesses of the sea. The fighting strength of armies was limited only by the manhood of their countries. Europe and large parts of Asia and Africa became one vast battlefield on which after years of struggle not armies but nations broke and ran. When all was over, Torture and Cannibalism were the only two expedients that the civilized, scientific, Christian States had been able to deny themselves: and they were of doubtful utility.[2]

This was a new kind of mechanized, total warfare featuring the goal of forcing the enemy to surrender unconditionally. After such large-scale, merciless killing, traditional Christian morality could not have the same authority it had had before 1914.

From one combat veteran of World War II, an artillery officer in the 89th Infantry Division of the U.S. Third Army in Europe from 1944 to 1945, I gained some sense of the effect that the war had on ordinary decent Americans. In the final week of my father's life when I, my wife, and our children were keeping round-the-clock vigils at his bedside, late one night in the stillness of his hospital room when I was alone with him he suddenly said, "I didn't mean to kill him." My father had been sleeping; so I thought he was talking in his sleep and went over to him. But he was awake and had been remembering shooting a German soldier in the closing days of the war when the battle lines were confused and the two of them had come upon each other suddenly and unexpectedly at night behind the lines. For thirty-eight years that memory of killing another human being face-to-face, even though the man was pointing a rifle at him, had gnawed at my father's conscience and filled him with unspoken remorse. In listening to the story (my father had never spoken to me before of his war experiences), I could see the spiritual damage done to men of ordinary good will when forced by the do-or-die circumstances of a war to kill other human beings at close quarters. Being an artillery officer, he had apparently had the experience only that one time. But it had left a wound on his conscience that had never quite healed.

Yet the United States had to participate in World War II. Otherwise, fascist governments would have forced Europe, Africa, Asia, and Australia into vassalage and after consolidating their hold on those continents would eventually have extended their dominion to the two American continents. But despite its efforts in World War II, the United States found itself after the war confronting, in the government of the USSR, a totalitarian state as guilty of terrorizing and murdering those who lived under its authority as any fascist regime.

Because of the twentieth century's two world wars and the fascist and communist tyrannies leading up to the second of them, uncountable numbers of European and Asian civilians including children had things done to them and had been forced to do things themselves in order to survive that would otherwise never have been part of their normal lives. These acts violated their humanity. Children saw parents assaulted and killed or dragged by state security police from their homes never to be heard from again. Millions upon millions suffered the miseries of starvation and forced labor camps. They helplessly watched acquaintances, strangers, and loved ones succumb to illnesses that went untreated because of the circumstances of war and the ruthlessness of tyrants. In the first half of the twentieth century it became a not-uncommon thing for supposedly civilized nations to reduce human beings to garbage—objects that could be disposed of by the hundreds and the thousands in anonymous mass graves. Hundreds of millions of lives were displaced in the world wars and tyrannies of the 1910s, 1930s, and 1940s that destroyed the honest, patient toil of uncountable millions. And tens of millions of decent young men and women brimming with health, venerable parents and grandparents, and innocent children and infants were killed in the wars and the death camps. Entire families, villages, cities, regions, and races were either entirely or nearly wiped out. Sixty years later, we still live with the moral consequences of those inhuman deeds.

In many parts of the world between 1914 and 1945, human life came to have value only in relation to its usefulness to the state. For many European Jews and Christians, as well as many American Jews and Christians, these events cast serious doubt upon their belief in the God prayed to by Abraham and Jesus. But it was not the will of the Almighty that filled the slave-labor camps of Joseph Stalin or the concentration camps of Adolf Hitler that mass-produced death. What did that was an abuse of the freedom that God has bestowed on mankind.

The feeling in the United States in 1945 among Americans who were not entirely caught up in euphoric relief over the end of World War II, and the desire to return to the normal American way of life and forget the rest of the world, was that something had to be done to prevent a third world war. Something had to be done to halt the spread of governments that had no regard for the sacredness of human life. The majority of Americans at the end of World War II, however, felt that America had fulfilled its duty again (as it had in the First World War) to make the world safe for democracy. It was time for Americans to get back to minding their own business and taking care of their families.

But in the aftermath of this war, the nations in southern, western, and northern Europe that had escaped the iron net of captivity that the Soviet Union had cast over the nations of eastern and central Europe needed the help of the United States to preserve their still-threatened and precarious independence if they were to stay free of communist dictatorship.

It is evident in retrospect that a conjunction of influences and circum-stances made the second half of the twentieth century a period of more direct danger to American culture than the first half of the century. Foremost

among these circumstances was a struggle that proved much more complicated for America to fight than a shooting, or "hot," war. The Cold War
with the Soviet Union had a dangerous military component, to be sure, but
it was primarily a struggle to defend American cultural beliefs against the
threat of an aggressive, intransigent ideology that aspired to become a global
culture. The defense of a culture is a much more problematic matter than
waging a military campaign because the dynamics of culture are not susceptible to command and control.

During the early years of World War II, between 1939 and 1941, Britain
and other countries in Europe looked to the United States for military assistance. And after Japan's attack on the United States at Pearl Harbor in
December 1941, the United States fully responded to that need with all the
might of her hard-working people and her young men's willingness to show
(as President Harry Truman said) "a ruthless enemy that they were not afraid
to fight and to die" in defense of their country and its way of life.[3] The sacrifices of Americans from 1941 to 1945 saved the world from Japanese and
German fascism. Then for more than forty years after World War II, American power was needed in the world to serve as a bulwark against the Soviet
Union's determination to reconstruct Europe and the rest of the world in the
image of Karl Marx's "scientific" prescription for man's salvation.

In the post–World War II period, the sympathy of some Americans with
the Soviet foreign policy of eliminating capitalism from the world and substituting communism in its place exposed the United States to attacks on its
culture from within its own borders. But there were few members of the
Communist Party USA. Alone, they and their fellow activists could never
have undertaken so daunting a task as a sustained internal attack on American culture with the goal of replacing it. However, the clamor of American
communists against U.S. "imperialism" resonated with a widespread feeling
in America at the time that went by the name of "isolationism."

In 1796 when the United States was a newly independent, third-rate
country with very little weight in international affairs, George Washington
had articulated that stay-at-home and tend-to-your-own-affairs sentiment in
his Farewell Address to his countrymen. The proper business of America, he
said in this valedictory, was development of the North American wilderness
and commerce with as many nations as possible. Washington advised his
countrymen to cherish their Constitution, build up their nation, and, above
all, avoid "entangling alliances" with European nations. This isolationism
(the term was coined during the First World War by British propagandists
who wanted the United States to cease its neutrality and become an ally of

Britain in her war with Imperial Germany) remained part of American foreign policy for a century after Washington published his Farewell Address.

And American isolationism was only reluctantly set aside. The first time was in 1898, in a brief overseas war with Spain in response to the sinking of a United States battleship at anchor in Spanish territory. The second time was in the third year of the First World War, after German submarines torpedoed ships carrying American citizens. This was a crucial moment in the war. Imperial Russia (the principal eastern ally of Britain and France) having dropped out of the war, it looked as though Germany would be able to concentrate its full military strength against France and Britain along the Western Front. But the army of one million fresh troops that the United States was able to rush to the battlefields in Belgium and France in 1918 to meet that menace turned the tide of battle, and led to an Allied victory in the war. Because of this American sentiment of isolationism, American participation in the Second World War was likewise tardy. Not until Japan's attack on American territory on December 7, 1941, and Nazi Germany's declaration of war on the United States a few days later—more than two years after the start of World War II in Europe, and four years after the war began in Asia with Japan's invasion of China—did the United States become a combatant in World War II.

But despite America's involvement in the two world wars of the twentieth century, sentiment for isolationism was still strong among Americans in 1950. In the first half of the century, the American people had dined twice at the table of international politics and had not much liked the taste of the fare or its price. Therefore, whenever American communists in the 1950s and 1960s accused America of imperialism and interference in the internal affairs of other nations, they could count on the accusation arousing the isolationist sentiment of many Americans. The communist allegation that America had imperial ambitions invoked the argument that other nations should be allowed to decide for themselves, just as the United States had done in 1776, the kind of government they wanted, without American "interventionism." Therefore, the United States should desist from its post–World War II foreign policy of containing communism. That this argument convinced some Americans was evident on one sign carried at an anti–Vietnam War demonstration in the late 1960s. Written in highly literate English, it read: "We must not continue to deny to others the principles of liberty & self-determination upon which this country was founded."[4] The politics of those Americans who regarded Marxism as the means to social justice, and who wanted the United States to refrain from containing communism, meshed with the sentiments of American isolationists who wanted no overseas entanglements. The motives of the two groups could not have been more different but the result was the same: protests against America's overseas efforts to contain communism.

The trouble with the communist argument about American interventionism, although it sounded reasonable and in keeping with the principles of American culture, was that self-determination for many nations following World War II was impossible without American military protection and economic aid. In the late 1940s and the early 1950s, Soviet agents actively interfered in the internal affairs of France, Italy, and other European countries. Without U.S. aid, Greece and Italy, and probably France, would have fallen under communist domination following the Second World War, not by the free choice of a majority of their citizens but through political subversion or military intimidation. Even with American support, remaining free of communist dictatorship in the late 1940s and the 1950s was for many nations a close call.

When America went to war in Korea in 1950 to repulse communist North Korea's invasion of South Korea, communist China intervened to hurl back the American forces that had not only retaken South Korea but had militarily occupied all of Korea as far north as its border with Red China. Once the Chinese attack had been stopped and the battlefront stabilized by American forces along the pre-invasion boundary between North and South Korea, there was little desire in the United States to continue the war. The American people were relieved that the fighting in Korea ceased in 1953 but dissatisfied with the result. Their history as a nation had accustomed them to expect decisive victories in the wars the United States engaged in. They believed that if you were going to fight a war, you should win it, not settle for a stalemate. After the seesaw of combat on the Korean Peninsula between 1950 and 1953, with 157,000 American casualties (58,000 of them battlefield deaths), the communist invaders from North Korea had been expelled from South Korea but not vanquished. The war ended where it had begun, at the boundary that had partitioned Korea following World War II. (As in the case of Germany, which had been similarly divided between capitalist and communist governments, the contrast between the prosperity and freedom of capitalist South Korea and the starvation and fear reigning in communist North Korea has made it perfectly clear which system works better. During the late 1990s, up to two million people starved to death in North Korea, where the infant mortality rate is currently 88 per 1,000 live births compared to South Korea's 8. Furthermore, in South Korea economic productivity is fifteen times greater than in North Korea, and the life expectancy of men is 21.5 years longer.[5])

The discontent of American isolationists with America's foreign entanglements was increased by U.S. involvement in Vietnam, a country that had also been divided after armed communist cadres in 1954 ousted France, the country's colonial master. As America's participation in the war between North and South Vietnam ground on and on through the 1960s and into the 1970s, America suffered 54,000 battlefield dead: about the same number as in the Korean War, which lasted only three years compared to the eleven years of America's military engagement in Vietnam. (The annual rate of American battle deaths in Korea was approximately 19,000 a year; in Vietnam, about 5,000. This contrasts with the estimated 400,000 South Vietnam soldiers who died in battle fighting the forces of communist North Vietnam.) Public support in the United States for this effort in Vietnam to prevent the communist takeover of another Asian country had been less to begin with than it had been for the war in Korea, and as the war dragged on and anti-American protests in the United States multiplied, that diminished support dwindled. By the late 1960s, it had fallen sharply as the counter-culture movement took hold on American campuses and organized incessant demonstrations against the U.S. presence in Vietnam. These protests often displayed national coordination, and the American media gave them coverage that magnified their prominence. At the same time, continuous daily and special television reports from Vietnam brought the violence of battle into American homes day after day, week after week, month after month, for years.

Discontent in America over the outcome of the Korean War had been mainly confined to the political extremes. The Far Right complained that the atom bomb should have been dropped on communist China to halt its military support for communist North Korea so that North and South Korea could have been reunited under a single democratic government friendly to the United States. The Far Left was unhappy that the invading army of North Korea had been expelled from South Korea and prevented from taking over the entire Korean Peninsula and creating a single "people's republic" friendly to Red China and the USSR. In the 1960s, the case was different. The Vietnam War polarized the middle of the American political spectrum. Before the withdrawal of the United States from Vietnam, most middle-class Americans either staunchly supported the war as a morally justified use of force to thwart the spread of communism or strongly denounced it as a waste of American lives and resources in what the antiwar protestors called an arrogant and immoral act of imperialism. By the late 1960s, not many Americans were undecided about the war.

Some Americans who opposed the Vietnam War went beyond verbal criticism. For the first time in American history, large numbers of middle-class college students became accustomed to expressing their political views through violence. Never before in the history of the United States had there been such widespread, violent political demonstrations against the government of the United States while hundreds of thousands of American servicemen were engaged in combat overseas.

More ominous for the future of American culture than the use of violence in the 1960s by middle-class youths to express their political opinions was the institutional politicization of higher education. Historically, America's colleges and universities had been institutions dedicated to the pursuit of knowledge, and students attended them in order to acquire the knowledge that would allow them to lead more productive, satisfying lives. But American colleges and universities ceased to be such institutions in the 1960s. They became instead seedbeds for political activism, social engineering, and "cultural change." Sometime around 1965 when America's military engagement in Vietnam steeply escalated, something intangible but quite real took place in American society: extreme reactions to extremism replaced cultural civility. This incivility has been and is a principal symptom of the culture war in America.

In the early and middle 1960s, America's cultural unity was furiously challenged from within in a way that not even the crisis of the Civil War duplicated. In the 1860s, the conflict had been over the cultural beliefs that God has given all men the same birthrights and that a written constitution, once agreed to and established, cannot be unilaterally abrogated. The origins of the Civil War derived from those two issues (slavery and constitutional law), and both had a resolution in the cataclysm of bloody war after all peaceful attempts to settle them had failed, the resolutions being the abolition of slavery by force of arms and the granting of citizenship to the former slaves through constitutional amendments. The cultural conflict of the 1960s was not like that. It was not limited to specific issues amenable to specific resolution. It was a sweeping condemnation and rejection of America. In the 1960s the United States per se was condemned and rejected by many young Americans. Its capitalist economy, its so-called imperialism and colonialism, its allegedly oppressive Establishment, its racism, and its "repressive bourgeois morality" were all denounced. No specific reforms, many young Americans felt, could remedy so many various categorical deficiencies. According to those who condemned and rejected American culture, it was necessary to construct a new culture.

For many persons who heeded this radical call for change, the righteousness of the need for change justified whatever had to be done to implement it. Riots, deceit, brazen lies, arson, armed robbery, aid and comfort given to an enemy of the United States in time of war, and even murder was justified if it advanced what the activists and radicals of the 1960s referred to as "the Revolution" or "the Movement." When one's intentions were pure, everything necessary to carry them out was righteous, regardless of how extreme the measures might be. At the University of Wisconsin, Madison, in 1969 and 1970, for example, during the height of the rioting on that campus and in the town of Madison (riots euphemistically renamed "actions" because in fighting for the cause of liberation from America's allegedly immoral culture, it was not useful to these activists to call things by their right names), there were hundreds of nighttime arsons. There was even a drive-by shooting at the home of a professor who was outspoken in his support of the Vietnam War. And at an all-university faculty meeting, the elected vice president of the University of Wisconsin student body told the assembled professors that they should not be upset by the violence because it was merely "another form of free speech."

On April 18, 1970, a rioting mob "trashed" the main business street in downtown Madison, the capital of Wisconsin, for the second time in four months. Plate glass windows of banks and stores were smashed. Movable property was hurled into the street. Parked cars were vandalized. And similar "actions" were "taken" in other parts of town by other "cadres," as the rioters sometimes referred to themselves. These actions included burning down a supermarket that was supposedly exploiting students. In the spring of 1970, there were daily battles for weeks between radicalized students (whom leftist faculty members fondly spoke of as "the kids") and the Wisconsin National Guard and Madison city police who had been mobilized to quell the rioting. In these battles, students used lengths of heavy chain, bricks, stones, and gasoline bombs as weapons; the police and guardsmen used clubs, rifle butts, and tear gas.

On the promise of anonymity, a reporter for the principal newspaper in Madison, Wisconsin, the *Capital Times*, taped and published an interview with three of the trashers—two young men and a woman—who justified their violence as an expression of a higher consciousness. Toward the end of the hours-long interview, one of the two young men said, "Even if the war in Vietnam ended, it wouldn't matter because there's a war to be fought right here [in America]. We're raising the level. Right now people are trashing out windows, next week they may be trashing pigs [killing policemen]."[6] One contemporary observer of the 1960s later recalled that what happened in America then was that "The concept of not being ashamed of even the worst things [was] introduced into American life."[7] Whatever was useful in intimidating the American government, ending U.S. military efforts in Vietnam, and eroding American culture was acceptable, was justified, because it would allegedly lead to peace, social justice, and liberation.

The orgy of political violence and hedonism that took place in the 1960s gave many young, middle-class Americans of that generation the heady experience of release from the normal constraints of their culture. It gave them a taste of "empowerment," of being a law unto themselves, of being self-righteously freer and smarter than their peers and elders, and of participating in a movement that had the betterment of all mankind as its purpose. Their consciousness had been, as they said, "raised." They no longer respected the norms of conduct representing the historical beliefs of their cultural ancestors, and they no longer saw their country in the way their parents and grandparents (the generations that fought World War II) did. They acted on behalf of all the poor and oppressed in countries throughout the world, including the United States, they said. They had been alienated from their cultural identity as Americans.

By the 1970s a virulent anti-Americanism had been injected into the cultural bloodstream of America by educated American young people who had become dedicated to the proposition that America was guilty of imperialism abroad and oppression at home and had to be stopped in the name of peace, social justice, and liberation. To be a true patriot, these young Americans were convinced, meant denouncing America and "working for change." After the United States withdrew its forces from Vietnam in 1973 and communists took over all of Vietnam, the political violence in America abated and opposition to American culture took other forms of intimidation.

The moral imperatives of those who gave active support to the leaders of the counter-culture movement that began on American campuses in the 1960s were simple: Question Authority, Don't Trust Anyone Over Thirty, and Do Your Own Thing. And as they repeated these slogans, the young activists seemed to feel they had discovered the secret of righteous living and had been liberated from all unrighteousness. But the difference between liberty and liberation is immense. Liberty assumes that all human beings have an equal and unalienable freedom that comes to them from God, who has endowed mankind with this freedom because without it there can be no morality, justice, or love. Liberty assumes that human beings are accountable for the consequences of the choices that they make. The concept of liberation, on the other hand, assumes that the majority of human beings are born into a condition of being dominated by a class of oppressors who manipulate institutions and moral codes as part of their oppression. It preaches that people must be liberated from their oppression by leaders who profess to love them (albeit impersonally and en masse), and who can teach them to identify, hate, and "disempower" those who are oppressing them. The oppressed learn from these benevolence-affirming leaders that their oppressors are responsible for everything bad that has ever happened to them.

To be liberated is to be entirely free of oppression, an oppression that can take many forms. It might be a law. It might be the civility of respecting the feelings of others by refraining from certain conduct and language. It might be an obligation to a stranger or a member of one's family. It might be a belief in, or what the liberated might call a "hang-up about," private property. It might be society's disapproval of one's taking habit-forming drugs or of one's particular "sexual orientation." It might be the demands of a "relationship" (the designation of what passed for love in the counter-culture movement). Oppression was anything that constrained a person and kept him from doing "his own thing" whenever he felt like doing it. In this view, liberation became the sum total of morality.

The unavoidable result of liberation, of course, is first of all moral relativism: the idea that every person can decide on their own what is right and wrong from moment to moment and situation to situation, without any acknowledgment of the right of other persons to expect anything (including dependability and honesty) of them. Liberation meant the breakdown of what made possible the traditional family, the fundamental institution of human society. And when the traditional family is rejected or abandoned, society loses most of its coherence. In the 1960s, the breakdown of "family life and sexual life and academic life and intellectual life"[8] was gleefully welcomed by those in the counter-culture movement as a preliminary step to getting rid of American culture in preparation for the construction of a new, "correct," liberating culture.

In the latter half of the twentieth century, American culture came under sustained assault by a comparatively small number of American left-wing extremists who disapproved of and opposed what America stood for, particularly its opposition to communism. They were joined in their protests by sizable numbers of disgruntled and disaffected groups within American society and by youths susceptible to the intoxicating idea of liberation. Opposition

to the Vietnam War was the catalyst for transforming American reform liberalism of the sixty years from 1890 to 1950 into the anti-American politics of
the counter-culture.

In American culture, interest in right and wrong has always been a central
concern. It was of course even stronger among young Americans who, being
young, were naturally idealistic. These factors played a necessary role in
alienating a good many young Americans in the 1960s from their native culture as they became convinced that America was a country whose evil ways
had to be changed. By making it appear that the U.S. attempt to keep South
Vietnam from falling under communist rule was immoral because it contradicted the American principle of self-determination, America's cultural enemies were able to turn the robust sense of right and wrong of young
Americans against their country. Instead of being the last, best hope of mankind, as Abraham Lincoln had called the United States during the Civil
War, the United States became in the 1960s for many young Americans "the
beast" that "ate its own children" and consumed other nations of the world
because of its insatiable "capitalist greed."

Fear was another factor in the success of the counter-culture movement
in the 1960s, especially in turning young American men into protesters.
These young men were told that they were doing the right thing by giving
in to the fear of dying or being maimed in battle. They should refuse (they
were told) to serve in an immoral war in a faraway country whose inhabitants
ought to be allowed to sort out their political future on their own. America's
young men were told that by not registering for the draft, or by running away
to another country in order to avoid the call to serve in the armed forces of
the United States, they would be saving not only their own lives but the lives
of millions of innocent Vietnamese. It was noble, they were told, to "make
love, not war."

Nearly every generation of Americans has made practical improvements
to America's political, social, and economic institutions. For many in the
generation that came of age in the 1960s, that normal cultural pattern was
transformed into a grandiose plan for creating a new culture. In the 1960s
the Cold War was (as the campus radicals said they wanted to do with the
war in Vietnam) "brought home." The result was the cultural war within the
United States of the past forty years.

But not all of the protests in the 1960s were hostile to American culture.
The civil rights movement of the late 1950s and the 1960s led by the Rever-
end Martin Luther King, Jr., one of the major events of the period, was a
long-overdue, positive reform in the American tradition of practical

improvement. It was not anti-American. Rather, it aimed at eliminating the demeaning Jim Crow laws and customs that segregated black Americans from white Americans. It wanted to achieve social integration and equal freedom for every American, regardless of color. As was also true of the reform movement in the 1840s and 1850s to abolish slavery, the civil rights movement of the 1950s and 1960s drew its strength from the Christian belief that God has given all men the same birthrights. This is the fundamental American belief that the Declaration of Independence proclaimed to the world in 1776, the belief in the equal right of all men to life, liberty, and the pursuit of happiness. These birthrights had been withheld from many black Americans when it came to their pursuing happiness in terms of a better job, better housing, or equal access to public schools, transportation, universities, motels, and restaurants. Even the right to vote granted in 1870 by the Fifteenth Amendment had in some cases been denied to black Americans.

The young Americans of the 1960s who rejected American culture accepted the Far Left's condemnation of the United States as a racist society. That conception of America overlooked the sacrifices and constitutional amendments that had extended to black Americans political freedom and a U.S. citizenship equal to that of white Americans. For left-wing extremists, it was as if the Civil War had never been fought and the Thirteenth, Fourteenth, and Fifteenth Amendments to the Constitution abolishing slavery and granting equal citizenship to black Americans had never been passed. For such extremists, the Jim Crow laws were the whole truth about America. To them, any talk of the belief that made the civil rights movement possible—the American belief in God-given, equal birthrights for all men—was just so much empty hypocrisy, not a cultural belief. They rejected American culture as irredeemably racist. They demanded something totally different than reform. They demanded liberation. They did not dream as King did of a reformed, better America that was more faithful to its cultural beliefs. The leaders of the 1960s counter-culture revolution in America hated everything about "Amerika." (This routine respelling of *America* by propagandists of the counter-culture movement—for instance, Jerry Rubin in his 1971 paperback *We Are Everywhere*—was intended to visually connect America to Hitler's Germany, a hard *c* in German being spelled *k*.) The anti-American radicals of the counter-culture movement rejected "Amerikan Kulture" as a "fascist, Pig Kulture." Its Establishment was "obscene" and "rotten to the core." It had to be replaced.

In the 1970s and 1980s, many of the young Americans who came of age in the 1960s and had been won over by the counter-culture's anti-American rhetoric entered professions and institutions that have historically had an influence on what Americans believe and how they act. They took up careers in law, television, public school teaching, entertainment, the arts, churches, consulting firms, libraries, social services, universities, foundations, government bureaus, think tanks, filmmaking, writing, publishing, journalism, economics, and corporations. Those who continued in the counter-culture movement in the 1970s and 1980s "worked for change" by founding organizations to "network" with other organizations that could be mobilized on specific occasions in the struggle for social justice, and they recruited the next generation to join them in working for change. As one critic of the counter-culture movement said at a get-together of former radicals in 1989: "The difference between the '60s and the '80s is that the radicals in the '60s were on the outside beating on the doors, demonstrating, trying to get in. In the '80s they're on the inside running the institutions."[9]

By rising to positions of influence and leadership in the above professions and institutions, and by setting up networks of activists, lobbyists, and opinion molders, the radicals of the 1960s and their followers in the next generation magnified the influence of their ideas. They also created a political atmosphere agreeable to their agenda in which laws, regulations, policies, and judicial rulings that supported the "correct" ideas of the counter-culture were encouraged. In a law-abiding democratic society like America, laws, regulations, and government policies are particularly useful in modifying behavior, the first step in changing cultural beliefs. The complex task of building a movement to replace American culture required a dogged, tireless, zealous commitment and determination of the kind that counter-culture activists seemed to have in abundance.

A book published in 1971 by a longtime leftist agitator and organizer on "how to organize for power" contained many of the concepts and tactics used in the 1970s and 1980s for "a pragmatic attack on the system."[10] Saul Alinsky's aim in his book *Rules for Radicals* was to create a movement "inside the system" that could produce a revolutionary change in American society. To do that, he said, large parts of the middle class would have to be moved to sustained action by "organizers" who used "conflict tactics" to "create discontent."[11] The first requirement in the process was the "reformation essential to any revolution," namely, to instill an "attitude toward change." People had to be persuaded that change was necessary and that they could bring it about, or at least they had to be persuaded that they should not stand in the way of change.[12] Getting people to participate in what Alinsky called "actions" made them part of a movement and gave them an appetite for more action.

Alinsky described in his book the "special training school for organizers" he established in his native city of Chicago. The students who attended it, he boasted,

> ranged from middle-class women activists to Catholic priests and Protestant ministers of all denominations, from militant Indians to Chicanos to Puerto Ricans to blacks from all parts of the black power spectrum, from [Black] Panthers to radical philosophers, from a variety of campus activists, S. D. S. [Students for a Democratic Society] and others.[13]

They came from all over the country, from "campuses and Jesuit seminaries in Boston to Chicanos from tiny Texas towns, middle-class people from Chicago and Hartford and Seattle, and almost every place in between." With evident satisfaction over what he had built, he added that

> For years before the formal school was begun, I spent most of my time on the education as an organizer of every member of my staff. The education of an organizer requires frequent long conferences on organizational problems, analysis of power patterns, communication, conflict tactics, the education and development of community leaders, and the introduction of new issues.

Alinsky stated that "Organization for action will now and in the decade ahead [the 1970s] center upon America's white middle class."[14] He advised middle-class readers of *Rules for Radicals* to "return to the suburban scene of your middle class with its variety of organizations from PTAs to League of Women Voters, consumer groups, churches, and clubs," and there "to search out the leaders in these various activities, identify their major issues, find areas of common agreement, and excite their imagination with tactics that can introduce drama and adventure into the tedium of middle-class life."[15] (The sixth rule in the chapter titled "Tactics" describes *"a good tactic"* as *"one that your people enjoy."*[16]) Other rules in his manual for change include these important principles: *"The real action is in the enemy's reaction,"* and *"The enemy properly goaded and guided in his reaction will be your major strength."*[17] Alinsky explained why these principles were so important: "Any attack against the status quo must use the strength of the enemy against itself."[18]

Such agitators as Alinsky in their attacks on American culture focused on the middle class because that class made and continues to make up the greatest portion of American society. The effect that these attacks (started in the 1960s and 1970s) had on middle-class beliefs and behaviors can be seen in the titles and subtitles of numerous books on America published in recent years: *The Disuniting of America, Coming Apart, The De-Valuing of America, The Death of the West, A Society in Chaos, The Tempting of America, The Unraveling of America, The Fraying of America, The End of Sanity, The Death of Common Sense, The Closing of the American Mind, The Collapse of the Common Good,* and *The Strip-Mining of American Culture,* to name only a few.[19] The substantives in these titles express a general sense of disorder and impending disaster: coming apart, devaluing, disuniting, unraveling, fraying, closing, collapse, end, death. And to anyone who has seen the broad, deep gouges and piles of sterile waste left behind by irresponsible strip-mine operators, the metaphor of strip-mining is a particularly vivid description of the ravages that have been inflicted on American culture. The present cultural landscape in America after four decades of assaults from the counter-culture does resemble the change left behind by a strip-mining company that has no interest in restoring the land before it moves on to its next operation.

America is a different country today, in the first decade of the twenty-first century, than it was in the 1950s. The difference is not a matter of changes in tastes or manners, changes that are to be expected with the passage of half a century. Rather, it is a matter of the disturbance of the deeply seated beliefs of American culture that have historically structured American society and given it stability, unity, and order. Many of the changes that have occurred in the United States since the middle of the 1960s are profoundly abnormal.

The nature of the counter-culture movement and its purposes were clear to Spanish philosopher Julián Marías who came to the United States several times in the 1950s and 1960s to teach at American universities. In 1970 he summarized the essence of what he had observed during his several visits, saying, "[E]xtremist criticism of the United States within American universities extends to the structure and organization of the country, the entire range of the laws, usages, customs, values, and way of life that make up American society. In short and above all, campus unrest is, to a high degree, what is called anti-Americanism." Julián Marías, from his European perspective, also perceived that this anti-Americanism did not originate with the Vietnam War but dated from "at least as long ago as 1945"—that is, the year the United States ceased to be the Soviet Union's wartime ally. He likewise perceived, again as an outside observer, that the anti-Americanism he saw in the United States in the 1960s "has played a part in the Cold War and dominated many of the Eastern countries, much of Europe and Latin America, and is now gradually gaining ground in this country. It has reached serious proportions with the younger generation that began to make itself felt in a historical way around 1964."

Julián Marías voiced what American observers had also perceived: that many young Americans of good will in the 1960s had accepted the Soviet Union's Cold War propaganda regarding the United States as the truth. But Marías's perceptions have a special credibility as those of a cosmopolitan observer, a fact that places what he wrote about America in the 1960s above any possible suspicion of partisan bias or prejudice. As a Spaniard, he had with regard to American politics no parochial point of view to advance, no ax to grind. His judgments about the 1960s were those of a foreign observer and a philosopher trained in rational analysis. And it was his considered judgment of the 1960s that

> If one examines carefully what radical students are saying, it can be seen that they are simply repeating with unquestioning willingness what older and more mature enemies of the United States were writing and saying for various reasons decades ago. The arguments of today's American groups are simply the transcriptions or translation into English of what was formerly being said outside the United States.

Marías also pointed out that the report of the presidential commission that had been appointed to look into the campus violence of the 1960s was too narrowly focused in its investigation.

> Without an awareness of the origins of the current anti-Americanism, it is very hard to diagnose the causes of campus unrest and to propose effective ways to deal with it. The report is inadequate because it rests solely on intra-American premises and considers only this country in its investigation, whereas the principal causes of the phenomenon lie elsewhere.

Marías attributed this "colossal oversight," as he called it, to the fact that there were "minorities of the extreme right" in the United States "obtusely obsessed with conspiracy, who try to explain everything in terms of subversive agents and the like," and the presidential commission on campus violence had wanted to avoid any association with that point of view because it was obvious that "the great majority of students implicated in [the agitation on American campuses] are not foreign agents or anything of the sort." This Spanish philosopher thought that the commission's refusal to look at the influence on American students of Soviet propaganda regarding the Vietnam

War prevented it from considering the role that foreign enemies of the United States had had in "the spreading of ideas that 'are in the air.'"[20]

One of the three trashers interviewed in Madison, Wisconsin, in 1970 angrily denied that any conspiracy existed among the rioters in that university town. "There's no [expletive deleted] conspiracy, man." The more articulate male in the trio agreed. "There's no conspiracy or pre-planning. . . . There doesn't need to be *any more*" (emphasis added). This remark implied that an ideological atmosphere of anti-Americanism had been created at the University of Wisconsin that automatically led to certain actions on the part of those who were moved by it. The female trasher of the threesome concurred by saying, "[People] just know [what to do]. They just know." But under the probing questioning of the reporter conducting the interview, the three trashers admitted that committees and teams called "affinity groups" existed in Madison. And when students took to the streets for a planned action, there were always persons among them who proposed the places to be "hit."[21]

The United States decisively won its Cold War with the Soviet Union. But while the elected leaders of the country were preoccupied with that struggle on the international scene, a movement was deliberately mounted in the United States to weaken the culture that unifies American society. The new Establishment, as the most influential participants in this movement are sometimes called, is now so ascendant that when the Soviet Union's collapse in 1991 signaled America's victory in the Cold War, there were no widespread public celebrations to mark the event because the new opinion makers frowned on any jubilation over the downfall of the Soviet Union. The new Establishment labeled such celebrations as "triumphalism" and criticized any expression of satisfaction over the disappearance of the USSR as "gloating."

In the 1950s, young Americans in college still conformed to the culture of their parents and grandparents. No significant number of that so-called silent generation of the 1950s rejected American culture. But the political violence on American campuses in the 1960s significantly diminished the number of practitioners of American culture in the subsequent generation (the so-called baby boomers), which happened to be the largest in American history. And that, in turn, prevented the full transmission of American cultural behaviors and beliefs to the generation that came of age in the 1980s.

One historian writing about the aftermath of the sixties has declared that as early as the 1970s the "hedonism" of the 1960s had been "absorbed" into American culture. Another analyst has observed that "we still live with the consequences of campus protest, political unrest, and the tearing apart of America's social fabric" that occurred in the 1960s. Writing in 1997, a third commentator judged that the 1960s counter-culture has become a "New Establishment" even though its project of replacing American culture has yet to be completed.[22] An American in government service during the 1970s and 1980s has said of this new Establishment:

> [E]lite and mainstream America now adhere to profoundly different sets of beliefs and values. The skepticism toward this country that once characterized many intellectuals and their ideological soulmates has turned to antipathy. Over the last two decades [1970–1990] they have waged an all-out assault on common sense and the common values of the American people. We now stand at a crossroads.[23]

That conclusion is a theme in commentary on late-twentieth-century America, namely that the antagonism between the battered but still standing culture of the majority of Americans and the ideology of the counter-culture movement has reached crisis proportions. More and more Americans now seem aware of the seriousness of the culture war that has been going on in the United States since the 1960s.

How heightened the strain has become between the beliefs of American culture and the ideas of the counter-culture movement is suggested in the following observations by one distinguished jurist, writing in 1990 about the politicization of American law:

> In the past few decades American institutions have struggled with the temptations of politics. Professions and academic disciplines that once possessed a life and structure of their own have steadily succumbed, in some cases almost entirely, to the belief that nothing matters beyond politically desirable results, however achieved. . . . It is coming to be denied that anything counts, not logic, not objectivity, not even intellectual honesty, that stands in the way of the "correct" political outcome. . . . The democratic integrity of the law, however, depends entirely upon the degree to which its processes are legitimate. A judge who announces a decision must be able to demonstrate that he began from recognized legal principles and reasoned in an intellectually coherent and politically neutral way to his result. Those who would politicize the law offer the public, and the judiciary, the temptation of results without regard to democratic legitimacy.[24]

The politicization that has made the law a tool to effect social engineering has happened in many other fields as well in the last few decades.

All but three of the twenty-three American writers represented in one recent collection of essays on education, the arts, science, the media, and public and private life in the United States conclude that ideas brought to the fore in the 1960s and the 1970s have thoroughly politicized American life. This collection of essays (published under the title *Dumbing Down*) chronicles and comments on what its editors call the "severe and demonstrable downward spiral of American life and culture" in recent decades. The final judgment of the editors of the collection in their introduction to the selections is plainly ominous: "American society, for some time fallen in disarray, has somehow begun sliding down a long, steep chute into nullity."[25] A slide into nullity may perhaps be overstating the matter somewhat. But there can be no doubt that America is in a severe cultural crisis brought on by the headway that the counter-culture movement has made since the 1960s among influential Americans. If the cultural damage is to be halted and repaired, a majority of Americans must understand the nature of this crisis.

The struggle between the beliefs of American culture and the ideology of the counter-culture movement is more momentous than any policy disagreements between political parties or the ups and downs of America's free-enterprise economy. Whatever the outcome of the culture war is, it will have repercussions, good or bad, for every American. And given America's singular political and economic importance in the world, it will also have consequences for the future of Western civilization.

CHAPTER THREE

Perfection vs. Practical Improvement

From as far back as the times of the pagan Greeks, folk stories have been told about a golden age in the distant past. The same idea appears in the much older Old Testament story of the fall of Adam and Eve from the perfect bliss of the paradise in which God had placed them. Narratives like Pandora's Box and the Garden of Eden describe a state of perfection lost through a wrong choice on mankind's part. In the eighteenth century, however, European intellectuals enlightened their fellow Europeans by informing them that the reverse was true. Perfection lay in the future. This reversal, from looking backward to a vanished golden age to looking forward in anticipation of a future perfection, represented a major reorientation in Western thought. It marked the beginning of what we refer to as "the modern world," with its belief in progress and its reliance on science as the means to achieve perfection, a belief and a reliance that were to become hallmarks of Western civilization during the nineteenth and twentieth centuries.

European philosophers of the Age of Enlightenment promised men they had only to use reason and science to achieve prosperity, peace, and perfect justice. Among enlightened Europeans, the Christian view of man as a creature in need of God's redeeming grace became passé: an outmoded thing of the past. Humanity might be flawed, but the fault did not lie in human nature. It lay in the social, economic, and political environments that civilization had created. Change those, and all would be well. The excitement of the Enlightenment ideal was that man could become his own savior and create a new world for himself. The science and rationalism of eighteenth-century Europe preached the good news that man is perfectible.

The eighteenth century was not, of course, the first time Europeans had dreamed of attaining perfection through reason and knowledge. Plato in the fourth century BC wrote of an ideal republic governed by a virtuous dictator (a philosopher-king), and two thousand years later, in the sixteenth century, Sir Thomas More likewise described a perfect society founded on reason. The title of More's book *Utopia*, a term compounded of two Greek words meaning when put together "no place," gave a name to this kind of fantasy literature: utopian. It was an apt coinage because More evidently never intended the perfect society he described in his book to serve as a plan for creating one. Eighteenth-century Enlightenment thinkers, on the other hand, did believe their ideas should be used to build a new society.

Jean-Jacques Rousseau (1712–1778) typified the new mode of thought by describing an original human innocence that civilization had corrupted, an innocence he characterized as man's "state of nature." Change man's institutions and educate him correctly, Rousseau argued, and the way to a bright future would open up. He overlaid the old, unenlightened story of lost perfection with a new, exculpatory modern story about the cause of evil. Evil did not arise from man's freedom to choose between what is inherently good and what is inherently bad for him. No, man's original nobility had been forfeited to a class of evildoers who wanted to dominate the rest of mankind. Evil was *class*-specific. It was not a capacity for wrongdoing latent in every man, whether rich or poor, humble or powerful, slave or free, male or female. Man was by nature good. Evil lay in the ruling class and its oppressive institutions.

The French Revolution, however, which was the initial application of Enlightenment ideas, did not bring peace, prosperity, and justice. Instead, it brought mass executions, the desecration of churches, the beheading of a French king, foreign wars, and three different constitutions in a period of five years. This turmoil lasted from 1789 to 1799. Then Napoleon's dictatorship, which culminated in his crowning himself Emperor of France, restored order but incited more than a decade of almost continuous warfare between France and the most powerful European monarchs as they attempted to dislodge this commoner who had usurped the French throne.

The revolutionaries in France had wanted to create a new way of life according to a rational plan. Napoleon, a brilliant autocrat, put some of that intention into effect by fiat rather than majority rule. And he was much admired by the French people for his genius and the uniform rationality that he imposed on such matters as weights and measures, finances, the administration of justice, and the centralization of government. Napoleon's victories on battlefield after battlefield brought memorable, if fleeting, glory to France, and some of his civil reforms remained as permanent parts of French life after he was overthrown. But neither the French Revolution nor Napoleon created a new culture. The French Revolution and its aftermath produced for France twenty-six years of internal upheavals and foreign wars, which ended only with Napoleon's expulsion from Europe and the restoration of the French monarchy. Not until the Third Republic, in the late nineteenth century, four generations after the French Revolution, did France finally achieve a republican form of government that lasted more than a generation.

The formation of America's democratic culture came about in a quite different way. Throughout the seventeenth and eighteenth centuries on the Atlantic coastal plain of North America, separated from the centers of European thought by an ocean voyage that could take up to three months to accomplish, an authentically new culture came into being gradually, generation after generation. There, on the verge of the North American wilderness and almost unnoticed, an unprecedented kind of society took shape, one made up of immigrants who had freely chosen to belong to it. It was composed of hundreds of thousands of dissatisfied Europeans who had individually revolted against life in Europe and found their way over the Atlantic to America where they encountered conditions of life far different from those in Europe's aristocratic societies. American culture was not created in accordance with a theory for perfection but through the steady dedication of these immigrants and their American-born descendants to practical improvements that were of great advantage to them. In their determination to better their individual lives in practical ways, these self-selected Europeans and their descendants demonstrated a mutual commitment to the pursuit of happiness. They undertook the brutal work of converting a wilderness into farms and towns not to create a new culture but rather to become property owners and to feed and house themselves and their families better and to be freer than people of their classes were in Europe. They wanted to lead more self-determined lives than was possible in Europe's rigidly structured aristocratic societies. In working to achieve their mutually agreeable individual purposes, their self-determining behavior produced a new society with a new culture.

Never before in history had there been a whole society predominately made up of self-selected immigrants from many countries, who had freely chosen to belong to it, and the descendants of such persons. The governments of France, Portugal, and Spain screened immigrants to Canada, Brazil, and Spanish America to ensure conformity to a single nationality and a single religion. Only the immigration policies of the British crown disregarded a would-be immigrant's nationality and church membership and permitted self-selecting immigration from diverse countries and religious denominations. These immigrants possessed a conformity that no government had imposed: they shared an ambition to improve their lives. Through their individual initiatives, their strivings from generation to generation, and their collective successes, this new society of immigrants from diverse countries of Europe, and their American-born descendants, created in the eight generations between 1610 and 1770 a new set of cultural behaviors and beliefs.

This new culture of the American people who inhabited the Atlantic coastal plain of North America first manifested itself to the world in the late eighteenth century in two unique state papers expressing American cultural beliefs: the Declaration of Independence and the Constitution of the United States of America. Nothing like them had ever been seen before in Western civilization.

Because a new culture had existed in America *before* the war for independence that came to be called the American Revolution—a democratic, self-determining culture distinct from the caste-conscious, know-your-place-and-stay-in-it aristocratic culture of England and the rest of Europe—this revolution had a unique result. All the other revolutions in the modern era, from the French Revolution, which followed hard on the heels of the American Revolution, to the twentieth-century Marxist revolutions, tried to force into being a new culture through political action based on a plan. Each of those revolutions had the problem of eliminating an existing culture and at the same time putting in place the desired new culture. The revolutionaries in America did not have that problem. They already possessed a new culture. They aimed solely at independence from the political authority of a European monarch. Therefore, there was no counter-revolution in the United States after the American Revolution, and no bloody struggle for power among the leaders of the American War for Independence, because an overwhelming proportion of Americans, including America's leaders, adhered to the belief-behaviors of the new culture, belief-behaviors that included belief in government by consent.[1]

American culture gave birth to the American Revolution and the republic of the United States of America. The American Revolution and the founding of the republic did not give birth to American culture.

Because America already had a new culture *before* 1775, a culture that the American Revolution confirmed and expressed rather than created, what came after the revolution in America was entirely unlike the aftermath of the French Revolution. The aftermath of the revolution in America was not twenty-six years of disorder and counterrevolution. It was instead the peaceful writing and ratification of the Constitution of the United States and the election of a congress and a president under the authority of that Constitution.

The American Revolution also differed in other fundamental ways from the French Revolution. The leaders of the French Revolution relied on rationalism and the power of the state to produce a new culture. The Founding Fathers who wrote the Declaration of Independence and the Constitution of the United States put their trust in God as the source of their rights. It was a cultural belief of Americans that the dignity that man possesses in his right to life, liberty, and the pursuit of happiness, as well as his right to government by consent, comes not from any government that human reason devises but from the natural law of the creator of man and nature. Man must make his government conform to that law. (Benjamin Franklin wryly remarks about reason in the first part of his *Autobiography* that it is "a convenient thing," since it enables one to "find or make a Reason for every thing one has a mind to do."[2]) The purpose of government, the leaders of the American Revolution said in declaring American independence, was to defend the equal and unalienable birthrights that God has given mankind.

Because American history has in large part been the history of civilizing a wilderness, American culture believes in practical improvements. The preamble to the U.S. Constitution promised only "a more perfect Union," not perfection. Among themselves the Founding Fathers spoke of the republican government they created in 1787 as "an experiment." Though imperfect, it has proven to be a practical plan for federal government. Under its politically unifying, pragmatic authority, thirty-seven new states, each having a republican form of government and a written constitution approved by the people of that state, have since 1787 been organized and added to the original group of thirteen states.

By that year, Americans had had more than a century and a half of experience in organizing communities in the wilderness of North America for the common good, and they had acquired a strong, practical sense of why rule by the consent of the governed was better than autocratic government. Americans accepted the Christian view of man's flawed nature (the propensity of all men, regardless of class or race, to sin). But they and their ancestors in America also had had the experience, for eight generations, of seeing that most human beings prefer to use their God-given freedom to treat others as they themselves would be treated, according to God's natural law, which was to their natural benefit. The founders of the American republic knew from experience that men love power and have to be curbed by a constitution that protects the majority from the tyranny of unscrupulous, power-hungry individuals and minorities. The same constitution would also have to protect individuals and minorities from the tyranny of the majority, while providing for the belief in rule by the majority.

The American conception of government was informed in basic ways by the Christian concept of man's mixed nature, but it emphasized the trustworthiness of human beings. Europe's aristocratic cultures, which were also Christian, stressed man's fallen nature. The cultural presumption in Europe was that unless the authority of the state was exerted to restrain men, the majority would inevitably do things inimical to social order. The democratic culture of Americans regarded human nature as sinful but also as trustworthy and capable of self-restraint.

The Constitution of the United States reflects the pragmatism of the American cultural belief that almost all human beings want to do what is right, but that men will abuse power when they have it. The constitution Americans wrote for themselves divided and balanced power among the various branches of the national government and between the national government and the states that made up the nation as a means of keeping any one of them from becoming overbearingly powerful. That way the men elected to office under the Constitution to serve those who had elected them would be kept in check, and the majority could rule. James Madison, the "Father of the Constitution," observed in regard to human nature: "If men were angels, no government would be necessary" (*Federalist Papers*, 51). He and his fellow delegates to the Constitutional Convention in Philadelphia that produced the Constitution of the United States in 1787 fully appreciated man's imperfect nature, but they were just as convinced that although men were not angels, neither were they demons who required constant monitoring and control of their behavior by government or a class of superiors in order to save them from themselves. The great debates surrounding the writing and ratification of the Constitution of the United States are replete with references to mankind's self-interest, fallibility, and love of power; but they also refer often to man's capacity for self-government, his willingness to perform public service, and his decent respect for the rights of others. James Madison, who attended every session of the Constitutional Convention, analyzed in his essays on the Constitution of the United States how the imperfections of human nature had been taken into account in writing it (*Federalist Papers* 10, 15, 38, 41, 51).

The debates on forming a national government for the United States were structured by the American cultural belief that because all men have the same birthrights from God they must be treated with respect. But the ambiguous nature of slaves, who were both human beings and property, nearly aborted the writing of a constitution. The delegates from the states where slaves were most numerous and slavery most economically important threatened to walk out of the Constitutional Convention in Philadelphia if the contemplated instrument for national government was going to deprive them of their "property." Only by conceding to the demand of these states that slavery not be abolished but be allowed to remain in any state that wanted to keep the institution, was a breakup of the Constitutional Convention prevented.

The constitution that was finally sent to the states for ratification, after four months of vigorous debate, was not agreeable in every one of its provisions to every convention delegate who signed it. And seventy-four years after it was ratified a terrible, bloody war had to be fought to eliminate slavery from American society. But other than that glaring flaw, it has proved to be practical. (In the convention's final session, Benjamin Franklin pleaded with his fellow delegates to sign the document they had devised, even though their individual judgments were not in all instances, as his were not, embodied in the final result of their deliberations and compromises.) Abraham Lincoln's Second Inaugural Address in 1865 shows just how much he, and in all likelihood millions of other Americans as well, believed that the Civil War was God's punishment of Americans who, by permitting slavery, had violated God's natural law of equal birthrights for mankind.

The cultural argument for independence that the founders of the United States set forth in their "unanimous Declaration of the thirteen united States of America" in 1776 manifests the political importance that belief in God had for them. It reads, with emphasis added:

> When in the Course of human events, it becomes necessary for one people to dissolve the political bands which have connected them with another, and to assume among the Powers of the earth, the separate and equal station to which the Laws of Nature and of *Nature's God* entitle them, a decent respect to the opinions of mankind requires that they should declare the causes which impel them to the separation.
>
> We hold these truths to be self-evident, that all men are *created* equal, that they are endowed by their *Creator* with certain unalienable Rights, that among these are Life, Liberty and the pursuit of Happiness. That to secure these rights [i.e., make them secure, protect them], Governments are instituted among Men, deriving their just powers from the consent of the governed. That whenever any Form of Government becomes destructive of these ends, it is the Right of the People to alter or to abolish it, and to institute new Government, laying its foundation on

such principles and organizing its powers in such form, as to them shall seem most likely to effect their Safety and Happiness.

[Then follows the Declaration's long middle section reciting the offenses of the British king against the God-given rights of Americans and the failure of every effort Americans had made to settle the discord.]

We, therefore, the Representatives of the united States of America, in General Congress Assembled, appealing to *the Supreme Judge of the world* for the rectitude of our intentions, do, in the Name, and by Authority of the good People of these Colonies, solemnly publish and declare, That these United Colonies are, and of Right ought to be Free and Independent States; that they are Absolved from all Allegiance to the British Crown, and that all political connection between them and the State of Great Britain, is and ought to be totally dissolved; and that as Free and Independent States, they have full Power to levy War, conclude Peace, contract Alliances, establish Commerce, and to do all other Acts and Things which Independent States may of right do. And for the support of this Declaration, with a firm reliance on the Protection of *Divine Providence*, we mutually pledge to each other our Lives, our Fortunes, and our sacred Honor.

The revolutionaries in France in their most important state papers did not invoke God—"the Supreme Judge of the world," the "Creator," "Nature's God," or "Divine Providence"—as the source of the rights of man. Nor did they declare men to be equals because the creator of man and nature had given them the same birthright of freedom. The American founders did.

A desire for perfection in human affairs is the enemy of patriotism and of every other kind of love. (Those on the Left in America fondly quote the saying by the eighteenth-century scholar Dr. Samuel Johnson "Patriotism is the last refuge of a scoundrel" without knowing of Johnson's extraordinary love of his country or realizing that he was condemning scoundrels not patriotism.) The idea of perfection is likewise the enemy of patience, tolerance, forgiveness, prudence, forbearance, and every good that contributes to mankind's daily well-being and peace. The desire for perfection taken to its extreme is the lust for uniformity and control. And that lust lies at the heart of the counter-culture movement's aim to replace American culture with a politically correct culture.

The proponents of perfection would have Americans believe that because Washington, Jefferson, and others of the Founding Fathers owned slaves, and because the constitution they approved in 1787 did not give women the right to vote, that there is no love of freedom or belief in any sort of equality in American culture. To be convinced by this condemnation of American culture is to believe that America has a culture that can be adequately and fundamentally described as racist and sexist. Perfectionists also condemn capitalism as a system of production and distribution because some capitalists are corrupt. If the great majority of students in a public school voluntarily participate in religious exercises that are offensive to the thinking of even one politically correct person, every expression of religious belief in every public school throughout the land must be suppressed. If a twelve-year-old boy sticks out his tongue at a girl who has refused to be his girlfriend, school officials must suspend him for three days for "sexual harassment."[3] That is the perfectionist mentality.

In Greek mythology, Procrustes was a giant who lived by the side of a road and made those who passed by his cave spend the night with him. He broke the legs of his guests who were too tall to fit into his iron bed; those who were shorter than the bed he stretched, using his gigantic strength, so they too would fit it. Political correctness is Procrustean in nature. It wants to force everyone into the same iron bed. How the counter-culture's Procrustean obsession with imposing rigid standards of behavior has affected American law since the 1960s is suggested in the following analysis:

> Rationalism, the bright dream of figuring out everything in advance and setting it forth precisely in a centralized regulatory system, has made us blind. Obsessed with certainty, we see almost nothing. We bolt a toy refrigerator to the wall and demand 42-inch-high railings without checking whether the day care center is a nurturing environment or the factory is actually safe. . . .
>
> Friedrich Hayek, the Austrian-American economist and Nobel laureate, devoted much of his brilliant career to describing how rationalism could never work. . . . The Soviet system of rules and central planning is doomed to failure, Hayek stated with confidence fifty years ago, because it kills the human faculty that makes things work.
>
> We too have deluded ourselves into thinking that government should only act through central, self-executing rules. Although for different reasons, we too have this egotistical belief that we can make government operate like a Swiss watch, tolerating no exception or uncertainty, and haven't made the connection to the centrally planned system that we so loathed. We have cast aside our good sense, and worship an icon of abstract logic and arbitrary words.[4]

Reason taken to extremes of theorizing abstraction without regard for practical considerations propels the counter-culture movement, whose insistent attempts to implement an idea of perfection mutilates tolerance, destroys good will, and aborts common sense. The price of that zeal for control has been an outbreak of preposterous lawsuits, increasing incivility, and disrespect for law in the United States.

Perfection is no longer something that an individual strives for in his personal life, as in the mastery of a skill or field of knowledge, the improvement of a product or service, or the attempt to be a more loving spouse or parent. The personal lives of individuals have no primacy and do not really count for much in the perfection the counter-culture movement aims to create. The counter-culture is concerned with the perfection of *systems*. The system is the morality. When the system is perfect, then the behavior of human beings (who are considered to be merely the products of their environment) will be perfect. That appears to be the counter-culture movement's idea of morality.

There are numerous ways people can be forced to conform to politically correct ideas without resorting to physical intimidation or violence. These include slander, humiliation, character assassination, control of language, conditioning through fear of sanctions, and the nonphysical abuse of hard-edged zeal. In the war against American culture, these methods have all been used. But the heavy-duty assault weapons for imposing politically correct behavior in the culture war have been government programs, bureaucratic regulations, and the law. Classrooms, boardrooms, churches, union halls, movie studios, television stations, press rooms, legislative chambers, libraries, courthouses, and even bedrooms have all become battlefields of the culture war. For the politically correct, the entire world is a war zone in the struggle for perfection.

The combative posture of politically correct activists could not be clearer. Our blueprint for a perfect society, they say, is faultless; you don't even have a blueprint. Our politics of political correctness is seamless; your politics of making practical improvements is patchy, not to mention partisan, mean-spirited, racist, unfair, insensitive, sexist, homophobic, and (most of all) stupid. To be politically correct is to be unrelenting and uncompromising. Any politics apart from the politically correct message is said to be hurtful to the poor, the homeless, the hungry, the old, the sick, children, women, and minorities. Only the counter-culture's politics helps people, despite the fact that political correctness devalues common sense, patriotism, a sense of community, politeness, good will, patience, individuality, prudence, personal loyalty, truthfulness, tradition, the family, and religious life.

The way perfectionist politics works is demonstrated by an event that took place in the early 1990s on the campus of the University of Pennsylvania. The incident involved a student newspaper columnist whose criticism of affirmative action programs offended the politically correct sensibilities of some black students at the university who protested Gregory Pavlik's incorrect views by stealing and destroying an entire printing of the campus newspaper in which his column appeared. University administrators did not punish this act of ideological property destruction of thousands of newspapers, even though it struck at the heart of what a university is supposed to represent: the unintimidated, free exchange of opinion and ideas. Instead, they ordered the campus policemen who apprehended the vandals to take classes in "sensitivity training"! In the fog of political correctness that now envelopes American campuses, policemen who regard theft as unlawful, without taking into account the political motives a criminal may have, need training to become more sensitive in their outlook. They must be made to understand that the impartial, equal protection they thought they were supposed to provide, as officers sworn to uphold the law, is not their primary duty. In politically correct institutions like today's universities in the United States, the primary duty of all officials and employees is to support political correctness.

One may be quite sure that if a left-wing journalist's ideas had been suppressed by someone's stealing the newspapers in which his or her column appeared, there would have been an unceasing yowl from the Left about censorship and the suppression of free speech. And there would have been a strident demand that the vandals be apprehended and punished. Had a group of students taken direct action against a newspaper columnist who published politically correct ideas, they would surely have been labeled "right-wing extremists." And the police who apprehended them would have been commended, not retrained. There would have been no expenditure of university resources for sensitivity training.

If further example is required, the University of Pennsylvania can supply it. Around the same time that the edition of the campus newspaper that printed Gregory Pavlik's columns was being destroyed, another student, who was white, yelled at a group of black female students who were being raucous outside the room where he was trying to study: "Shut up, you water buffalo!" And for this spontaneous protest against the disturbance of his peace, Eden Jacobwitz was nearly expelled for racial harassment from the University of Pennsylvania. Only after the incident had received widespread publicity was the ridiculous accusation of racial harassment dropped.

These cases received national attention in the press. Worse incidents never made the national or even local news. For instance, in 1990 Father Charles W. Polzer, an ordained priest, historian of the early Southwest, and director of an ethno-history center at the University of Arizona, felt compelled to cancel an announced public lecture on Christopher Columbus after Native American activists forced their way past his secretary and confronted him in his office with the threat that if he went ahead with the talk, people would "get hurt." Polzer's offense? He had had the audacity to think of giving a public talk on Columbus's discovery that the Atlantic Ocean could be crossed from Europe, a voyage of exploration that fundamentally changed mankind's knowledge of the world's geography. But to think well of Columbus and his accomplishment was (and is) not politically correct. The only view of Columbus that the counter-culture will tolerate is that he led a genocidal, slave-dealing invasion of Europeans against the unwarring, slavery-free, environmentally-friendly inhabitants of the pre-1492 Americas. Therefore, Polzer had to be silenced. He had to be intimidated and forced to cancel his lecture, and he was.

Threats similar to those made against Father Polzer also prevented Linda Chavez, a former member of Ronald Reagan's White House staff and president of the Center for Equal Opportunity, from giving a speech at the University of Arizona. Who made the telephone threat that caused her to cancel her scheduled talk at the last minute was never discovered. At the appointed time in the auditorium where she was supposed to have delivered her speech, Mexican-American activists marched up and down the aisles of the auditorium carrying signs denouncing Chavez's betrayal of her race (la Raza). Finally, one of the protesters took the podium and announced to the audience that had shown up for her talk that it had been canceled. Some years before this, the well-known conservative William F. Buckley, Jr., was whacked in the face with a cream pie at the University of Arizona while leaving the podium after giving a talk. Such an outrage declares very clearly: "I was close enough to you to have done you bodily harm, and someday maybe I or somebody else with my politics will do just that." This kind of intimidation is very effective in discouraging any speech that expresses ideas contrary to the ideas of the counter-culture. But most often on today's politically correct campuses, it seems that invitations to speakers whose views are politically incorrect are simply not extended; thus such intimidation is seldom necessary.

In contemplating such matters, one immediately notices that left-wing extremists do not apply to themselves the concepts of sensitivity and tolerance that they insist their opponents respect. The use of double standards is inherent to the counter-culture movement because it is intent on destroying American culture. The counter-culture cannot use the same standard to judge both its own ideology and the beliefs of the American culture that it wishes to destroy.

Let us continue in the anecdotal vein to present unpublicized examples of how the counter-culture movement imposes its ideas. In 1990 all twelve professors on the creative-writing staff of the University of Arizona were called into the office of a vice president of the university and accused as a group of having "created a hostile sexual environment" for their students. When the professors naturally asked for particulars—the who, the what, and the when of the charge—they were told that that was "privileged" information that could not be divulged. Two of the professors understandably brought suit against the university for defamation and obtained favorable findings of fact from the Arizona Attorney General's office to use in their case. But the suit never went to trial. Dr. Annette Kolodny, the dean involved in the case (who as a graduate student at the University of California, Berkeley, in the 1960s was one of the leaders of the Vietnam War protests on that campus), had no evidence to present in court to prove that there had been even one instance of sexual harassment, let alone that the twelve professors were collectively guilty of creating a hostile sexual environment. After the professors who had taken legal action had expended a great deal of their time, money, and energy to defend themselves against a false accusation, the university settled out of court. The settlement barely covered the cost to the professors of their defense against this slander.

Most persons of course, when faced with the necessity of expensive legal proceedings to exonerate themselves from false accusations, are cowed by the prospect and back down. Mere accusation can usually achieve the purpose of intimidation. And a false accusation against an individual or group for an alleged workplace violation of some shibboleth of political correctness, once the accusation has been made, intimidates everyone in that class of persons. The threat is most effective when it is false. Everyone then understands that a person does not have to have actually done something reprehensible to be accused; therefore, everyone tries to be super-careful to obey the politically correct regulations, and to neither do nor say anything that could possibly be construed as politically incorrect. Once that sort of atmosphere has been created, and it is widely known that any hint of politically incorrect behavior will result in an accusation and sanctions, everyone then knows how they are supposed to behave, and as a result freedom of speech and common sense go out the window. Then, people start reporting each other for any and all appearances of violating politically correct behavior in order to curry favor with the managers of the politically correct regime. This sort of atmosphere of anxious conformity to an ideology is especially harmful at an institution like a university that is supposed to respect and foster freedom of thought and serve the search for truth rather than foster some program of social engineering and cultural change.

One more example of how the idea of perfection is imposed by the counter-culture movement. In June 1991 at Duke University, Larry Nelson, an assistant vice chancellor, was screening candidates to fill a position and made the observation to a subordinate who was helping him in the interviewing process that one of the candidates they had interviewed seemed to have "homosexual mannerisms." Six months after the position was filled, a confidential memo that included Nelson's remark was leaked to a weekly give-away newspaper known for its leftist views, which published excerpts from the memo. This prompted the president of Duke University to order an investigation into the matter. The investigation found that sexual discrimination had not affected who got the job and that the position had been offered to the best qualified candidate. Nonetheless, Nelson was punished by a month's suspension without pay (in effect a fine of thousands of dollars), required to take a course in sensitivity training, and ordered to perform community service at a local soup kitchen. The identity of the person who gave the memo to the newspaper never became public.

In light of these events, a Duke University professor of law, Donald L. Horowitz, was moved to write a letter, published on February 17, 1991, in the *Durham Herald–Sun*, on the draconian punishments that the university had imposed on one of its administrators for a remark made in private and in confidence and which, furthermore, had not affected a hiring decision. Professor Horowitz noted in his letter that such administrative behavior "smacked of the Chinese cultural revolution, of reeducation . . . in thought reform camps." And, he declared, "It is difficult to think of anything less appropriate for a university than to compel indoctrination."[5]

The atmosphere of political correctness at American universities and colleges today should not be principally attributed to left-wing extremists, however. The burden of responsibility for the situation rests primarily with university and college administrators who either agree with, and therefore welcome political correctness, or who are afraid to treat left-wing violators of free speech with the rigor with which they would treat anyone else who committed such excesses. Administrators fear criticism from left-wing zealots. They fear being labeled racist, sexist, or homophobic. And the special protection that politically correct behavior gets from cowardly administrators is giving America's future leaders (the undergraduates presently attending

American universities and colleges) the idea that they had better conform to the ideas of the counter-culture movement if they want to succeed in the world. Whatever particular subject they may be individually studying, all of today's undergraduates are getting an education in political correctness.

One often hears from the Left of the horrors of the so-called McCarthy era when for three months in 1954 Senator Joseph McCarthy conducted hearings in Washington in which he accused hundreds of Americans in positions of influence and authority, including high-ranking members of the State Department, of being communists or communist-sympathizers. However, the politically correct new Establishment has applied exactly the same tactics of false accusations and name-calling in institutions of higher education and other institutions in America, and is intimidating millions of young persons by these culturally damaging tactics. And these developments are not receiving even the amount of media coverage and reporting that the McCarthy era still receives. The disparity is inexplicable, considering the magnitude of political correctness and its much longer duration. The McCarthy era lasted less than a year before Senator McCarthy's fellow senators censured him and he lost his credibility. The false accusations, character assassinations, and browbeating by left-wing extremists today have been going on for decades and have become institutionalized. Now nearly every university and college has a well-staffed Affirmative Action Office to impose racial, ethnic, and gender quotas and to ensure conformity to that aspect of political correctness known as diversity, which is little more than a political spoils system.

As the sexual liberation, disrespect for property, and drug use promoted by the counter-culture movement in the 1960s to break down the belief-behaviors of American culture have become more widespread, greatly expanded campus police forces have become necessary to deal with such behaviors as rape, theft, vandalism, and substance abuse. The increase in police forces on the campuses of American universities reflects a general trend in American society. Gated communities and private uniformed police forces used to be quite rare in the United States; today such communities are common, and private police are visible everywhere in buildings and parking lots across America. Many ordinary businesses, not just large corporations, now find it necessary to hire uniformed guards to protect their customers, personnel, and facilities.

As American culture has been weakened, traditional moral standards have declined, and lawsuits have increased. The new morality is the promotion of political correctness. Politically correct regulations and laws have come to serve functions once performed by the common sense of right and wrong derived from the moral tradition of Christian ethics. In the last three decades of the twentieth century, the trend in America has been Less Morality, More Law. And a whole new field—expertise in secular morality—has had to be created to fill the void left by the decline of Christian morality. "Ethicists," as these secular experts are called, are now commonly hired as columnists and consultants in the print media to instruct business executives, members of various professions, and the general public on correct behavior.

Such phenomena were not part of American life before the 1960s. Nor were billboards and other advertisements offering the services of lawyers in evidence until recently. The ads that lawyers now place in the telephone directory of a city of 600,000 can run to 100 pages, many of them half-, full-, and even double-page ads, often in color. After decades of politically correct "victimology," almost everybody seems to be a victim deserving of recompense. Justified by the Procrustean standards of counter-culture perfectionism and stimulated by the astronomically high sums won by trial lawyers in suits against individuals and corporate America, more and more people feel the need to register a complaint and to take someone to court to get what they (the plaintiffs) "deserve."

Once political correctness has created an atmosphere of fear and intimidation, the perfectionist mentality and the programs it initiates are from that point on immune to criticism so far as the Left is concerned. Any proposal to curtail or abolish affirmative action, for instance, brings down on the head of the proposer a barrage of name-calling. Instead of engaging in debate, the Left engages in indignation. Anyone who dares to criticize or challenge politically correct doctrines and programs is dismissed out of hand as a sexist, a racist, a homophobe, or a fascist. Criticism of leftist ideas, so far as the Left is concerned, is taboo. Only by being protected by double standards that place them above criticism can politically correct ideas prevail. Larry Elder has astutely discussed this phenomenon in *The Ten Things You Can't Say in America*.[6]

Ideas that should not be criticized, according to the Left, include racism among people of color (only Americans descended from European stock can be racists); the responsibility of the poor for some of the poverty in their lives; the exemption of politically correct persons (even if they are rich) from the charge of greediness (only the politically incorrect can be greedy, an attitude that makes it expedient for Hollywood celebrities and many other wealthy persons to be politically correct); the responsibility of addicts to overcome their self-destructive behavior;[7] the proposition that every workplace and institution should reflect the composition of the population as a whole (except in the armed forces and professional sports, where individual competence is, as it should be in every endeavor, the primary consideration in hiring, firing, and promoting); the idea that money spent by the federal government is the root of all good; the usefulness of multicultural, bilingual, and sex-education programs in public schools; a mother's right to kill a healthy baby growing in her body (a woman may be said to be a mother from the moment she becomes pregnant, because from that moment on she is nurturing a human life); the celebration (not just tolerance) of homosexuality; and the suppression of religious belief in public places (supposedly in the name of religious freedom and the separation of church and state). Those are among the things that the Left considers closed to discussion. A debate requires respect for one's opponent. Persons who are politically correct and active in promoting the counter-culture rarely exhibit such respect.

The desire for systematic perfection played a minor role in the cultural history of America prior to the last four decades. But it has existed ever since twenty thousand Puritans settled around Massachusetts Bay in the 1630s to create a society under the authority of a single church, membership in which would be a requirement for voting and holding governmental office. But such planned perfection—in that case, a theocracy—did not work in America where the freedom and opportunity for individuals to pursue their own interests beckoned from every thicket and vista of the unsettled wilderness, and by 1692 the excesses of the Puritan experiment in theocracy ended in failure with the Salem witch trials. The impulse to institute perfection did not, however, vanish with the collapse of the Puritan theocracy. Various utopian communities were organized here and there across America during the 1700s and 1800s, but most of these communities did not outlive their founders.

In the late nineteenth century, the spirit of perfectionism manifested itself in a remarkable way in a novel written by a descendant of seventeenth-century Massachusetts Puritans. The novel Edward Bellamy (1850–1898) wrote envisioned a fully perfected society. His utopian fiction, which became a nationwide bestseller, exemplifies the desire to impose systematic control over individual freedom that typifies today's counter-culture. Bellamy titled his work (published in 1888) *Looking Backward, 2000–1887* because it described the wonderful society that he imagined could exist in the United States by the year 2000. *Looking Backward* is a classic embodiment of the mindset that looks to the future for the advent of a permanent golden age. In Bellamy's fictional society, perfection has been achieved, and the reader looks back from the vantage of that enlightened perspective on the benighted days of the late nineteenth century before perfection had been attained.

Looking Backward addressed a problem known in the 1880s as "the Labor Question." This was the decade that saw the rise of the Standard Oil Company and the United States Steel Corporation, the organization of big labor unions, strikes that often turned bloody, the use of "corporate armies," and the appearance of an organization of coal miners turned terrorists that called itself "the Molly Maguires." What should be done in an age of huge, impersonal corporations to secure the rights of American workers? Bellamy coined the terms *nationalize* and *nationalization* in formulating his thinking on that question. In the perfect future society that he envisioned, the federal government has taken over (nationalized) all industry and agriculture and runs the country's economic system as a single corporation for the good of the people rather than for profit. Capitalism is no longer permitted in the America of the year 2000 that Bellamy imagined. The government issues everyone a credit card each year, and whatever goods and services a person consumes are charged against this "generous" allowance that is the same for everyone. There is no private property. Nor is there unemployment, poverty, taxation, illiteracy, an army, a navy, or any wars. There are no banks, lawyers, classes, political parties, general elections, or state governments. (Municipal governments are responsible for "comfort and entertainment.") Likewise, private education, buying and selling, advertising, public or personal debt, and private savings accounts are not permitted. Insanity, suicide, and crime have become almost nonexistent, and the rare offenses against one's fellow citizens and the system that do occur are regarded as "atavism" and treated as mental illness.

Comprehensive laws have established this system, and Congress meets only once every five years to make minor adjustments to it. (No law can be voted on in the session of Congress in which it is proposed.) An "international council" has been formed of representatives from Australia and the nations in Europe and the Americas that have adopted the new economic order, and the development of "a federal union of worldwide extent" is underway. In short, "the science of wealth and happiness" has triumphed in the United States because everything has been organized under the authority of the national government, which employs everyone. The U.S. Constitution has been abrogated, because the previous system of intrafederal and federal-state checks and balances is no longer needed. All power has been concentrated in the executive branch of the federal government.

In the America of the year 2000 that Bellamy imagined in 1887, education is free and compulsory up to the age of twenty-one. Then every American male and female enters the lowest rank of either "the industrial army" that produces all the goods and services in America (except food), or becomes a worker on one of the government's nationalized farms. (Point 8 at the end of the second chapter of Karl Marx and Frederick Engels's *The Communist Manifesto*, published forty years before Bellamy's novel, speaks of "industrial armies" being established with the advent of a communist culture.) After three years of service as common laborers in the industrial army or on one of the government's collectivized farms, each worker chooses the occupation he or she wishes to work at and is best suited for. (In the new social order, women have perfect equality in their choice of occupations, but a separate "woman's corps" in the industrial army, with its own regulations and commanded by its own elected female general, has been deemed necessary to take into account the menstruation and "maternal duties" of women.) The state requires only twenty-five years of labor service from everyone. And because the system provides "cradle to grave" (Bellamy's phrase) welfare, average life expectancy in America has gone up to eighty-five years. Thus most workers after their retirement can look forward to forty years of leisure for "refined pursuits." (It is perhaps worth noting that in this regimented society, bad manners are liable to punishment meted out by a judge.) Individuals who demonstrate extraordinary competence and have been promoted to the highest of the nine ranks of labor are not required to retire, however, after their twenty-five-year stints of compulsory national service, but can be elected by their peers to five-year terms as the judges and managers of the system. When their managerial or judicial terms expire, one of these gifted workers is elected president of the United States for five years (renewable once).

Edward Bellamy liked this vision of a perfect future. And apparently so did a good many other Americans who bought his novel, which had a remarkable sale of over one million copies when the population of the United States was only sixty-three million. Within a few years of its publication, more than 160 clubs had been organized nationwide to discuss the ideas in *Looking Backward*. Likewise, a monthly magazine (*The New Nation*) and several newspapers were established for the explicit purpose of promoting Bellamy's vision of a socialist utopia and convincing the reading public that it was attainable if only enough Americans of good will would commit themselves to the effort of making it happen.[8] And in the 1892 national election, a political party that had been founded under the inspiration of the ideas set forth in *Looking Backward* elected the governors of three states.

The popularity of this utopian fiction probably stemmed from the fact that the perfect "equality of condition" that it described was said to have been brought about without any bloodshed through the peaceful process of nationalization. By gradually eliminating capitalism, the national government had arranged a totally rationalized economic system that delivered to Americans everything they needed, when they wanted it, without injuring anyone by its production and distribution.

In the final pages of *Looking Backward*, a sermon delivered by a Boston minister (the novel is set in Boston, the capital of Bellamy's native state) points the moral that the author wanted to make certain every reader of the novel understood. In this sermon, the minister tells us that the new society represents "[the effects of] a changed environment upon human nature." He explains to his listeners that America was "founded on the pseudo-self-interest of selfishness," which appealed solely to "the antisocial and brutal side of human nature," and that that old society has been replaced by "institutions based on the true self-interest of . . . the social and generous instincts of men." This sermon contains the kernel of the Marxism that so attracted Edward Bellamy. He saw no horrors and only good in a totally regimented society and a planned culture. His was the politics of every other revolutionary since Jean-Jacques Rousseau: change the environment of human beings, and all will be well with mankind.

This sort of thinking also animated the counter-culture movement of the 1960s, whose seedbed was the decades between the world wars of the twentieth century when the Soviet Union was organized, the then new social science and political science departments in American universities were attracting public attention, and John Dewey wrote his *Liberalism and Social Action* calling for social engineering. The image of a future socialist utopia that Edward Bellamy presented to the American reading public in the late nineteenth century in his popular utopian novel *Looking Backward* represents the unending allure of the idea of achieving perfection someday. (Seymour Martin Lipset and Gary Marks explain in *It Didn't Happen Here* why socialism has never taken root in the United States and become an ordering principle of American society.[9])

In the nineteenth century, however, Bellamy's fellow New Englander Nathaniel Hawthorne (1804–1864), who was also a descendant of seventeenth-century Puritan ministers in Massachusetts, represented the mainstream of American cultural history when he satirized in several of his short stories the pernicious nature of utopian schemes for perfection. Hawthorne regarded human nature as flawed and fallen. Perhaps at some earlier time in his history, man may have had a perfectly noble nature, but the cause of sin in the present day could not be traced to any environmental deficiency. That cause, Hawthorne was convinced, lay in man himself. Hawthorne's short stories, "Earth's Holocaust," "The Celestial Railroad," and "The Birthmark" particularly expose the folly of relying on science and technology or any systematic change to the political, economic, and social environment as a remedy for man's disposition to sin. A more transcendent remedy than socialism, government, or science was necessary, Hawthorne thought, to redeem mankind from its sinfulness.

CHAPTER FOUR

Class Struggle vs. the Responsible Individual

The flaw in the revolutionary's concept of planned perfection is that no one can be sure a permanent, utopian perfection is humanly attainable. The revolutionary must accept on faith that salvation through political action is possible. And to protect himself from any doubt on that score, he must be uncompromising in his dedication to the correctness of his faith.

The revolutionary hates the existing culture and loves the perfect culture in his mind. His dilemma is that while it is easy to hate what is, it is not so easy to love what does not yet exist. A saintly Christian, Muslim, or Jew does not have to create God's perfection and can be joyous, content, and thankful in his contemplation and worship of God's perfection, as long as he does not disturb his peace of mind by trying to force his faith on others. The notion of "a Christian revolutionary" is self-contradictory because the saintly are at peace with their God, even in the midst of persecution. A revolutionary, on the other hand, is never at peace, never full of praise, thanksgiving, or grace, because the revolutionary loves an idea that has no present reality. His idea of a perfect future requires from him unrelenting effort to bring it about.

Dedicated revolutionaries find happiness in accusing their enemies (i.e., whoever disagrees with their intention to create perfection) of being mendacious, atavistic, and unintelligent. In other words, they find happiness in belittling people with different ideas than theirs. They have nothing but scorn for whoever thinks peace and justice are possible without a revolutionary change in culture. As the history of twentieth-century communism shows, the dedicated revolutionary is quite willing to wade through blood to reach the land of promised perfection. If that is required, so be it. Whatever blood must be shed is justified by the revolution's good intentions.

To construct a culture according to the blueprint of a revolutionary ideology, whole classes of persons within a society must be induced to reject the cultural norms of behavior in their society. These classes must be alienated from their culture and made to transfer their allegiance to the idea of the new culture. In other words, to initiate and sustain a counter-culture movement, whole classes of persons must become conscious of class grievances. They must be made to feel they have suffered injuries at the hands of other classes of persons. Otherwise there can be no class struggle. And without class struggle, there is no chance of building the projected new culture. Raising class consciousness is therefore the indispensable first step in the long march to the planned future. To put the matter in the simplest terms, the culture war is a war of class hatred.

But the revolutionary method of arousing class hatred encounters serious problems when applied to American culture and its history. From the beginning of its history, the overwhelming majority of America's population has descended from immigrants who left their grievances behind them in Europe (and elsewhere) to start life over again in America. America represented for them the chance to build a better future for themselves as *individuals*. The self-selected immigrants who came to America by their own free choice came as hopeful individuals in search of opportunities to improve their individual lives. Among the things they fled in leaving Europe were the limitations of the class-membership that typified Europe's aristocratic cultures. They wanted to belong to a new society that would encourage their *individual* aspirations of self-improvement and their ambition to rise in society. They did not undergo the trauma of leaving their native place for the chance of staying in the same class of society they belonged to in Europe.

In Europe before the twentieth century, birth defined one's class membership. And the ruling classes in European societies consisted of men and women who thought of their blood (or descent) as "noble," while everyone else's blood (and descent) they said was "common." These ruling classes looked upon anyone who was not of their class as inherently inferior. But in America there was no ruling class based on birth. There were no leisured men and women with titles who lorded it over everyone else and lived off the labor of others because of their supposedly noble blood. In the American wilderness, everyone had to work. To have high social standing meant doing something useful. Being born into the highest rank of society did not define respectability. Nor did it convey any inheritable entitlement to govern.

Even if an immigrant failed to achieve through his accomplishments a higher social status in America than he had had in Europe, even if he and his offspring remained on the lowest rung of free men, immigration to America was usually worth the effort and the sacrifices it required. Because the demand for manual labor in America historically has exceeded the number of available laborers for hire, the wages paid to laborers have historically been higher than in Europe. (The shortage of available laborers for hire was one of the principal causes of the introduction of slavery into America; see my *American Beliefs: What Keeps a Big Country and a Diverse People United*, 54–59, for a discussion of that development.) Moreover, food was more abundant and cheaper in America, taxes were lower, and land was available for purchase at a much lower price than in Europe. Thus, even immigrants who remained in the lowest economic class of free men in America were better off than persons in the lowest class in Europe. And immigrants to America, or their offspring, who were diligent workers usually did improve their lives to some degree and not infrequently rose to a higher place in society than they or their ancestors had been born into in Europe. For all of these reasons, plus the much greater religious and political freedom to be found in America, immigrants kept coming to America in increasing numbers, even after attempts were made in the late nineteenth century to limit immigration. Immigration to America has in fact been the largest movement of human beings to a single destination in the history of the world.

The slaves brought by force from Africa to America and their descendants never comprised anywhere near a majority in American society, as slaves did in Brazil for 350 years. Complete statistics are unavailable prior to the first U.S. Census in 1790 but reliable estimates indicate that slaves probably averaged 12 percent of the American population from the 1660s when chattel slavery was institutionalized in colonial Virginia until the institution's abolition in the 1860s. In being the only class of persons in American society whose social status was fixed by birth, slaves were an anomaly in American culture. The first black immigrants to America were from the islands of the Caribbean; they came as freemen and contract workers (indentured servants) as did about half of the white immigrants in the seventeenth and eighteenth centuries. These self-selected black immigrants were motivated by the same desire to improve their lives that motivated white indentured servants.[1] But once slavery was established, the slave minority in the American population could scarcely hope to improve their social standing through their labor and an accumulation of savings. Slavery was un-American because self-determined improvement of one's lot in life was the purpose of immigration to America.

Yet even under the handicap of chattel slavery, a few slaves did work their way out of slavery and achieve the status of free men. To give slaves with special skills such as cabinetry and brick-making a reason to do good work, which increased the value to their owners of their for-hire labor, such slaves were often allowed to keep a small portion of the money they earned for their master or mistress. And some of these highly skilled slaves, through extraordinary self-discipline over the course of many years, saved enough from their meager earnings to purchase their freedom from their owners. Once free and able to work for themselves, these exceptional, self-emancipated former slaves then often saved, much more quickly, further sums from the earnings of their self-employment to purchase loved ones out of slavery too. Although there were never many of these self-emancipated former slaves, the fact that there were any at all demonstrates the reality of the opportunities in America for anyone with enough imagination to see them and enough diligence to take advantage of them. Most importantly, however, the accomplishments of these extraordinary individuals who overcame their enslavement proved that the immigrants brought to America from Africa against their will were not an inferior class of human beings fit only to be kept in permanent bondage.

Social classes of course existed in America. But in America (except for the slave class), class membership was not fixed. Individuals were continually rising to a higher class than that into which they had been born, while persons born into the higher classes could fall below those of their birth. It was by no means a foregone conclusion that a person born in poverty in America would remain poor or that someone born to the middle or upper class would remain there. The freedom that led to upward social mobility could also lead downward. Life in America was not a one-way street assuring every American of a more prosperous, higher social status. Living in American society was no guarantee of a particular outcome. Rather, the extraordinary freedom this society offered was merely the most important circumstance that allowed a wider range of opportunities to be pursued in America than in other societies.

From the historical circumstances of life in the society of self-selected immigrants and their descendants that developed in America between 1610 and 1770, certain habits of behavior arose expressing the beliefs of the more than 85 percent of the society that was free. The following ideas, by being acted on during those eight generations, became cultural beliefs:

Improvement is possible.
Opportunities must be imagined.
Society is a collection of individuals.

Achievement determines social rank.
Every person's success improves society.
Every person is responsible for his own well-being.

These historical beliefs comprised a principle of responsible individualism. As long as a majority of Americans in each generation acted upon this cultural principle, it would be impossible to maintain the sort of class hatred necessary to sustain a class struggle because no strong class consciousness could be maintained when the principle of responsible individualism was acted upon. Therefore, in the attempt to alienate young Americans from their culture, the first imperative of the counter-culture movement in the 1960s was to discredit these six cultural beliefs and to propose ideas antithetical to them.

The ideas that the counter-culture has proposed and since the 1960s has induced a considerable portion of the American people to accept as true are the following:

Improvement is impossible without government help.
The government must provide opportunities.
Society is a collection of classes.
The privileges of birth determine social rank.
Those who succeed do so by oppressing others.
Society is responsible for everyone's well-being.

In recent decades too many Americans, especially those who occupy positions of influence, have accepted these counter-culture ideas. Consequently, the counter-culture's principle of collective responsibility is on its way to replacing American culture's principle of individual responsibility.

To make the counter-culture ideology plausible required rewriting America's unique history, a history that includes millions upon millions of individual success stories and the creation of a continent-sized nation from a Stone Age wilderness in just three centuries (1600–1900). The new history of America produced by the counter-culture movement is based on the ideas of class-dominance, oppression, and victimization. This revision of American history began to be promoted in the 1960s and 1970s. Once American history became a "myth" and enough influential Americans had accepted the idea of victimization as the whole truth of that history, and once that idea had been institutionalized in American public schools, colleges, and universities, this new, revised concept of American history promoted a sense of class struggle.

The lowest economic class of persons in American society was a natural recruiting ground for class consciousness. But, as noted, the poor in America in most cases did not think of their poverty as a fixed, inescapable condition. Many of them aspired to become property owners or to otherwise improve their lives, and most worked hard to do so. This has been especially true of immigrants and their children. Also, some of the American lower class had once belonged to the middle class, and hoped to regain that status. It has made little sense to most Americans to defer their individual ambitions and commit themselves to working for a cultural change that allegedly was the necessary preliminary to improving their lives. American culture's emphasis on individual striving and individual responsibility made the American lower class an unreliable source of recruits for class struggle.

Something more fixed than economic status was needed to create the class consciousness necessary for class struggle in America, something more explicit, stable, and unequivocal than class as defined by comparative wealth and poverty.

Biological categories fit that need exactly. The first biological group that might be recruited as a class for the class struggle was, naturally, the descendants of the former slaves. Up to 1970, most black Americans for five generations (1870–1970), regardless of their individual talents and achievements, had been largely excluded from integrated participation in American society. The three amendments to the Constitution that had abolished slavery and given black Americans equal civil rights with white Americans were ratified in 1865, 1868, and 1870. But black Americans had nonetheless been generally subjected to social segregation and economic discrimination. Therefore, they as a biological class had ample reason to be fed up with the status quo in America in 1970. But the civil rights movement led by Martin Luther King, Jr., that began in America in the late 1950s and continued until his death in 1968 was not based on class hatred. It was based on Christian forgiveness, and it asked only that black Americans be allowed the same chance to prove themselves as individuals that white Americans had historically enjoyed. That movement, unlike the counter-culture movement, was an appeal to the individual consciences of their fellow Americans.

Martin Luther King's foursquare American belief in individual responsibility and equal freedom, however, was hijacked by a call for "black power" and "black separatism" after his assassination in 1968. A militant left-wing organization that called itself the Black Panthers urged armed revolt and set the tone for an aggressive racism among black Americans. The Panthers were committed to black segregation and black racial preferences. Theirs was a spirit little different from the white segregation and white entitlements that King had preached against, most memorably in his "I Have a Dream" sermon delivered in 1963 to a mass audience gathered in front of the Lincoln Memorial in Washington, D.C., and via television to the nation at large. The racism of the Black Panthers was the antithesis of the objectives of King's civil rights movement.

But even if every black American could have been roused to hate every white American as his oppressor, which was of course never a possibility, the black Americans in the United States would still have fallen well short of the number of class-conscious haters that the counter-culture movement needed to sustain a class struggle. To accomplish that revolutionary goal, something at least on the order of 20 percent of the American population would have to be alienated to some degree from their American culture. And in 1970 black Americans made up only 11.1 percent of the nation's population; thirty years later, in the U.S. 2000 census, they were still only 12.1 percent of the population.[2]

The historical grievances of Americans who descended from the aboriginal inhabitants of the central part of North America that became the United States of America offered another biological recruiting ground for the counter-culture movement. But again, even if every American of aboriginal ancestry could have had his consciousness "raised" to the point of class hatred of their fellow white Americans, they comprised just under .004 percent of the population (783,000 out of 203,200,000 people in 1970).[3] The combination of the two biological groups—Negroes, Afro-Americans, or African Americans (the designation changed as the class consciousness of these Americans was raised another notch), and Indians, Amerinds, or Native Americans as they were variously referred to by the Left before Native Americans was settled on as the politically correct reference—still fell short of the necessary numbers needed to sustain an assault on American culture. Nor could a sufficient recruitment be had from raising the consciousness of Hispanics or Latinos as they were called—with their bewildering array of sub-groups: Mexican Americans, Central Americans, Cuban Americans, and so forth—who were of several races and mixes of races. (It is interesting to note in this regard that in the 1970 U.S. census Latinos or Hispanics do not appear as a category of persons. They had not yet been invented as a biological-political category.)

The big breakthrough for the counter-culture movement came in the 1970s. It was then that the single-largest biological segment of the American population—104,640,000 females (51 percent of the population in 1970)—

became politically defined as a minority. In 1973 a radical political action group, the National Organization of Women (NOW), published a twenty-one-page manifesto titled "Revolution: Tomorrow Is NOW." Part II, section A.8 of this manifesto demanded that the federal government's General Services Administration, Small Business Administration, Department of Commerce, and "all such federal programs, now or in the future, define the word 'minority' to include women of all races." And this demand was soon enacted into federal law, because a majority of congressmen were anxious to prove they were not sexist. (The complete text of "Revolution: Tomorrow Is NOW" may be found as appendix 2 in Phyllis Schlafly's *The Power of the Positive Woman*.[4])

The consciousness of American women began to be raised in the 1960s, but it was not until the 1970s that militant feminists increased the number of biologically defined minorities in the ranks of the counter-culture movement to the point that making a sustained assault on American culture became possible. With a sizable portion of this "minority," which was really the largest segment of American society, recruited into the ranks of the counter-culture movement and aroused to self-conscious militancy, a large enough coalition of biological classes—disaffected blacks, Indians, Hispanics, and women—existed to seriously attempt the replacement of American culture. And at the heart of this coalition's protest was the idea of an eventual equality of condition. It was typical of counter-culture tactics, however, that the up-front demand was an appeal to something American: equality of opportunity.

The protest was made first for black Americans, female Americans, Indian Americans, and Hispanic Americans, and later on for homosexuals (perhaps as much as 4 percent of the American population), homosexuality both male and female being said to be an unalterable, irresistible biological condition. Occasionally, demands were also made in the name of Asian Americans, who were, however, as recent immigrants, generally too enamored with America's individualistic culture of hope and opportunity to participate in the counter-culture movement that cast women, blacks, Hispanics, and homosexuals in the role of victims of oppression.

The biological-political melodrama of victimization, of course, required a villain. White male Americans were cast in the biological-political role of victimizers, and as a biological class were identified as the dominant oppressor of all other biological classes in America. For this reason, they had to have their power to oppress wrested from them, and the biological classes they oppressed had to be empowered. That was the scenario of the melodrama of victimization. And according to the radical feminists who promised to militantly confront the dominant class and liberate women from their condition of victimization, men generally, regardless of their race, were oppressive as lovers, as husbands, as fathers, and even as providers and protectors. Since truth was of no concern to the counter-culture movement, unless truth happened to coincide with its political goals, there was nothing amiss in this gross falsification of American history that made all males the enemies of every other person in society (even their wives and daughters). It was politically necessary, and therefore correct. The idea of a biologically defined class oppressing other biological classes created the necessary class-consciousness for class struggle. Truthfulness was irrelevant.

The counter-culture movement demanded group rights and group entitlements. Not surprisingly in a culture such as America's, with its emphasis on individual striving and success, anyone who fell short of these cultural expectations might be attracted to an ideology that rejected individual responsibility and made society responsible for a person's failures. Furthermore, it was certainly true that prejudice (the prejudging of individuals according to some class stereotype) had undoubtedly denied, on the basis of pure prejudice, some meritorious individuals the chance to pursue happiness on their own individual terms. So the accusation of the counter-culture movement against American culture that it excluded some biological classes from opportunities that should have been theirs had some legitimacy, even though the categorical villainy attributed to white males as a biological class was flagrantly untrue.

Who were the recruiters for this culture war who enlisted women, blacks, Indian Americans, Hispanics, and homosexuals in the class struggle? These leading militant activists dedicated to the replacement of American culture were, apart from some European socialists who had immigrated to America around the time of World War II, native-born Americans. They were the ideological heirs of Edward Bellamy (d. 1898), Jack London (d. 1916), Eugene V. Debs (d. 1926), W. E. B. DuBois (d. 1963), and Norman Thomas (d. 1968). In other words, they were American socialists who believed in the necessity of creating a new political and social system in America, either through peaceful means, as in Bellamy's novel *Looking Backward*, or, as imagined in Jack London's novel *The Iron Heel*, through the use of guns and dynamite.

World War II had put on hold the New Deal programs begun in the 1930s in response to the Great Depression. The *new* New Deal undertaken in the 1960s and 1970s was in important ways a reprise of the 1930s New Deal. It depended on the same kind of programmatic federal initiatives, enormous expenditures of public money, and federal controls to redress social wrongs and achieve wholesale social justice. But the scale of the spending and the range of initiatives in the New Deal of the 1960s dwarfed the New Deal of the 1930s. Furthermore, the new New Deal of the 1960s had no connection to any economic crisis, as the old New Deal had had. The Great Society and War on Poverty programs of the 1960s, as they were called, aimed to create a new society in a time of prosperity through the massive redistribution of tax dollars.[5]

By 1993 the new New Deal that began in 1965 with the Great Society initiatives of President Lyndon Johnson had expended *5.4 trillion dollars* on social welfare programs. (Supposing a billion dollars to equal a volume of money the size of the Empire State Building, 5.4 trillion dollars would be the island of Manhattan with 5,400 stacks of money that big on it.) This unimaginable amount of money was "some 70 percent greater than the price tag for defeating Germany and Japan in World War II, after adjusting for inflation."[6] Not even the wealth of the United States could sustain such fantastic outlays of money indefinitely without financial ruin, and by the late 1990s the scale of new welfare commitments began to be reduced somewhat. The reduction was needed not only because increasing the size of the federal welfare pot could not continue indefinitely, but even more importantly, because the so-called War on Poverty and the Great Society that the social welfare programs initiated during the presidency of Lyndon Johnson had led "only to higher spending and escalating social problems." By subsidizing "non-work and non-marriage" for thirty years, the federal government achieved "massive increases in both."[7]

The words *victim* and *victimize* came into widespread use in America roughly between 1965 and 1985. It was in those two decades that American society and its history were redefined in the thinking of a significant number of influential Americans. For them, American society was no longer a collection of individuals striving to improve their individual lives in self-determining, practical ways. It became, instead, a society of aggrieved, biologically defined classes of victims united only by their hostility toward a biologically defined ruling class that was their common enemy. This enemy was defined with great clarity. Militant feminists at the outset of the counter-culture movement called the enemy "male chauvinist pigs." As the movement to replace American culture with a politically correct ideology gained adherents and strength, the oppressive enemy was given the blander, broader label of "dominant white males."

The totality of the counter-culture movement's rewriting of American history had a breathtaking scope. Naturally, those who want to depict American culture as oppressive never comment on the fact that over sixty million immigrants representing nearly every race, language, and nation on earth—both men and women—have chosen to come to the United States, this alleged land of oppression, during the past four centuries. Nor do they take into account the fact that the rate of immigration is increasing rather than diminishing. How could this be? Why would tens of millions of immigrants have kept on coming, both legally and illegally, over a period of so many successive generations, in search of opportunities that those who reject American culture say do not exist? That fundamental question is inconvenient to the ideology of victimization, which insists that America is a land of oppression. Yet the volume of immigration to America is indisputable. So is the fact that a great many of the immigrants and their offspring succeed in America—otherwise the immigration would not have continued nor would America have acquired the largest middle class of any nation in the modern world. But because these salient facts do not conform to the politically correct vision of American history as a story of endless oppression, they have to be denied or ignored. Similarly, the fact that slavery, cannibalism, and warfare all existed in America before 1492 is politically incorrect and must be denied or ignored. The most politically correct idea is that Columbus and the white, male Europeans who followed him across the Atlantic after his first voyage to America introduced these evils to the Americas. To counter-culture activists, the American continents were a sinless paradise before the coming of Europeans. Neither is there in the counter-culture version of American history any useful truth in another salient fact of American history, the fact that the descendants of the tens of millions of immigrants to America representing innumerable ethnicities and languages chose to meld into a single nationality speaking one language. The unifying effect of American culture is likewise inconvenient to mention.

These paramount features of American history—the unprecedented volume of migration to America and the melding of persons of many cultures and languages into a unilingual new society having a single, unifying culture—have no usefulness to persons on the Far Left and their sympathizers.

The reclassification as either a victim or a victimizer of everyone in a society that in 1970 numbered over 200 million was stupefying in its enormity as a revision of American history. Today, with the current population of the United States well on its way to becoming 300 million, it is even more so. This is prejudice on a colossal scale and with a vengeance. Every trace of individuality disappears into the vortex of the idea of victims and victimizers and the need for a biological-political class struggle. The uniqueness of individuals and their life stories no longer counts for anything. All individuality is swallowed up by the abstract ideology of oppression and victimization and disappears, just as America's history of assimilating the world's largest migration into a new society, with a new culture, vanishes into nothingness.

In the 1960s and 1970s, America was transformed for political purposes from a land of opportunity into a land of oppression. This new image of America agreed with Karl Marx's analysis of European history as class struggle. Almost overnight, Marx's allegedly scientific understanding of history became American history. And the truth of American history became myth. Suddenly, American history reflected only the kinds of ills analyzed in Marxist theory. Suddenly, there was nothing about American history to distinguish it from Europe's history of ruling classes determined by birth; unwritten constitutions; differentiated group rights and privileges; inquisitions; pogroms; political purges; executions for religious heterodoxy; chronic wars between princedoms, dukedoms, and nations; and recurring famines, peasant uprisings, dynastic wars, and religious wars. Suddenly, there was nothing at all distinctive about American history to differentiate it from that history, which tens of millions of lower- and middle-class Europeans over the course of the seventeenth, eighteenth, nineteenth, and twentieth centuries had fled to build a new life for themselves and their descendants in America. Suddenly, anyone who proposed that the history of the United States differed fundamentally from the history of Europe was guilty of something the American Left called "exceptionalism." This term had been part of the vocabulary of the Left in the 1930s (see John Dos Passos's memoir *The Best Times*, chap. 5), and it came back into use among American academics in the 1970s. "Exceptionalism" was the label the Left put on anyone's claim that American history is an exception to the history of other countries in North America, Europe, and South America. The politically correct view of American history has been that it is just what Marx had said the history of Europe was: class struggle.

The idea that a nation with the largest and most prosperous middle class ever seen in history is a land of oppression is, of course, preposterous. It is also full of inherent contradictions. From the perspective of political correctness, white men are oppressors unless they happen to be Hispanic, in which case they are oppressed. Black American males are both victims in being black and oppressors of women in being males. Asian Americans are sometimes said to be among the oppressed even though they exhibit an extraordinarily high level of achievement and are generally prosperous and upwardly mobile. Male homosexuals belong at one and the same time to the categories of the oppressed (homosexuals) and the oppressors (men). All black Americans, Hispanic Americans, Indian Americans, and female Americans, if they are not homosexual, are "homophobic." And women—regardless of whether they are white, black, Hispanic, married, single, widowed, divorced, impoverished, rich, lesbian, or "straight"—become a vast sisterhood, united by their victimhood, that must rise up as one against their wicked male oppressors. (Within this minority, which in fact is the largest segment of the American population, there are, it has been said by radical feminists, categories of "minority women" who suffer "double oppression."[8]) The supreme contradiction perhaps lies in the fact that a large portion of the activists in the counter-culture movement have been white males. But their correct politics has exempted them from being treated and referred to as belonging to the biological-political class of oppressors.

Of course, each of these biological-political classes has within it persons who are poor and persons who are rich. But poverty is no longer necessarily the principal sign or defining characteristic of being oppressed so far as the ideology of the counter-culture movement is concerned. America is a rich country whose huge middle class has historically been well-off, and in the history of the United States this largest class of persons in American society has not been in a permanent condition of poverty. Hence, it has been expedient to identify the oppressed in biological terms. Oppression in this movement is a state of mind and a biological condition. If a person belongs to a biological category other than white males, then he or she is oppressed. If persons within one of the biological classes that are allegedly oppressed by white males are unaware of being oppressed, then they have to be taught that they are. That, of course, is the point of sensitivity training and consciousness raising and of the various women's studies, black studies, and gay studies programs that have been introduced into American schools and institutions of higher learning since the 1960s.

At both ends of the redefinition of America as a land of oppression are other biological categories—children and the elderly—that are also allegedly victimized. Besides their general victimization as children, female children are, predictably, as females, also victims of sexual harassment and bullying by their fellow children who are male. And (at least theoretically) elderly males dominate elderly females.

The revisionist idea of America as the land of oppression was wonderfully total. Because of its uniformity, one might almost call it scientific. But it produces a great many inanities: a high-school student who, because he bears his blue-eyed Cuban mother's maiden name as his middle name, is classified a Hispanic and consequently given a federally-funded bus pass to get back and forth to school because, according to political correctness, as a Hispanic he must be oppressed and in need of help, even though both of his parents have PhDs and are middle-class homeowners; an upper-class black family's children, who have had every advantage of an expensive private-school education, being given preference in admission to Ivy League universities because presumably at least some, if not all, of their 128 great-great-great-great-great grandparents were slaves, and consequently, persons with that biological background, no matter what their parents' actual achievements might be, need preferential treatment; or, a couple of elderly retirees worth millions of dollars who have their medical care subsidized by the federal government just because of their age. These indiscriminate reductions of individuals to biologically defined classes make sense only as the indispensable accompaniment of counter-culture ideas.

Regardless of race, gender, age, or sexuality, anyone who resists the classification of individuals into oppressed biological categories is regarded as an enemy and mercilessly subjected to verbal abuse by the Left. The reason for this contradiction is plain: anyone who insists on their individuality poses a serious threat to the all-encompassing paradigm of victims and victimizers. They have to be denounced for their deviant thinking and betrayal of their biological-political classification. No American today could expect to receive a respectful hearing if, for instance, she dared to declare in a public meeting that sexual harassment regulations have harmed both women and men because of the suspicions and antagonisms they have aroused. And even a lesbian would be hooted down if she said that many young Americans are being given, just because of their race or "ethnicity," high-school diplomas that will get them admitted to state universities when in truth they lack the skills and knowledge needed to pursue a higher education. A black American, whether male or female, would likewise be derided if he or she pointed out that there is no evidence at all that diversity in workplaces or in classrooms improves job performance and learning. (No one acquires a better knowledge of mathematics or English from studying them with a diverse mix of fellow students.) And if a Hispanic woman were brave enough to declare in public that bilingual education is an impediment to success in America and ought not to be publicly funded, she would certainly be denounced. Such a bold speaker would be shouted down as soon as the politically incorrect nature of her remarks became evident.

The most scathing scorn of the Left is reserved for those who refuse to be cast in the role of victim. Imagine a black American male denying that he is oppressed and that every member of his race needs special help to succeed in the world. Disgraceful! Such persons are traitors to their biological-political class. They are un-racist!

Faced with the vehemence of political correctness, only the strongest-minded persons openly criticize the scenario of victimization that has been scripted and directed by the Left and that continues to be applauded by those who fear the consequences of not applauding it. A large part of the American public, however, may either be only vaguely aware of the implications of this political morality play or may think it too silly to deserve their attention. They may in some instances tolerate it as a fad that will eventually pass away, like other fads, and that does not therefore (they think) seriously affect them or do anyone any lasting harm. Such judgments are a mistake.

As absurd as the melodrama of victims and victimizers is as a distortion of American history, it has nonetheless been enacted into law and institutionalized at an enormous cost in both money and distorted social relations. It has caused, is causing, and will continue to cause serious cultural damage in America until people stop applauding it as the whole truth of American history. The changes that the Left has been able to make to American law and the Left's tireless repetition of its ideology have conditioned most American politicians and a good many other people of good will to think only in terms of class struggle. Even though in their hearts most Americans know that the politically correct melodrama of victims and victimizers is a stage-production of Marxist theory, they remain uncritical of it because they do not want to be called racist or sexist if they denounce it.

Left-wing intimidators have been especially effective, it seems, in gaining the support of the party of Franklin Delano Roosevelt (the Democrats) which in the early decades of the twentieth century showed a proclivity for villainizing the uppermost echelons of the American upper class. But some members of the party of Theodore Roosevelt (the Republicans) have not been behindhand in embracing the Marxian rewriting of American history as a tale of misery and oppression that cries out for social justice and a wholesale redistribution of wealth. In the morality play of victims and victimizers, plain justice has little significance. What the counter-culture movement calls for is social justice. According to its ideology, American culture has been found guilty of racism, sexism, homophobia, and general oppression. Anyone who reveres and acts on the beliefs of American culture is a right-wing extremist.

If a story is to engage tens of millions of people, it must have a simple, clear plot. The scenario of victims and victimizers certainly has that. There is, however, something more basic, more universally appealing in the Marxist revision of American history than its mere simplicity, and that is the inclination of human beings to put the blame for their deficiencies and troubles on someone else. I first became aware of this inclination in 1967 while teaching a literature class at a men's prison outside Fox Lake, Wisconsin. After meeting over the course of several months with a dozen or so inmates at this medium-security prison, I found that all of them wanted to talk with me on a personal basis during the break we took halfway through each three-hour class. And sooner or later, all of them talked about their "rap"—why they were in prison. Their stories varied, but each had a consistent theme: exculpation. It was not their fault they were in prison. They had had an abusive, alcoholic father. They had had an abusive, drug-addicted mother. They had grown up in a bad neighborhood among bad influences, and so on and so forth. The most frequent self-justification they offered, however, in explaining why they were in prison, was that they had had a bad lawyer. Their lawyer had not done his or her job, which was to get them acquitted of the charge they had been found guilty of in a court of law that had been conducted according to long-established courtroom procedures designed to safeguard them against miscarriages of justice. None of them denied doing what they had been convicted of doing. That question never came up in their conversations with me. They simply did not take personal responsibility for how their lives had turned out. And these were not unintelligent men. Some of them had committed white-collar crimes involving financial intricacies beyond the comprehension of most persons.

The uniformity of the exculpation theme manifested by these convicted felons taught me one of the big lessons of my life. I had to admit to myself that I, too, had a tendency to blame either circumstances or the actions of other people whenever I had done something blameworthy, though I never had the least difficulty in taking full credit to myself for any of my praiseworthy actions. The culture war launched in the 1960s, insofar as it has succeeded, has played on this tendency of our human nature to blame others for our failure to live up to the behavioral expectations of our culture.

In American society, success has been historically prized and culturally encouraged; and one of the most important beliefs of American culture in regard to success has been the belief that every person's success benefits society. That belief had its origin on the American frontier, where any improvement a family made to the farm they were carving out of the wilderness was a step toward the common good of creating a civilized community. The counter-culture movement has turned that belief on its head. It proposes the contrary idea that anyone who succeeds must have done something bad to someone to achieve their success. In the melodrama of victims and victimizers, honest, useful work cannot be the cause of success. This change, whereby success is a sign of villainy rather than diligence and accomplishment, and all prosperity is undeserved and evidence of the exploitation of others, appeals to anyone who might have failed to achieve success. In the view of the counter-culture movement, any dissatisfaction that individuals have or any economic disadvantage they might feel is the fault of those who dominate, exploit, and oppress them.

In the latter decades of the twentieth century in America, it became politically correct to think that no one is responsible for their own shortcomings. A whole new outlook on personal responsibility has taken root in America as a result of the Left's constant relegation of individuals into biological-political classes to serve its ideology of class struggle, which holds that successful people have wronged unsuccessful people. Belief in individual responsibility has become another myth to be discarded along with the myth that America is an exceptional country because of the extraordinary freedom and opportunity it has historically offered for individual achievement. Now, unless everyone succeeds together, and no one succeeds much more than anyone else, everything is unfair. Young Americans are now being taught in public schools to regard competition as something harmful, not as something rewarding and socially beneficial. Success and the competition that leads to it are now shameful to many Americans. And after the term *elitism* took on a derogatory political meaning, eminently successful persons were among the quickest to denounce being wealthy, lest they themselves be labeled "elitist." According to proponents of the idea of victimization, individual success is detrimental to society because, they assert, the competition needed to succeed hurts people.

American culture was created by a society made up of individuals who wanted to be successful, who were determined to take responsibility for their lives, and who intended to improve their personal circumstances in practical ways. By their immigration, the self-selected immigrants to America demonstrated their determination to improve their lives. But as part of the betterment of their own lives, they had to work cooperatively with others to civilize the wilderness they had entered and to develop the young society they had joined. That improvement benefited everyone. The common good (civilizing the wilderness) was the good of each. Everyone's self-interest powerfully coincided with everyone's social interest. Every member of this society, in performing the arduous work of establishing a civilization in a wilderness, had an obligation to pull his own weight. Teamwork was vital to getting the job done. And helping persons "down on their luck" who wanted to pull their own weight again was a practical imperative as well as an obligation of Christian charity.

These mutual interests produced a dynamic, future-oriented, wealth-producing, compassionate society with an extraordinarily high rate of personal success (as well as the inevitable failures). This society of course developed a distinctive culture, which included in its set of beliefs the conviction that the individual contributes most to society when he takes responsibility for his own welfare and extends personal help to other individuals who may be in trouble.

The counter-culture's ideology of victimization, which makes society collectively responsible for whatever happens to people and whatever difficulties they may get into, reverses the belief of American culture that makes individuals responsible for both their own well-being *and* the good of society. The counter-culture has also reversed American society's orientation to the future. The politics of the counter-culture emphasizes the past. Giving priority to historical injustices ignores the general success of the American enterprise and the capacity of American culture to progressively reform itself. This exaggeration of and constant dwelling on historical wrongs, however, is essential to the counter-culture's efforts to delegitimize American society and its culture.

The Left's version of the American past, which makes such great historical wrongs as slavery and racial discrimination the whole history of America, justifies its project of replacing American culture. And of course the present incomparable general prosperity and extraordinary freedom of American society have, in the thinking of the counter-culture, no connection to the cultural beliefs that Americans have historically acted on. The Left's version of the American past as oppression, however, does not and cannot explain the general well-being of American citizens that shows so favorably in comparison to conditions in the lives of the citizens of other countries. The greatest truth about American history is the fact that the diverse immigrants who came to America starting in the early 1600s loved freedom enough to uproot themselves from their native places to go in search of it. The second greatest truth is that the freedom they found in America and their hard work made them prosperous. Neither of these truths has any importance in the revision of American history effected by the counter-culture movement's adherents and its sympathizers. Furthermore, from the multitude of Christian denominations that these immigrants brought with them emerged the belief that God can be legitimately worshipped in many churches. That belief produced a society of extraordinary religious tolerance.

The many voluntary associations of persons that typify American religious and civil history created a society like no other in history, and one whose motto, One From Many (E Pluribus Unum), truly does represent the general cultural history of America. In the latter twentieth century, those who have wished to subvert, destroy, and replace American culture have denied that truth. They have aimed to institute, through manipulating the legislative and judicial powers of the federal government, the idea that individuals are not responsible for themselves. They have wanted to make as many persons as possible dependent on (rather than independent of) the state. The counter-culture movement favors wealth redistribution, not wealth production. In the society that the Left wants to create, no one would be responsible for pulling their own weight, improving their life, helping other persons, or making a personal contribution to the general welfare. In that perfect future society, the responsibilities of the state would be all-encompassing.

The drift away from American culture's belief in the responsible individual toward the idea of society's responsibility is the essence of socialism. In the attempt to effect progress through the power of the state rather than through the dynamic energy of freely associating individuals having common interests, the American cultural principle of responsible individualism has come to be seen as an impediment to progress. The idea of social responsibility has been seductively promoted by calling for a "compassionate" government. But no state in history has ever been compassionate. That is a behavior that only persons, not governments and their policies, are capable of. To regard compassion as a government responsibility is one more example of the corruption of words that has been wrought in the culture war by the Left's incessant ideological message.

Under the counter-culture movement's principle of social responsibility, the solution to human problems has been invariably more laws, more government spending, more government regulation, more social programs, more intrusions into the lives of individuals, and a devaluing of belief in independence, freedom, self-determination, and personal responsibility. And the worst of it is that government welfare programs have often aggravated and increased the problems they were intended to ameliorate. For example, in 1963 about one out of every fifteen babies born in America (6.5 percent) were illegitimate births; in 2000—after thirty-five years of programs that shifted the responsibility of a man for getting a woman pregnant from the man to the government by making government aid to unwed mothers available—one in every three babies born in the United States (33.2 percent) is now born out-of-wedlock.[9] In *A Nation of Victims: The Decay of the American Character*, Charles J. Sykes notes as a matter of fact that "In the 1960s, the political and moral stature of the victim was transformed and made attractive to an increasingly wide array of groups who rushed to grab a piece of the action for themselves. This rush was accelerated by the creation of an elaborate array of programs, privileges, and entitlements that were specifically attached to various groups' victim status."[10] He also notes that a "chain reaction of new demands and expanded grievances" began in the 1960s.

American society in the 1960s and 1970s became an immense insurance company for victims, and it still is. The premiums on the insurance are the federal taxes that American citizens pay and the IOUs that the federal government writes in borrowing money to pay claims that exceed the funds that can be extracted from productive citizens through taxation. This is akin to Karl Marx's famous slogan defining communism: "From each according to his ability, to each according to his needs," which the preface to the Constitution of the USSR in force at the time the USSR collapsed echoed in proclaiming that "the law of life" is the "concern of all for the good of each and the concern of each for the good of all." But experience has shown repeatedly that unredeemed human nature, without the help of a much higher power than the state, cannot produce enough saintly men and women to make living by such socialist slogans a practical basis for behavior in a society. And the total coercion that the Soviet government exerted during its existence offers ample evidence of the force that is needed when giving society primary responsibility for the individual.

In the second half of the twentieth century, the government of the United States became mired in satisfying the escalating needs of groups that had had their consciousness of their victimization raised. Under the politically driven welfare system that resulted from the idea of victimization, there was little attempt to make government frugal or efficient. The United States—a land where the majority of people were allegedly exploited—was enormously productive, and the productivity of the American people could be taxed and used as collateral for borrowing. There did not seem to be any limit to the money available for government programs and social engineering. And the federal government did not dole out benefits just to people who were comparatively poor. It collected vast sums from the middle class and then redistributed it back to them as the government saw fit. Influenced by the ideology of the counter-culture movement, the government decided who was deserving and who was not. By the end of the twentieth century, 40 percent of personal income was being taken on average by taxation and redistributed to various categories of persons as prescribed by a socialist principle of social responsibility. The U.S. government's plan for the welfare of individuals resembles, in the way it works, the confinement of a mass of grasshoppers in a glass jar. If left in their unnatural confinement inside the jar, the grasshoppers will suffocate. But they will die en masse. And according to the teachings of socialism, that is the correct way for everything to happen.

The counter-culture movement does not represent any real justice or progress. On this basic point, one commentator has made the following observation concerning what has happened in America since the 1960s in regard to correcting racial prejudice:

> To reform centuries of white entitlement, we do not enforce the democratic principles it violated. Instead we grant precisely the same undemocratic entitlement to minorities and women in the name of redress. We use the old sin to correct its own damage. But this difference is not as great as it seems, because in both cases we allow the mere claim (of oppression or of white superiority) to become a currency of entitlement. This claim does not have to be supported. The child of well-to-do black parents gets preference in college admissions without any evidence of oppression, just as whites were once preferred without any evidence of superiority. Group membership alone seals the advantage.[11]

Along the same lines, an investigator of radical feminism has this to say about "children's liberation," perhaps the most dangerous aspect of the feminist movement:

> The movement to "liberate" children from their parents has been an integral part of the Women's Liberation movement and one look at a radical feminist newspaper such as *Off Our Backs* leaves little doubt as to the reason why the feminists want the little ones liberated from their parents. Children pick up values from their parents and grandparents, and the only way to mold a truly revolutionary child is to separate the child from his parents at birth or shortly thereafter. In their own words, the liberators tell us, "We believe . . . that child care from birth is the responsibility of a whole society and not the exclusive responsibility of individual women. . . . Therefore our struggle for free, universal child care is a part of the larger struggle to create an entirely new society."[12]

Radical feminist activists see the role of homemaker as demeaning (feminists have all but obliterated the term *homemaker* from American speech). They want women to be free from bearing children and child care; hence, their demand for government-subsidized abortion and day-care centers. They insist that every woman, even females who are yet minors, has the right to kill the baby developing inside her at any stage of the baby's growth. They reject and denounce the belief that "the overriding psychological need of a woman is to love something alive."[13]

Had the immense sums expended on welfare programs in the second half of the twentieth century resulted in immense benefits to society, they would have been worth the expenditures. But the spending has not appreciably improved the conditions it was intended to ameliorate. At the beginning of 1966, the year in which the cost of federal welfare programs zoomed upward as the War on Poverty in the United States got into high gear, 14.5 percent of Americans were considered to be living below the poverty line set by the federal government to define who is living in poverty.[14] In the year 2000, thirty-four years later, the official poverty rate was 11.7 percent.[15] This 2.8 percent reduction in poverty was accomplished by spending *more money than was spent in fighting World War II*. In other words, there has been nothing even close to a cost-effective connection between social welfare spending in the United States in the second half of the twentieth century and the social benefits it has actually delivered.

Since 1950, the relationship between the individual and society in the United States has become skewed. All the demands are now on society. Society has been stripped of its right to demand anything of individuals. Activists in the cause of social justice, as Marvin Olasky has observed, now contend that "anything short of unlimited tolerance is injustice to the oppressed." From "the perspective of 1990," Olasky judged that "the social revolution of the 1960s has not helped the poor," and that "Every time we tell someone he is a victim, every time we say he deserves a special break [and] every time we hand out charity to someone capable of working, we are hurting rather than helping."[16]

Perhaps the three Laws of Social Programs identified by Charles Murray, the author of *Losing Ground: America's Social Policy, 1950–1980*, best summarize the reasons why hostility between classes of people has been the main outcome of the social welfare programs of the latter twentieth century rather than any overall improvement of American society.

1. The Law of Imperfect Selection. Any objective rule that defines eligibility for a social transfer program will irrationally exclude some persons.
2. The Law of Unintended Rewards. Any social transfer increases the net value of being in the condition that prompted the transfer.

3. The Law of Net Harm. The less likely it is that the unwanted behavior will change voluntarily, the more likely it is that a program to induce change will cause net harm.[17]

Those who paid for the social transfers of trillions of dollars over the last forty years are justified in resenting the expenditure of their taxes on government programs that have had no appreciable improving effect. And some of that resentment has rubbed off on the recipients of the funds when no resentment had previously been felt toward them.

Under the influence of the morality play of victims and victimizers, the consciousness of belonging to some biological class is on the ascent in America and consciousness of being an American is declining, along with the sense of the uniqueness of each person's individuality. If these trends are not halted and reversed, perhaps every vestige of the individual responsibilities of the American citizen and his obligations to American society will eventually vanish, leaving only contentious groups in interminable conflict with each other, groups whose members will be more focused on their entitlements and their unproductive group rights than anything else.

Should that point ever be reached, then the American cultural principle of responsible individualism will have been destroyed, and American society will have become dysfunctional. The conditions will then exist for a new culture of total government control over society. Government of the people, by the people, and for the people will have vanished from the Earth. The day of the responsible individual will have ended in America and the day of society's comprehensive responsibility for every individual's happiness will have arrived. At that point, the United States would cease to be a great nation.

CHAPTER FIVE

Liberation vs. Equal Freedom

Equality in American culture is the conviction expressed in the Declaration of Independence that every human being has been created by God, lives under the same natural law of moral obligations, and has been given by their creator the same unalienable rights to life, liberty, and the pursuit of happiness. (The clauses in the Declaration of Independence that state "all men are created equal" and that they are "endowed by their Creator with certain unalienable Rights, that among these are Life, Liberty and the pursuit of Happiness" refer of course to human beings, both men and women. Any other reading would require us to believe that the Founding Fathers thought the creator did not equally endow women with life. The American dictionary closest in time to the writing of the Declaration of Independence, Noah Webster's *A Compendious Dictionary of the English Language*, published in 1806, gives "a human being" as the first meaning of the word *man*; the second being, of course, "a male.") The liberty, or freedom, spoken of in the Declaration is part of equality because no human being has more of this freedom than any other human being. Equality is when every person possesses the same rights and liberty.

Individuals are unequal in their interests, capacities, and personality traits, which are unique to them as individuals. Individuals differ in what each can do and wants to do. A tall person can do things a short person cannot, and vice versa. Some people have an interest in caring for plants, others in flying airplanes. This person has a talent for sculpting, that person for managing a business. Some differences in capacity to do certain things are determined by inherent characteristics (such as gender) and some by circumstances (the possession of wealth, for example). These individual and categorical differences necessarily mean that each person is free to do somewhat different things in the sense that they can do or are interested in doing them. Children categorically cannot do many things adults can do; no one but Mozart could have done what Mozart did; women can nourish human life in their bodies but men can't. The great principle of equality, however, which underlies all of this variation, is the acknowledgment that your unalienable rights as a human being define my rights and my unalienable rights as a human being define your rights. As God's creations, we are equal in having the same worth in his eyes and are equals in each other's eyes because we have the same birthrights from the creator. That is the nature of human equality in American culture.

Because liberation separates freedom from equality, it changes the relation between freedom and equality. It gives each person the right to do whatever pleases him or her without limit, and without consideration of the equal rights of other human beings. Liberation empowers or enables certain *groups* to redress wrongs committed against their group, or their ancestors in the past, by committing the same wrongs against other groups in the present. Liberation liberates individuals from other individuals and categories of human beings from other categories. Such freedom affirms only itself. It does not affirm a common humanity. It negates the rights of others by making each person or group morally autonomous, rather than equal in their obligation to please their creator by obeying his natural law and revering the equal birthrights he has given every human being. Liberation grants to each person or category of persons a separate standard of judgment. It separates freedom from equality in order to destabilize American society and its culture for the purpose of building a counter-culture.

The following observations about the 1960s show what happens when freedom is divorced from equality and becomes liberation. They were part of a conversation on the condition of American society that I had some years ago in Tucson, Arizona, with Vivian Gornick, a writer from New York City who was visiting the University of Arizona. Because I found her remarks on the 1960s uncommonly insightful, I asked her to write them down for my use in the study of American culture that I was working on, which she kindly did. This is what she said:

> In 1968, my then-husband and I, like everyone else in America between the ages of 20 and 40, were running away from home. New Mexico was one of the major destinations of this generation of self-styled free spirits, so we headed for Taos. We settled into an adobe house with nothing in it but electricity (no plumbing, no running water) in a valley fifteen miles above the village, and very quickly came to

know all the other "runaways" in the neighborhood. Actually, a remarkably interesting lot. Three generations of bohemians were gathered here—people who'd come to Taos in the twenties and thirties, as well as the forties and fifties, and now the sixties. But it was only the children of the sixties who had decided to live out their ideas of freedom-from-bourgeois-society communally.

When we got to Taos we discovered that the entire area—from Santa Fe to the Colorado border—was dotted with communes. The communes were filled with people from all over the country who had grown up in cities, towns, and villages, ranged in education from college professors to high school drop-outs, came from families that were loving as well as dysfunctional, church-going as well as atheistic. All, however, were united in a common longing to live in a state of unfettered freedom. It was agreed, from the very beginning, that the commune would be free of all structures of obligation and of hierarchy. No one would do anything that he or she did not want to do: ever. Each day would be a day in which one followed one's impulses, consulted one's desires, acted on honest inclination. Such was the belief in natural inner balance that it was honestly assumed that social equilibrium would establish itself without direction, rule, or command, and thus the commune would easily achieve a peaceable and workable scheme for daily living coupled with spiritual uplift.

What actually happened was a kind of benign anarchy set in. Benign soon turned malign. To begin with, without assignment of tasks, it was often true that the common chores of cooking, cleaning, working the fields or the small cottage industries that each commune had set up, became so muddled an affair that there were evenings when no meal was prepared, days when no clean clothes were available, months when unscheduled and erratic farming produced no income. Even worse, the impulse to sleep with whomever took your fancy led to promiscuity and adultery, and this soon became intolerable. Men and women alike discovered—with the jolting power of original discovery—that such behavior was too painful to live with (but not before many marriages went smash and otherwise good communards deserted). Then the matter of scientific and medical distrust was encouraged to such an indiscriminate extreme that women nearly died of unexpected complications in childbirth, and children often went unattended until they too, came to the brink of life-threatening illness. Oh yes, the children. Since they were being cared for by the commune but not really raised by anyone, many of them began to resemble juvenile delinquents. On one commune three of them actually burned down the communal dining hall, and faced their elders with a blankness of expression that was eerie, and no explanation for why they had done what they had done.

But the communes did not go under in the sixties and seventies—and herein lies their historical value. Instead of dissolving out, their people learned from their own experience. In the year I lived in New Mexico, I watched the communes undergo the most astonishing and moving self-reformation to the needs of the common interest. In order to have the good, free life within, it was understood, one had to re-discover the values of nationhood—which included habits of responsibility applied to work, loved ones, shared social tasks, community civility. And they did. It was a remarkable thing to watch, and unforgettable. All this happened thirty years ago, but the meaning of what I witnessed on the New Mexico communes in 1968 has never left me.

Vivian Gornick's reminiscences clearly demonstrate that freedom is not to be confused with doing whatever one pleases.

Freedom is the right to do whatever you want to do all the time only if you happen to permanently live apart from every other human being. (And even then there are certain imperatives of hygiene that a hermit must obey to live a healthy life.) Whoever lives in society with other human beings has to acknowledge that each person's rights are limited by the rights of other persons and that certain reciprocal obligations, proprieties, and duties must be observed if one is to be a member of society. Freedom must not be mistaken for liberation, which destroys society by separating equality from freedom. Freedom and equality must exist together. Freedom is anarchy unless it is joined with and limited by respect for the equal rights of others. We have not been given freedom by our creator to do whatever we please. We have been given freedom to choose to do of our own free will what is right in the nature of things and therefore pleasing to God as he has created us and the world. That is the natural law of God's creation. If there were no free will, there would be no right or wrong. Without choice, there could be no goodness.

The prohibition of certain conduct in the Ten Commandments is not what makes that conduct wrong. Rather, conduct that the Ten Commandments prohibits (adultery, blasphemy, stealing, murder, bearing false witness, coveting what belongs to another) is wrong in the nature of things in being harmful to us as God has created us and in violating the way he has intended human beings to live in society for our own good. The conduct the Ten Commandments enjoins (worshipping God, Sabbath-keeping, honoring one's parents) is right for the same natural reason, because it is beneficial to us. Do unto others as you would be done by is God's natural law. No one wants to be lied to, stolen from, murdered, and so on. Therefore, no one should do such things to another person. They are contrary to the way we ourselves naturally want to be treated and should be treated by our fellow man. Each of us is God's creation—the same as every other human being.

Perhaps the most striking observation in Vivian Gornick's reminiscent observations about the New Mexico communes is her description of the effect that the irresponsible behavior of liberated adults had on children. The eyes of the three children who burned down the communal dining hall were morally blank. They could not explain why they had done it because in the atmosphere of liberation in which they had been immersed they had no operative examples of right and wrong to imitate. They saw neither prohibitions nor obligations in the behavior of the adults among whom they lived, and they had not been told do this but do not do that. All they saw in the conduct around them was whim and impulse. Inevitably, they picked up on and imitated what they perceived. It was destructive but fun to burn down the dining hall. Adultery is also destructive fun, a surrender to impulse without any other consideration. The Ten Commandments—God's law for mankind—is a standard for knowing what makes liberation so destructive. It is in the nature of God's creation that no human being has a *right* to injure another human being by breaking God's commandments.

Children who are being raised by everybody (society, the village, the commune) are, in effect, being raised by nobody and so lose their humanity. This is because to be properly raised, a human being must be loved, which requires self-sacrifice. Societies, villages, and communities do not sacrifice themselves for their members. Only persons will sacrifice themselves for other persons because of the love they bear them. Families offer both protection and love because they are created by loving adults who are willing to sacrifice and care for their children, for the elderly members of their family, and for each other. Groups do not love. They provide only safety, strength, and familiarity. The closest thing to a loving family is the fraternal bond formed by soldiers in combat, which is likely to last for the lifetimes of the members of the combat team that have faced death together and been willing to sacrifice themselves for each other.

To become a part of humanity, a child needs to live with adults in mutual respect and love. As children mature morally and physically, they learn from the adults who love them the habits of thought and conduct that will contribute to their own welfare and the welfare of society. When a child sees in the adults he lives among the behavior of self-respect and respect for other people, he internalizes those values. If instead of the example of such behavior, he sees liberated, selfish behavior, he cannot develop beyond the amoral, self-centered stage of infancy. He remains morally infantile even though he matures physically. This has nothing to do with any hierarchy of authority, whether it be a male or a female hierarchy. It has everything to do with the reciprocal obligations and restraints of natural law. To ignore the moral duties that the principle of equal freedom imposes is to ignore the basic needs of human nature.

Belief in equal freedom is one of the principles of American culture—the others being belief in practical improvement (see chapter 3) and belief in individual responsibility (chapter 4). The immigrants who ran away from England in the early 1600s to live in the wilderness of North America learned these principles the hard way, from scratch, through experience, and in the same way as the runaways to the communes in New Mexico that Vivian Gornick describes. Those initial generations of Americans in the seventeenth century passed down to their children, through the example of their behavior, their belief in practical improvement, in individual responsibility, and in equal freedom; and those children, in their turn, passed the beliefs on to their children through their behavior, and so on, generation after generation. That process of transmission continues today. It is among the things we mean by American culture. It expresses the historical experience of a people who created in a Stone Age wilderness a new society with a new culture and found while doing so that equality is an essential element of freedom.

The first progression of nine generations in American cultural history began with the first permanent English settlement on the Atlantic coastal plain of North America and came to a close with the first government elected under the Constitution of the United States. The midpoint in this 180-year progression of nine generations between 1610 and 1790 was the year 1700. The American population in that year (1700) was approximately 250,000 souls. During the next progression of nine generations, 1790–1970, America rose from a newly formed nation to a position of preeminence in the world. The midpoint year in this second progression was 1880. By then the population of the United States had grown to 50,000,000—two hundred times what it had been at the midpoint of the first progression of nine generations. America is now in its third progression of nine generations. The midpoint year in this progression, which started in 1970, will be 2060; and were the rate of population growth of the twentieth century to hold (which it probably won't), there would be around 500,000,000 Americans in 2060.

One fundamental cause for the historical burgeoning of the American population was the opportunity to own land in a country whose economy for the first 250 years of its history was principally agricultural. The comparative ease with which a man could acquire land in America and support a family by farming meant that marriages could be formed at an earlier time in life than was generally the case in Europe. This prolonged the childbearing years of married women and increased the number of children that they could bear and raise. Also, the abundance and comparative cheapness of food in America resulted in better nourishment and better chances of healthy births and infant survival. As early as 1751, Benjamin Franklin wrote an essay titled "Observations Concerning the Increase of Mankind, Peopling of Countries, etc." on the effect that these fundamental American conditions (affordable land and abundant food) were having on the growth of the American population.[1] However, by themselves these conditions could not have produced America's prodigious population increases (a doubling every twenty years during the first two centuries of American history after viable colonies had been established) had there not been the high volume of immigration to what was to become the United States of America in 1776.

Besides the opportunity it offered to acquire property, life in America also attracted immigrants because of the equal freedom it offered. To choose to go to America was to choose to live in a society that had no hereditary ruling class, no group that believed it was a superior breed of human beings entitled to special group privileges. There was no class of free men in colonial America with rights distinct from the rights of other classes of free men, no class that from generation to generation kept ownership of almost all land and positions of authority in the hands of its members. The absence of an aristocracy in America with special rights pertaining only to their class was attractive to tens of millions of free men and women in the lower classes of Europe and other continents and convinced them to leave their native countries for America in order to find a society that offered them equal freedom.

Socialism makes society responsible for the welfare of each person (a variant of the aristocratic ideal in Europe of noblesse oblige that made the ruling class responsible for the well-being of classes beneath them). The self-selected immigrants who populated America, however, believed they were responsible for themselves. They did not wish society or any class in society to be responsible for them. Their immigration was their first step in taking responsibility for themselves.

Since the doctrine of strict materialism that Marxist socialism is based on excludes belief in God, it cannot offer an equality founded on belief in God. It has only an equality of condition to offer. Marxists regard religion as a ruse of ruling classes to get other members of society to acquiesce in their inequality of condition. In the 1960s, however, through a concept called "liberation theology," socialism tried to attract Christians to the ideas of making society responsible for everyone's welfare and of establishing an equality of condition. Liberation theology claimed that Christ was a socialist and said that Christians should work to create a culture in which the state would provide an equality of condition. In the 1980s, prominent Marxist socialists, including the communist dictator in Cuba, Fidel Castro, endorsed liberation theology.[2]

Acknowledging the same creator, living under the same moral imperatives, and having from God the same birthrights to life, liberty, and the pursuit of happiness were the definitive components of the belief in equality among Americans that integrated multitudes of immigrants from diverse nations with different languages and religions. Belief in this kind of equality allowed the varied individuals of America's immigrant society to relate to each other as equals, regardless of their diversity. In accordance with the American cultural belief in equal freedom, each free man and woman in American society had, as God's creations, an equal worth, and therefore deserved equal respect. The condition of the slaves that existed in this society for two centuries contradicted these cultural beliefs. Because the slaves were considered property, their humanity was compromised in civil law, though never in natural law. But belief in the cultural principle of equal freedom has been the rule in American history; slavery was the exception. And as long as American culture endures, the principle of equal freedom will remain an indispensable component of it.

In American culture, morality depends on individuals accepting responsibility for the consequences of their choices. The counter-culture is trying to create a collective morality that makes social conditions responsible for the behavior of individuals and groups. In this view of things, morality is constituted not by individual choices made in accordance with a divinely ordained moral law but by decisions made according to the prevailing, impersonal social conditions, or environment, that individuals find themselves in. This new morality has an exclusively political rather than a religious foundation. As the counter-culture movement in America in the latter half of the twentieth century has transferred responsibility for the consequences of one's choices to society, the number of laws and the frequency of lawsuits have increased by leaps and bounds. Even happiness has become a responsibility of society.

Spanish philosopher Julián Marías also remarks on this phenomenon in the epilogue to his second book about the United States in the 1960s. During one of his visits to teach at an American university, he noticed a marked tendency among young Americans: they were denying their *right* to pursue happiness, even though "happiness has always been probable and frequent in the United States, perhaps more so than in most other countries." The denial of the right to be happy, Marías said, was also observable in European societies during the same period:

> Expressed in different ways, this is what Western man is hearing. Because so many things are wrong, because there is pain, sickness, poverty, oppression, and vice, some conclude that we have no right to be content, much less happy. Notice that they do not say we *cannot* be happy, but rather that we *should* not be. We must be unhappy, even though our circumstances may be favorable, because there is always someone less fortunate. . . . Today many think they have to protest against everything that is bad, regardless of whether or not it affects them. And since there is always something wrong somewhere, protest becomes a permanent and normal *condition* of life. . . . The present American generation, which has just begun to play a role on the stage of history, is being persuaded that it ought not to be happy, not even to the degree to which it can be. Under the pretext that not everything is right, it is told it should behave as though everything were wrong.[3] [This is the counter-culture idea that unless everything is *perfect*, everything is wrong; see chapter 3.]

Forswearing the right to pursue individual happiness because "everything is wrong" and needs to be put right by political action, marks a radical departure from American culture. As Marías notes, Americans have historically been "resolutely on the side of happiness" which is preeminently an individual pursuit. Indeed, in the judgment of this Spanish philosopher, Americans have carried the pursuit of happiness to the point of believing that they have "a duty to be happy" and that it is "a breach of ethics not to appear to be so."

Acceptance of the idea that society is responsible for the happiness of every person is contrary to the beliefs of American culture. But the idea was spreading in the 1960s among well-meaning persons in Europe and the United States. Many young Americans in the generation that came of age in the 1960s had been persuaded, Marías wrote, to make "protest the rule in the midst of what must be considered—in view of the true state of the world—[their country's] incomparable example of well-being, justice, freedom, and prosperity." Marías concluded these observations in 1970 by pointing out that during his nearly two decades of repeatedly visiting the United States, "Almost everything *real* is better than before, but there is a budding belief that it is worse, and if people continue to believe it, it *will* be worse." Nonetheless, he had "high hopes for the whole world." But he believed the world would be better in the future only if the United States, the most influential Western country of the twentieth century, continues to believe in and act on man's inherent "right to search for happiness."[4]

The pursuit of happiness, as everyone knows, is one of the unalienable birthrights of mankind mentioned in America's Declaration of Independence. As a society established by immigrants who were unhappy with their lives in Europe and in search of a better way of life, America has in a quite real sense been dedicated from its inception to the pursuit of happiness. And anyone who gives the matter a moment's thought must realize that happiness is by its very nature "a personal affair," and that "No form of society, no political constitution or government, can guarantee or grant happiness."[5] Socialists, as Edward Bellamy's utopian novel *Looking Backward: 2000–1887* makes clear, want to reorganize society in so perfectly rational and scientific a way as to bestow uniform happiness on everyone as a permanent condition. The surrealistic nature of this project (not only in terms of the perfection it envisions but also in terms of substituting government programs and regulations for the striving of individuals to be happy), is another radical difference between the counter-culture and American culture.

The realization of collective happiness necessitates one of two recourses: either (1) a reconstruction of human nature, which is an impossibility, although those who believe in the perfectability of man now seem to be working themselves up to undertaking the task of reconstituting human nature through genetic manipulations, or (2) the creation of "a dictatorship of virtue," perhaps for a considerable length of time. This wonderfully accurate phrase, dictatorship of virtue, which epitomizes so much of the spirit of the counter-culture's politics, is from Richard Bernstein's book *Dictatorship of Virtue: How the Battle Over Multiculturalism Is Reshaping Our Schools, Our Country, Our Lives* (New York: Vintage Books, 1995).

But, even if a (theoretically temporary) dictatorship of virtue could mass-produce happiness, following a painful transitional period of say four generations in which American society would be radically reorganized, the question naturally arises: Would the elite planners and managers needed to carry out such a project relinquish their authority once social happiness had been obtained? And who except this elite would be in a position to say when the requisite degree of happiness had been attained? Would not those self-righteous directors become incurably addicted to the idea of their virtue and to wielding their power to implement the great new society they envision? That outcome is all too likely, if we judge by the histories of the Soviet Union, Nazi Germany, and other totalitarian socialist regimes in the twentieth century. A disinterested, socialist exercise of power, without any purpose other than achieving an equal happiness for all, is so improbable that a reasonably mature person can scarcely contemplate the idea without a smile. But perhaps the chief obstacle to the realization of a dictatorship of virtue is that no human being or political party possesses the godlike ability to perceive what is best for everyone at all times and without exception.

A dictatorship of virtue cannot succeed because it contradicts the way the world and human beings have been made. No group of human beings—no matter how vain they may be of their supposedly superior intelligence, knowledge, perception, and judgment, and no matter how much empowerment they may acquire for the alleged purpose of doing good en masse and ending human suffering—can ever deliver even an approximation of wholesale happiness. Twentieth-century history has conclusively demonstrated, however, that even the attempt to create a dictatorship of virtue can cause enormous havoc in trying to achieve this end. Because their promise to achieve happiness en masse *makes the virtuous dictators happy*, they ignore the possibility that their social policies could be wrong and that they are causing a great deal of unhappiness, not uncommonly among the very persons they claim to be dedicated to helping. This is the kind of menacing good intentions that Henry David Thoreau undoubtedly had in mind when he wrote in *Walden*:

> If I knew for a certainty that a man was coming to my house with the conscious design of doing me good, I should run for my life, as from that dry and parching wind of the African deserts called simoom, which fills the mouth and nose and ears and eyes with dust till you are suffocated, for fear that I should get some of his good done to me,—some of its virus mingled with my blood. No,—in this case I would rather suffer evil the natural way.[6]

Persons intent on acting the part of ungentle saviors, and who are hell-bent on seeing social justice done once and for all, give little consideration to the resistance that the nature of things, especially human nature, poses. Progress for them is liberation from restraints. They cannot abide the thought of there being any insuperable barrier to a perfect society with a perfect culture. Such persons must, it appears, cling to their titanic illusion that no reality can sink their great ship of good intentions. To them it is obnoxious to be told that man does not live by bread alone or by reason alone, even though their own spectacularly irrational project demonstrates the latter truth. And the fact that a movement to force into being a perfect society with a perfect culture has been strenuously pursued in the United

States—a country where the roughly 12 to 15 percent of the population living below the federal government's official poverty line are richer than most people in most nations of the world—demonstrates that bread is not the main issue for the counter-culture movement. The main issue for the counter-culture movement appears to be the correctness of its virtue.

For those who would tear American culture apart and rebuild it according to their idea of perfection, any degree of imperfection is intolerable. No one should be left free to pursue happiness on their own. Society must march together, in unison, toward the perfect future, even if that perfection lies at the foot of a cliff. Those who want to engage in social engineering are bothered, it seems, by the idea of unprogrammed happiness. But seeking happiness en masse causes unhappiness for anyone who seeks to be happy in their own way, which is the only way that happiness can truly be obtained, if it is to be had at all.

But, it has been objected, does not society have a collective moral obligation to see that everyone is supplied with food, shelter, and education because without them, what chance does anyone have of attaining happiness? In response to that question, it should be asked, May not the habits of dependence consequent to being supplied with these fundamental necessities prevent happiness and make it meaningless? One might also ask whether people who have enough to eat, adequate shelter, and plenty of education are thereby assured of happiness because of those felicitous conditions. Experience would seem to indicate otherwise. A person may be materially quite well-off and still unhappy, even miserable to the point of committing suicide. The widespread modern belief that the primary causes of self-destructive and antisocial behavior lie in material conditions ignores the moral and spiritual imperatives inherent in God's creation, which man must live by if he would be happy. Time and time again in the twentieth century, it has been shown that demolishing slums and putting their inhabitants into new housing does not automatically reduce the incidence of self-destructive and antisocial behavior among the former slum inhabitants. Nor does affluence automatically eliminate self-destructive and antisocial behavior among the rich and well housed. And who has observed an invariable connection between the level of a person's education and the possession of a good character or peace of mind? Are persons with PhDs happier, more virtuous human beings than persons with bachelor degrees, or are persons with bachelor degrees necessarily better persons than high-school dropouts? The point may be stated thus: Virtuous individuals produce good environments, not the other way around.

Forty years ago, James Burnham analyzed the thinking that typifies leftist ideologues. His understanding of the disdain that ideologues have for the world as it is and of the ideologue's passion for the abstractions of his ideology still rings true. In trying to decide whether someone is an ideologue, Burnham wrote in 1964, "we may be fairly sure we are dealing with an *ideology* and *ideological thinking*" when "certain ideas about man, history and society" seem to those who hold them "so manifestly correct that opposing them is a mark of stupidity or malice."[7] (In the U.S. presidential election of 1992, the Democratic Party indeed confronted its Republican opponents in exactly these terms, with the harsh slogan "It's the economy, stupid.") For an ideologue, any opinion at variance with his ideology is unintelligent. Those who do not conform to the ideology are enemies of mankind. Deviance from the correct political ideology is evidence of mental and moral deficiencies. Hence the assumptions and reasoning of whoever disagrees with an ideologue can be derided and dismissed by him out of hand, once he perceives their deviance. Right and wrong become merely matters of political prejudice, or prejudgment, entirely unrelated to objective truth. In short, politics determines truth.

For the ideologue, reasoning is always an exercise in prejudgment. His mind is closed to independent reasoning. He derives his conclusions from the ideology he so passionately embraces. Should unusual circumstances present themselves, the elite keepers of his ideology will tell him what to think. Independent thought would put the seamless virtue of his ideology at risk, and he does not dare to take that chance, which might cost him his place in the comforting ranks of the virtuous. ("The rebel angels fly in ranks," it has been shrewdly observed.)

In my own case, living in Cuba in the summer of 1960, a year and a half after communist revolutionaries took power there (a revolution that I, like most Americans at the time, misunderstood and supported), made me doubt somewhat the correctness of my then-liberal bias. Events on the campus of the University of Wisconsin, Madison, where I was a young professor during the Vietnam War protests of the late 1960s (especially the attempt by leftists to firebomb the main library as part of their campaign to shut down the university) increased my doubts a great deal. Listening to Senator Paul Laxalt's speech nominating Ronald Reagan as the Republican candidate for president in 1980 made me question the truth of what I, as a staunch Democrat, had heard and believed about Reagan's record as governor of California and about Republicans in general. A summer teaching behind the Iron Curtain in communist-ruled Poland in 1981, after a general strike by Polish workers the previous summer had given the lie to the claim of Polish communists that they represented the working class, was my final lesson in truth vs. ideology.

Once the ideas that comprise an ideology have been accepted, facts have no value until and unless they are assessed in terms of the ideology and are found to corroborate it. Anything that does not correspond to an ideological description of reality can be ignored or its validity denied. The ideology is, in other words, a self-contained substitute for reality. Take the ideology of Freudianism for example. Among its ideas are the so-called Oedipal complex (the proposition that adolescent male children subconsciously want to have sexual intercourse with their mothers and on that account are subconsciously hostile to their fathers as sexual rivals), and the related Freudian concepts of either acting out or repressing subconscious urges. A boy kills his father: he is, according to Freudian ideation, *acting out* the subconscious Oedipal urge of all boys to kill their fathers. The boy does not kill his father: he is therefore *repressing* his Oedipal urge. Either way, no matter how the boy acts, he has an Oedipal complex, and his behavior proves it because he is either acting out or repressing his complex. It is a beautiful setup. That is undoubtedly why Freudianism remains attractive to ideologically minded academics today, even though it has long since been discredited as an effective clinical therapy.

Marxism has the same irrelevance to reality for anyone willing to look beyond theory to results. For a believing Marxist, the implosion of the Soviet Union in 1991 meant nothing. What occurred during the three generations of communist rule in the USSR was not the application of Marxism, they say. It was Stalinism that was put into practice in the USSR; Marxism has yet to be tried. If Marxism had been tried in the USSR, there would have been a wonderful result rather than incalculable suffering and the deaths of the approximately twenty million politically incorrect people who were "liquidated," that is, murdered under a government controlled by the Communist Party of the Soviet Union.

To take another case: the fact that Cuba under the rule of Marxist ideologues has been a military dictatorship for a longer period than any other country in the history of Spanish America,[8] or the fact that the Cuban people have lived under strict food rationing for more than forty years, or the fact that oxen are now being used to plow fields in communist Cuba, or the fact that the average worker in Cuba is now making $120 a year[9]—none of these facts matter to a Marxist ideologue. To such a person, Cuba is what the Communist Party of Cuba and its American sympathizers continually proclaim it to be: "a participatory democracy" governed by "popular power." And Fidel Castro is the supreme leader (*el máximo líder*) in the struggle against American imperialism. The miserable Cuban economy that countless Cuban workers have risked their lives to escape during the past forty-five years has not been caused, the communist leaders of Cuba say, by communist central planning and control. No. The U.S. embargo on trade with Cuba has caused the decline. Yet before the collapse of the Soviet empire, Cuba traded with the Soviet Union and all its satellites in the Eastern bloc, and it is still able to trade with those countries today, as well as with China, Spain, Canada, Mexico, and many other countries. Nevertheless, communist ideology demands that the oxen now being used instead of tractors to plow the fields in Pinar del Río and Camaguey provinces be explained in terms of the U.S. embargo. Such regressive agricultural practices can have no significance apart from the *ideology* that makes U.S. imperialism responsible for all of the world's ills.

Cuba remains for its ideological admirers in the United States a liberated, enlightened, progressive country because their ideology tells them that it is. They dismiss the fact that Cuba's economy has been depressed ever since communists took over Cuba in 1959. The further fact that the Cuban regime is a brutal, one-party dictatorship that suppresses individual initiative and disregards human rights is likewise insignificant to them. Cuba's economic problems, so far as they are concerned, are entirely attributable to the refusal of the United States to enter into trade relations and thus include Cuba within the sphere of its allegedly evil capitalist system, which Cuban communists and their supporters in the United States are busy denouncing. That is the reasoning of an ideologue. An ideologue of the Marxist persuasion, just as in Freudian ideology, has it both ways: Yankee capitalism is evil, but until the United States lifts its embargo and allows Cuba to participate in that evil, Cuba cannot be expected to prosper.

James Burnham, in the chapter "Ideological Thinking" in his *Suicide of the West*, has a number of revealing illustrations of this way of thinking, but perhaps the most telling one concerns the commentary that a journalist wrote about a simple report from Peru. That report read in its entirety:

[January 13, 1963] Lima, Peru—Five persons died early Wednesday in clashes between police and striking peasants at two sugar mills near Chiclayo, in northern Peru. The clashes occurred after strikers attacked and sought to burn down the Patapo and Pacula mills, inflicting heavy damage.[10]

A syndicated newspaper columnist named Ralph McGill, whom Burnham characterizes as "an intransigent and orthodox liberal," fashioned the following commentary out of that simple report:

> Drawing on our general knowledge of South American conditions, we can assume, with some confidence, that feudal conditions obtain in Chiclayo. We may be rather certain that low wages, long hours, and poor working conditions prevail. Agriculture in Latin America is almost everywhere depressed. Its workers live in poverty and wretchedness. Their political status is prejudiced. Illiteracy is the rule. Health conditions are primitive. The story is an old one. It is, however, no older than the familiar one of police *vs.* strikers in an area where labor has no bargaining rights. The two paragraphs out of Chiclayo would, if amplified, help us to understand why President Kennedy's intelligent plan for assistance to Latin America [the Alliance for Progress] is inoperative. It depends, for a beginning, on reform by land-holders and industrialists in Latin America. Killing hungry and desperate men is hardly a reform.

These elaborate assumptions about a factual report intrigued Burnham; and he decided to investigate the events at Chiclayo, an agricultural center on the north coast of Peru.

The first thing he discovered was that McGill's column bore a strong resemblance to a *New York Times* editorial on the violence at Chiclayo. The *Times* editorial had also spoken of it as "a protest, the specific motivation of which was less important than the general discontent" of peasants who were "learning that their poverty, illiteracy and disease are based on social injustice." McGill had evidently taken his cue from the *New York Times*. The second thing Burnham learned, from a friend of his who had lived in Peru, was that Chiclayo was in "one of the relatively more advanced parts of Peru," that the sugar mill workers there were "relatively well paid," and that the mills themselves were rather modern, not primitive operations.

Burnham got the same story from "several other persons with firsthand knowledge." But he was not satisfied and sought further information. He discovered it in testimony given on February 18, 1963, by Edwin M. Martin, President John F. Kennedy's assistant secretary of state for Latin-American affairs, before the House of Representatives Committee on Foreign Affairs:

> In Peru we have another dramatic example of the increasing tempo of communist-inspired subversion and violence. For the past several months, in an agricultural area of the Andean Department of Cuzco, communist agitators, many of whom were trained in Cuba [Castro's communist regime was in its fourth year by this

time], have been responsible for the forceful seizure of lands, armed attacks, and considerable bloodshed. Last December, Castro-Communist agitators subverted a strike at the smelter of the American-owned Cerro Corp. at La Oroya in the central Andes, seized control of the installation and caused about $4 million worth of damage. Early in January, following a strike that had been settled between the management and the legitimate trade union leaders, Communist agitators persuaded workers on two Peruvian-owned sugar plantations near Chiclayo on the north coast, to damage installations and fire canefields—about a million dollars of damage in all.[11]

Burnham thus found out from his investigations that every point in McGill's commentary was wrong—oppressed workers living in conditions of feudal poverty, heartless latifundios keeping their workers illiterate and refusing to let them organize labor unions to bargain for their rights, and so on. The truth of the matter was that the workers at the sugar mills where the five deaths and the arson took place were not starving illiterates living in feudal servitude, because the mills where they worked were comparatively modern affairs that required skilled workers. The workers had a labor union. They were accustomed to bargaining for their rights and higher wages, and had in fact just settled a strike through their union representatives when the communist-inspired violence at Chiclayo occurred. Ralph McGill's column was incorrect as history, though it was ideologically correct. Other events in Spanish America in the 1960s might have fitted the prejudices of McGill and the *New York Times*. But not the events at Chiclayo.

Liberation theory separates freedom from equality. It also separates facts from ideas, and insulates ideology from the consequences of its application. In applying an ideology to a society and its culture, no matter what happens, the ideology is never proven wrong for those who believe in it. Unlike a historical culture, whose beliefs have been tested in the crucible of experience by being acted on by generations of a people and found useful, an ideology springs full-blown from the mind of its creator. After the founder of an ideology dies, his disciples perpetuate his creation. To doubt the ideology would leave them without their identity as true believers. Thus, an ideology can never be self-correcting. It must run its course until events beyond the control of the keepers of the ideology discredit its claims (as happened during the general strike of workers in communist-ruled Poland in 1980), or until even its disciples tire of its uselessness (as seems to have happened, at least in part, in 1989 to 1991 during the disintegration of the Soviet Union).

The "communards," as Vivian Gornick called the young Americans who ran away to the communes in the upper valleys of the Rio Grande watershed in the 1960s, were not ideologues. They were acting on their American culture, doing the same thing their cultural ancestors had done in the seventeenth century in leaving Europe for the wilderness of the Atlantic coastal plain of North America. They were looking, as individuals, for freedom. And they found it. They also found, as their cultural ancestors had found in the seventeenth-century seaboard wilderness of eastern North America, that if they were to live together in a civil society they would have to treat each other as equals and do unto one another as they would be done by. And after awhile—a year or two or three—many of the runaways to northern New Mexico in the 1960s, having rediscovered the validity of natural law and their American culture, rejoined American society. But some of them didn't. They joined the ideologues of the Left to war against American culture.

The protest of the ideologues in the counter-culture movement in the United States is total. Like their hero Fidel Castro, their identities are as revolutionaries intent on establishing a new culture. They know the truth of their ideology and nothing else. No experience, no argument, no amount of data, no contrastive examples, will ever dissuade them from believing in it. They can never change their intention. Protest, opposition, and conflict are for them a way of life. They feel that there can be no justice for anyone until there is social justice for everyone. Such a revolution is interminable. It has no foreseeable end because total social justice is humanly unattainable, just as universal happiness is unattainable.

The communards of the 1960s believed in themselves as individuals and saw themselves as a community of individualists. When they came together as a group, they manifested the American cultural belief that a society is a collection of individuals and that a majority decides. They made decisions affecting the group according to the tried and true, historically tested American belief in majority rule. If experience proved a decision to be impracticable, they reformed it by further discussion and another vote in which the will of the majority was decisive.

Ideologues operate in a different way. Everyone must conform to the decisions of the ideological group's leaders. There must be no diversity of opinion, no deviance. This is called "democracy by consensus." It works as follows: a meeting is held, and the leaders of the group present a matter for discussion and decision. The leaders (who have decided beforehand on what they want done) make it clear in their presentation of matters for decision what they think should be done. Once that has been clarified, and any question or concern that a member of the group might have has been addressed by the leaders, one of the leaders calls for a show of hands to see who agrees with them. There are no written bylaws of procedure, no precisely worded motions made and seconded according to rules of order derived from parliamentary experience. Nor are there any amendments moved and seconded, debated, and voted on, one at a time, before the final vote is taken on the motion, a vote that will either carry or fail by getting majority assent rather than unanimous approval. In democracy by consensus, everything depends on the authority of the leaders, who have explained to everyone who joins the group at the time that they join that all decisions will be made by consensus. And what that means is that anyone who cannot go along with the consensus has to leave the group. (The show of hands is to see if everyone agrees with the leaders.) No one can remain in the group unless they are willing to abide by this consensus. Anyone who wants to remain in the group knows that he is supposed to raise his hand in agreement with the leaders, and there is seldom any dissent. If there is a dissenter in the group, that is, someone unwilling to raise his or her hand in assent, there is further discussion focusing entirely on the dissenter's opinion. If after this the dissenter still disagrees with the consensus, then he or she is ousted from the group—not for the remainder of that meeting, but permanently. This procedure of governance in the Soviet Union was known as "democratic centralism."

That is the way the meetings of Nuclear Free State that I attended for a couple of months in Tucson, Arizona, were conducted. There were three leaders, two men and a woman, and the group's decisions were always unanimous. In being a participant in (or, more accurately, a useful idiot in!) this Marxist political action group, I had my brief career as an activist (except for some picketing I did, and am still proud of, in North Carolina during the civil rights movement in the early 1960s). I quite stupidly in 1979 believed what was said in the movie *The China Syndrome* when the nuclear engineer played by Jack Lemmon tells an activist journalist played by Jane Fonda that if the nuclear power plant where he works ever "melted down" (the China Syndrome) it would "take out an area the size of Pennsylvania." Since I was born and raised in Pennsylvania, I thought that this was a horrible possibility and that America's nuclear power industry should be shut down. It took me a couple of months of meetings to discover that the leaders of Nuclear Free State were not interested in shutting down the nuclear power industry in Arizona or any other state. Their real purpose was to agitate for the elimination of America's nuclear weapons through unilateral disarmament.

I left the group the evening a mysterious young man, who was anonymously introduced by the leaders of Nuclear Free State simply as someone "just returned from South America," spoke to us in learned detail, using printed charts and colored graphs worthy of a Department of Defense briefing to illustrate his points. His subject was America's arsenal of nuclear weapons and the need for America to disarm. After the meeting, I asked this young man whether he wanted the Soviets to disarm too, and he said that socialist uses of nuclear energy were different from capitalist uses because socialist uses were "for the people." Only capitalist nuclear weapons and engineering had to be eliminated. (This was a few years before the accidents at Three Mile Island in Pennsylvania and Chernobyl in the Soviet Union demonstrated to the world the great difference between the safety features of capitalist and communist nuclear power plants.) After that conversation, I attended no more meetings of Nuclear Free State.

After several decades of the counter-culture movement, the most liberated people in America today are visible on the streets of every middle-size and large American city. They are the social derelicts euphemistically called "the homeless," who live a day-to-day, hand-to-mouth existence, separated from all social obligations. Theirs is a completely liberated lifestyle, one that is guaranteed to be self-destructive and to cause problems for them and society. Homeless men and women are free to die prematurely. Their way of life reflects the nasty, brutal, dehumanizing reality of living each day liberated from the American cultural principles of equal freedom and individual responsibility that make men responsible for themselves and that oblige them to contribute to the good of society.

The harmfulness of ideologies is also evident in the effects of radical feminism. Women's liberation, it must be said, is a lie. It is the liberation of *men* that has been accomplished by radical feminism. Men have been freed by the sexual revolution of the 1960s from responsibility for their sexual behavior, and multitudes of women have paid the price for their liberation from being honored as wives and mothers in the institution of marriage (which "woman's lib" regards as a kind of slavery). They have been freed from enduring mutual commitments. Now, instead of marriage, they have "relationships."

Ideology is detrimental to healthy social relations. To those in the service of an ideology, neither society as it exists nor the personal lives of individuals within that society are of any importance whatever. What is sacred is the ideology. That is why an ideologue sees abortion as liberation. What happens to human beings (including themselves) does not matter. Everything revolves around the ideology. The counter-culture movement opposes the family, patriotism, and religion because these represent rival loyalties that are more important than ideology. As noted earlier, those who have been captivated by an ideology regard anything that does not conform to its pre-scriptions as malicious and stupid. But everyone who does conform to the thinking of the ideology is automatically virtuous and intelligent. One has only to be absolutely loyal to the ideology to be automatically smart and righteous.

An ideologue would never believe that poverty is relative to needs. Yet a wealthy man who does not live within his means is in the same psychological distress and economic condition as the man constantly dependent on others for food and shelter. As Henry David Thoreau, one of the sagest Americans ever to author a book, said in 1854, "[A] man is rich in proportion to the number of things he can afford to let alone."[12] We are each of us responsible for our own happiness and our own poverty or wealth. How, then, are we responsible for the self-indulgence of our neighbors that may cause them to be in want, whether they live in a mansion or a hovel? Nor should we be responsible for the sins of our ancestors or the sins of our children past the age of their majority. There are limits to our individual liabilities. And if we go through life feeling sorry for ourselves because our parents did not dis-charge their parental responsibilities toward us as we think they should have when we were children, and if we blame them or society for any fault in our lives, what sort of adults are we? Are we not in a state of permanent infancy, entirely lacking in responsibility for ourselves?

Our cultural ancestors came to America to leave their past behind them and to take responsibility for building a better future for themselves and their children. It is culturally un-American to hold present generations account-able for what generations long since at rest in the earth may have done. We might just as well puff ourselves up and call ourselves great because we had ancestors who did great things. We have no right to take credit for what they did; nor should we allow anyone to hold us accountable for any wrongdoing of theirs.

The greatest slavery is surely what enslaves the soul, what robs a person of his equal freedom as a human being created by God. In the latter half of the twentieth century, a thralldom of that sort that called itself "liberation" insinuated itself into the American way of life. Once the idea of this libera-tion became fashionable and embracing or at least tolerating, the ideology of the counter-culture movement came to be regarded as smart and virtuous, and then the movement picked up adherents among those who wanted to think of themselves as more intelligent and more moral than other people. At this point it gained a momentum that it still has, though the momentum has of late been noticeably slowing.

Wanting to be morally justified is a strong tendency of human nature that affects people in every class of a society. When the counter-culture movement became chic in the 1970s among intelligent, educated Americans and came to be associated in the minds of many persons with being against racism and sexism, it was then that it became a serious threat to American society and its culture.

CHAPTER SIX

Bending: A Means of Cultural Subversion

Turning a culture's strength against itself is what I am calling "bending." And a good deal of bending has occurred during the counter-culture movement in the United States.

What strengths of American culture have been turned against it? The American responsiveness to right and wrong. The indispensable U.S. Constitution. The American belief in freedom. The American belief in helping others. The American belief in equality. The American belief in a government of laws.

The Spanish conquests of Mexico and Peru afford extreme examples illustrative of the powerful effects bending can have. These phenomenal conquests of populous empires by a few hundred determined, disciplined soldiers led by insightful and undauntable commanders were accomplished because both Cortés and Pizarro perceived the respective strengths of the Aztec and Inca empires and used them to effect their conquests.

When the small troop of infantry and cavalry commanded by Hernán Cortés entered the Valley of Mexico in 1519 and beheld the Aztec capital of Tenochtitlán, it was one of the biggest cities in the world.[1] (Under its present name, Mexico City, it is still the world's second-largest metropolis.) The seventy-eight temples, palaces, and state buildings of the city, including the two-hundred-feet-high pyramid of its main temple, were erected on land-fill around rocky islets in the midst of the large lake that then existed in the valley. Three fortified causeways and thousands of canoes brought supplies and tribute to the great city every day from the territories the Aztecs had conquered across central Mexico from sea to sea. The variety and quantity of goods for sale in Tenochtitlán's daily market surpassed the amount of mer-chandise brought from all over Europe to Spain's annual fair at Medina del Campo.

How could a paltry military force like the one Cortés commanded con-quer this center of Aztec power? It was done by perceiving and taking advan-tage of the history of the Aztecs' relations with the other civilized peoples of central Mexico, with whom they had dealt harshly in subjugating them. With the willing aid of these Mexicans who hated the Aztecs, Cortés ordered a squadron of ships constructed, disassembled, and carried in pieces to the lake, where he had the thirteen vessels reassembled, launched, and armed with cannon. Using this flotilla, Cortés cut off food and supplies to Tenochtitlán. What had been a source of protection—the city's isolation in the midst of the lake—made it a death trap once the Spaniards had control of the lake. Famine followed by pestilence killed most of the city's population that did not die in battle trying to break the siege by the Spaniards and their Mexican allies. With the fall of Tenochtitlán in 1521, the Aztec empire col-lapsed.

A decade later, in Peru, the same sort of thing happened. Again a bold, perceptive Spanish commander of a quite small expeditionary force used a great civilization's own strength to overthrow it. The Inca empire was as advanced as that of the Aztecs and of far greater extent. It ran for more than three thousand miles along the Pacific coast of South America and stretched inland up the western slopes of the Andes, across the wide tablelands of the central Andes, and down the eastern side of the cordillera to the jungles of the Amazon Basin. The Inca empire's thousands of miles of paved roads tra-versed every sort of terrain and spanned dozens of Andean gorges with sus-pension bridges of up to five hundred feet in length. Precisely engineered irrigation systems distributed water, sometimes over distances of hundreds of miles, to arid regions throughout the empire, and made them into productive agricultural land. In the palace-temple of the imperial capital at Cuzco, a garden of plants and trees sculpted in gold, complete with insects and birds on their delicate twigs and leaves, dazzled the beholder. There were twenty life-size statues in gold of llamas and their attendant shepherds in this gar-den, in tribute to the millions of state-owned llamas that yielded the Inca emperor immense resources of wool and meat. The Incas' imperial wealth was also reflected in the fortress at Cuzco constructed of colossal blocks of cut stone weighing up to sixty tons. Within the formidable walls of this mighty fortress, which could accommodate the city's entire population, were abundant sources of water and storehouses stocked with enough *charqui* (dehydrated llama meat), dried corn, and *chuñu* (dehydrated potatoes) to withstand a prolonged siege. But Francisco Pizarro, commander of the Spanish expeditionary force to Peru, did not have the military wherewithal to lay siege to Cuzco. Instead he invited the Inca emperor, who was worshipped by his subjects as a god, to meet with him at Cajamarca. And there, in that Inca city, on November 16, 1532, in a do-or-die ambush that slaughtered hundreds of the emperor's unarmed retinue and routed the rest, Pizarro and his soldiers who numbered only around 270 infantry and 30 horsemen (the Incas had never seen horses) took Atahualpa prisoner. The overconfident god-emperor of a realm the size of Western Europe with a population numbered in the millions had mistakenly considered himself safe from assault by such a tiny band of invaders.

The power of the Inca empire lay in its centralized authority. By capturing Atahualpa and issuing orders through him, Pizarro mastered that power. Centuries of orderly succession to the Inca throne had acculturated hundreds of thousands of bureaucrats to obey the emperor's orders, and the empire's millions of peasants were accustomed to obeying these imperial functionaries (an estimated one for every ten subjects of the emperor). Pizarro conquered the Inca empire by turning the power of the Inca state and the central religious belief of its culture (obedience to the god-emperor) against it. When the Spaniards finally executed their imperial prisoner, they created a vacuum of power in a society whose culture depended on a hierarchy of authority, and then they filled the vacuum.

Similarly, as one commentator has said, the counter-culture movement has used "freedom and democracy to undermine the foundations of freedom and democracy."[2]

Americans in the past half-century have been made to feel that their country's history is contemptible because it is not immaculate. They have been made to feel ashamed of their society's incredible wealth, as if it were immoral for any society to have as many people who are as well-off as America's extraordinarily hard-working middle class. (It is from their ranks that most of America's millionaires have emerged, generation after generation.) Americans have been made to feel shame that slavery once existed in their society, a century and a half ago, as if America's unprecedented wealth was mainly the result of slave labor instead of free labor. (One must look at the history of Brazil for an example of a New World society whose wealth was based on slave labor.) Americans have been made to feel ashamed that there is any poverty in their society. Americans have seen their belief in freedom bent into the idea of liberation and their belief in the equality of human beings as children of God bent into a demand for equality of condition. They have seen laws bent into social engineering and justice bent into social justice. They have seen progress through practical improvements bent into stagnant bureaucratic systems of regulation and control. They have seen personal responsibility bent into social responsibility. They have seen their culture's belief in individuals pursuing opportunities that they imagine for themselves bent into group entitlements and a demand that opportunities be provided by government. They have seen America's historic diversity of immigrants that has made Americans a praiseworthy "race of races" (as the poet Walt Whitman called Americans) bent into diversity quotas. They have seen freedom of speech bent into the freedom to say only what is politically correct.

Bending in America in the second half of the twentieth century has been attacking one's political opponents as immoral and unintelligent while asserting the fairness of whatever suits one's own political ends. Bending has been creating divisiveness and calling it justice. Bending has been advocating tolerance while being stridently intolerant. Bending has been saying that truth is relative while claiming for one's own views an absolute correctness. Bending has been inventing novel rights while abolishing long-established rights. The tools of bending are misrepresentations, half-truths, double standards, and deceit.

Here are specific illustrations of bending. A *New York Times* column by Anna Quindlen on June 13, 1993, titled "A Political Correction," justified the theft of an entire run of a university newspaper (see description of this incident in chapter 3). Since Quindlen herself is a newspaper columnist, one would have thought she would have been unequivocally opposed to censorship of this kind. And she did, sort of, disapprove of it.

> During the last few months there has been gnashing of teeth about pilfered student newspapers at various institutions of education spirited away in the night by students who found certain free speech objectionable and so imprisoned it. [Besides the theft of newspapers at the University of Pennsylvania, an edition of a conservative student newspaper at Dartmouth had also been stolen.] This is no good. The right to free speech must include the right to objectionable free speech. That is the overarching argument, and I buy it. But [there is always a *but*—that is where the bending begins] the uproar implies that these students are being insulated from counter orthodoxy, thought-policed in liberal bastions. Let's let real life intrude for a minute among ivory tower discussions of hate speech, free speech and the now ritual complaint that variations from some P. C. [i.e., politically correct] party line are put down.

Quindlen then gave four examples of "real life": the murders of a homosexual and a Japanese exchange student, the failure of some food-servers to provide black Secret Service agents the same attention as their white fellow agents, and a U.S. senator's remark that he would not vote to confirm a "damn lesbian" for a high-ranking federal job. This juxtaposition suggested that it would be well to restrict complaints to serious matters like homophobia and racism and stop making an "uproar" over such trivial matters as "pilfered" newspapers "spirited away in the night." Quindlen's final *but* made this point quite clear:

> There are complaints that because of incidents like the one at Penn, students feel
> inhibited about airing their opinions on campuses that have become oversensitive
> to minority groups. But let's remember that there are good inhibitions, and there
> are bad inhibitions. If people can no longer discuss their differences, that is bad. If
> people make fewer racist jokes, that is fine.

Thus, she bent press censorship—when it was correctly motivated—into a "good inhibition." How stealing newspapers might inhibit racist jokes was not explained.

Consider this further instance of bending by another politically correct, syndicated columnist, Molly Ivins. Her column in the *Arizona Daily Star* for June 17, 1994, titled "Amid Irrelevant Political Debate, We Ignore Increasingly Divided Nation," bent criminal activity into a career choice.

> [A]ll our wringing of hands about the decline of the family, the rise of illegitimate
> births, teen-age crime and gangs (all of which the right wing now says can be cured
> by abolishing welfare), stems from the fact that more and more Americans have
> neither jobs nor hope nor opportunity. Hard work will not get them ahead; it will
> leave them further behind. No wonder many of them are choosing crime; it's obviously more remunerated, and they're not stupid.

According to this voice from the Left, crime when committed by someone out of work can be justified quite simply: it pays, stupid! Yet when unemployment in the United States ran as high as 30 percent nationwide during the Great Depression of the 1930s, there was no commensurate rise in the crime rate. How could that be if crime is merely a career choice in response to a depressed economy? Perhaps it was because seventy years ago there was still a widely respected, intact moral tradition of right and wrong based on the Ten Commandments that discouraged illicit conduct and because most Americans in the 1930s still belonged to extended families that could provide some support when times were bad. It should be obvious to anyone who is not an ideologue that "choosing crime" as a career is not a choice that society is obliged to prevent unemployed young men from making by providing them with more remuneration than they could earn through working. Molly Ivins's claim that "hard work would not get [Americans] ahead [but] leave them further behind" is an outstanding example of ideological bending.

And what are we to make of the reasoning that bends burning the symbol of America into the virtue of free speech? But since the 1960s, that is what has happened. U.S. senators, and justices of the Supreme Court, now regard burning the American flag in public as nothing more than freedom of speech. This bending authorizes the same vitriolic and total hatred of America that one sees whenever a mob in a foreign country burns the American flag. This is not the free criticism of government that the free speech clause in the First Amendment was written to protect. To claim constitutional protection for flag burning as freedom of speech is to bend the Constitution into an instrument to attack America and protect expression of intense hatred of the country. If burning the flag is merely freedom of speech, then so is a cross burning by Ku Klux Klansmen (which of course it is not). If burning the flag is a "speech act," it undoubtedly falls into the category of what the Left calls "hate speech," the same as a KKK cross burning.

Those who bend the meaning of words have especially concentrated on the First Amendment of the Constitution because they know that in the United States the Constitution is revered and that Supreme Court interpretations of it will be obeyed. (The Constitution is revered and obeyed in American culture because it is indispensable to the existence of the United States: no Constitution, no United States.) The Supreme Court decision in *Roe v. Wade* that made abortion a constitutional right of women provides a foremost example of bending the Constitution. The Court found in that case in 1973 that it was unconstitutional for a state government to prohibit abortion during the first three months of a pregnancy. Once that ruling was handed down, however, it was bent, and then bent again and again, until now killing a full-term, fully formed baby emerging from the birth canal (in what is euphemistically termed "partial-birth abortion") has become a constitutionally permissible and protected choice.

The defenders of *Roe v. Wade* justify a woman's decision to abort the developing human baby in her body at any stage of the baby's development as "a woman's right to choose." Thus the idea of choice (the essence of freedom) becomes the issue, not *what is chosen*, which is the true moral and legal issue in any exercise of freedom of choice. Reasoning in the way the federal courts have reasoned in regard to abortion, one might justify murder or car theft or rape or any criminal act that was premeditated as merely a choice that someone makes, if what is chosen is disregarded. (Remember Molly Ivins's reasoning in her column regarding crime as a career choice that young men make because they are out of work and are "not stupid.") But apparently those who insist on a woman's right to choose with regard to abortion do not want her to make an *informed* choice. From 1995 to 2003, abortion clinic operators, with the organizational backing of NARAL Pro-Choice America (NARAL is the abbreviation for the National Association to Repeal Abortion Laws) and its supporters, including such prominent feminist activists as Tipper Gore and Hillary Clinton, opposed on the lecture circuit, in the media, and through the courts all the way to the Supreme Court an Indiana law requiring a pregnant women who was seeking an abortion to be shown pictures of her baby's stage of development and counseled on abortion procedures. The statute also required that the woman after receiving this counseling then wait eighteen hours before making her final decision as to whether to have the abortion. The Supreme Court when it finally decided the case in February 2003 upheld the constitutionality of the Indiana law. The reaction of the president of NARAL Pro-Choice America, Kate Michelman, to the ruling was to continue denouncing the Indiana statute as "an outrageous law" that left many women "without access to abortions or certainly places a heavy burden, an undue burden, on a woman's right to choose."[3] It is difficult to see, however, how the Indiana law denied women "access to abortions." But when you're interested in bending the truth you're not interested in speaking the truth.

In bending to suit its purposes such important beliefs of American culture as freedom and constitutionality, the counter-culture movement regularly engages in censorship. Long lists of politically incorrect words and their politically correct substitutes have been devised to guide writers and the publishers of books on politically permissible language. Feminists in the counter-culture movement, for instance, have banned the use of *man* in the sense of "human beings" because the word also means "a male," and therefore its meaning as "human beings," they say, is sexist. Yet using the word *man* to mean "human beings" goes back to the beginning of the American republic. (See the entry for *man* in Noah Webster's *A Compendious Dictionary of the English Language*, 1806.) The great lexicographer Webster in his monumental *American Dictionary of the English Language* (1828) traced the word *man* as meaning "human beings" to Sanskrit, the oldest written language providing evidence for the beginning of the Indo-European family of languages to which English belongs. (The earliest extant Sanskrit texts are nearly four thousand years old.)

Even more arbitrarily and again for purely political purposes, radical feminists in the counter-culture movement have even proscribed as sexist those words in which *man* appears as a syllable. The following is a sampling from published lists of words that have been declared sexist and biased because they include the syllable *man*, and whose use has therefore been prohibited for anyone who does not want to be labeled sexist: airman, anchorman, chairman, congressman, councilman, doorman, draftsman, fireman, foreman, garbageman, groundsman, journeyman, junkman, letterman, lumberman, mailman, man-hour, manhunt, man-made, manpower, middleman, milkman, newspaperman, plainsman (politically correct substitute: *plains dweller*), policeman, postman, pressman, repairman, salesman (*sales representative* is the politically correct substitute for both this word and saleswoman), seaman, serviceman, snowman (*snowperson* is the politically correct term), spokesman, statesman, strawman, and yes-man.[4]

The only word having *man* in it as a syllable that radical feminist have made little headway in suppressing is *woman*, an old, old word in English whose etymological origin is a man (i.e., a human being) with a womb (see entry for *woman* in Webster's *American Dictionary of the English Language*, 1828). Radical feminists have tried to obscure that etymology by demanding that the spelling of *woman* be altered to *womon* or *womban* to eliminate the hated sight of the allegedly sexist syllable *man*.[5]

Of course, except for *woman*, in none of the words just cited that have the syllable *man* in them—businessman, doorman, serviceman, and so forth—is gender necessarily a part of the meaning. And if gender is part of the meaning of a word having the syllable *man* in it, the context of its use will usually make that significance clear. The word *chairman*, for instance, means only a human being who presides over a meeting or an organization. Yet by categorizing it as sexist, feminists have almost eliminated its use.

Among agencies and publishers that have promulgated politically correct word-lists to govern language use are the American Institutes for Research (*AIR Principles for Bias, Sensitivity, and Language Simplification*, 2000), Educational Testing Service (*Sensitivity Review Process: Guidelines and Procedures*, 1992), Harcourt Publishers (*Striving for Fairness*, 2001), Harcourt Horizons (*Editorial Guidelines*, 2001), Houghton Mifflin (*Eliminating Stereotypes*, 1981), the Massachusetts Department of Education (*Guidelines for Bias Review of the Massachusetts Comprehensive Assessment System*, 1998), Macmillan, McGraw Hill (*Reflecting Diversity*, 1993), National Evaluation Systems (*Bias Issues in*

Text Development, 1991), and the New York City Board of Education (*Promoting Bias Free Curriculum Materials: A Resource Guide for Staff Development*, 1988).[6] Many more publishers, agencies, professional associations, and corporations besides these have taken on the role of language policing through their published lists of so-called sexist, racist, or otherwise insensitive and biased words. Supposedly words like *chairman* and *congressman* offend women. But what the creation of bogus lists of insensitive words and their allegedly more sensitive substitutes truly serves is the counter-culture movement's interest in fostering class consciousness and a sense of victimization among certain groups. Language policing is now, after forty years of counter-culture rhetoric, common practice in America in education, business, and everyday speech.

The counter-culture movement has even convinced a few Americans that it is insensitive of them to use the terms *American* and *America* to refer to themselves and their country! The argument is this: inhabitants of the United States of America have unfairly appropriated the word *American* to refer only to themselves and the word *America* to refer only to their country, unfairly, that is, because *America* can refer to the entire Western Hemisphere. Every inhabitant of North and South America, the language police say, is an American. This critique of the supposed insensitivity and arrogance of Americans is, of course, a self-contradiction. For if the inhabitants of Argentina, Brazil, Canada, Mexico, and other countries in the Western Hemisphere have the right to call themselves Americans (which they surely do if they want to), then so do inhabitants of the United States of America, and for the same reason: they too inhabit America, in the continental meaning of the word. As to the charge that Americans have unfairly expropriated the continental meaning of *America* for their exclusive use, should they refer only and always to their country formally as the United States of America? In being the only country to incorporate the continental name *America*, the inhabitants of the United States of America have a natural right to abbreviate their country's name to either *the United States* or *America*. If someone thinks the United States, the first nation in the post-1492 Western Hemisphere to revolt against European rule and win its independence, had no right to call itself the United States of America, such a person is too ideological to be reasoned with.

Why is language being policed, and why are so many Americans participating in it? It is being done for the same reason that there is only one candidate per office in a communist election: to exercise power (even to the point of requiring that a snowman be referred to as a *snowperson*) and by exercising that power to strengthen it.

Language policing is not a trivial matter. When a word's use is prohibited, its meaning dims. And when behaviors, objects, and concepts are no longer spoken of in the way they once were, they eventually lose their former meaning. A vocabulary that is politically defined reinforces the politics that does the defining. In countries with communist governments, for instance, ideologically correct language is the only language allowed. And the enforcement of politically correct diction conditions people's minds to think in terms of the communist party line. It is the politics of the counter-culture movement in America that explains why such words as *housewife* and *homemaker* are seldom used anymore. It also explains why *God* and *Satan* appear on the list of prohibited words promulgated by the Association of Education Publishers.[7] *Housewife, homemaker, God,* and *Satan* do not represent politically correct ideas. They are words that make possible traditional modes of thought.

Language policing in America succeeds by bending kindliness. When kind-hearted and decent people are told again and again that a certain vocabulary shows insensitivity and bias and that another set of words that are allegedly unbiased and sensitive must be used, they begin censoring their own language and the language of people around them. They willy-nilly become a part of the counter-culture movement's language police (also sometimes referred to as "the thought police," because language is inextricable from thought). Using politically correct diction becomes a badge of sensitivity. It distinguishes kind persons from everyone who is supposedly insensitive. And in a society like America's, where people take leave of each other by saying "Have a nice day," few people want to be thought of as insensitive, so the politically correct vocabulary soon catches on and becomes standard diction in everyday discourse. Language policing in the name of sensitivity enforces the idea that certain groups in society have been victimized and must therefore be shown special linguistic consideration. To do otherwise is to be guilty of racism, sexism, homophobia, or some other psychological aggression in the victims and victimizers melodrama that the counter-culture movement has scripted as the truth of American history.

Only in a society where sensitivity is already prevalent, however, can language policing catch on. For if it were true that America was as insensitively racist, sexist, and homophobic as the counter-culture claims it is, how is it that an appeal to sensitivity could be effective? Only a sensitive person is bothered by being told it is insensitive to use certain words. A callous person wouldn't even know what you were talking about if you told him his language was insensitive. And if he did understand you, he wouldn't much care (being insensitive) what you thought of him. Only persons who are not racists care about being called that. A racist if you called attention to his prejudices might think you were complimenting him for being forthright, because he regards his prejudices as nothing but the unvarnished truth.

It should also be noted that language policing involves a double standard. Activists in the counter-culture movement insist that other persons not use words that they have identified as offensive to the groups whose consciousness of being victims they are trying to establish. But they themselves claim, *as their right of free speech*, the public use of four-letter words that are highly offensive to the sensibilities of a majority of Americans. Double standards are fundamental to the process of bending. There is the standard pertaining to the beliefs of American culture, and there is a second standard representing the politically correct ideas of the counter-culture. The Left either attacks or ignores the former standard by insisting on the exclusive applicability of its standard, while denying that any double standard of language-use exists.

The free speech movement on the University of California, Berkeley, campus in 1964, which is credited with giving the counter-culture movement its initial impetus and national publicity, exemplifies the counter-culture movement's double standard when it comes to language. The free speech movement started the use of obscenities that is now commonplace in public contexts. One newspaper article that I recall on the free speech movement at Berkeley carried as part of its coverage a photo of a young man sitting cross-legged on the ground unsmilingly staring at the camera and holding a hand-lettered sign on which he had cleverly written, "PHUQUE." The word epitomized the scorn he and other participants in the free speech movement at Berkeley had for the principle of middle-class decorum and for middle-class standards of language propriety. But in 1964 he considered it prudent to present the word in a phonetic spelling. Now, forty years later, that word (spelled nonphonetically) regularly appears in novels and in the dialogue of feature films made by Hollywood for national and international distribution. The word's use in public still discomforts and offends a majority of middle-class Americans. But nowadays, at the beginning of the third generation since the free speech movement gave the counter-culture movement its initial impetus, Americans are becoming less sensitive to seeing and hearing it in public contexts. Even some children and women now use the word in their speech so as not to be thought of as children or women in the traditional way. To many females caught up in the ideology of women's liberation, being a lady has little or no meaning, and unlady-like behavior, including the use of vulgar and obscene words in public, is engaged in as a sign of their liberation.

Besides language, politicized art is another important means of bending Christian cultures. Those who object to granting the status of art to putrid carcasses of turkeys or to a nude woman covered in chocolate ("a living sculpture") are dismissed by the counter-culture movement as prudes or puritans who want to impose their idea of art on everyone else. The real imposition, however, in the examples of alleged art just mentioned, is the substitution of putridness, obscenity, vulgarity, or prurience for the idea of art. Despite the Left's insistence on the idea that no one can say what is or is not art, there is such a thing as decadence. And decadence is not necessarily in the eye of the beholder.

If art is to have a humanizing purpose, it ought to be in the service of excellence and beauty, not sordidness and ugliness. That has been the traditional theory of art in Western civilization. The counter-culture movement's idea of art is that it should challenge and "deconstruct" a people's inherited cultural beliefs. The civilizing decorum and humanizing effects traditionally served by Western art have been put aside by artists in Europe and the Americas intent on insulting conventional decorum and the sense of what has been in the past thought of as civilized decency in Western countries. Politicized art deliberately assaults normative standards of decency with the intention of destroying them. Pornography serves the same purpose by stimulating lust at the expense of sexual affection and tenderness. When the French Revolution began the destruction of the ancien régime of Europe during the Enlightenment, the modern idea of the artist as a "poor but free spirit" was born among the coteries of artists who gathered in the cafes of eighteenth-century Paris. This was the idea of the artist as a bohemian liberated from "the bonds of the greedy and hypocritical bourgeoisie." Artists then wanted to be "whatever the fat burghers feared most" and to look at the world "in a way they couldn't see."[8]

Trends in literature, painting, film, music, dance, sculpture, and architecture in the United States after the Second World War reflected an increasing hostility toward American middle-class sensibilities and the traditions of Western civilization. More and more frequently, artists rejected the artistic concepts of harmony, balance, restraint, unity, and symmetry that had distinguished the arts in Western civilization since the Renaissance, and much of which had been devoted to Christian themes. Avant-garde artists favored asymmetry, abstraction, dissonance, incoherence, excess, and eccentric "self-expression." In the years following World War II, architectural design became in some instances intentionally out of plumb and even dysfunctionally whimsical. What passed for music was sometimes little more than monotonous, thudding rhythms that overwhelmed the melody, if any, and what was called singing was sometimes little different from shouts and screams. (Electronically amplified music of that kind can reach decibel levels that cause hearing loss, even deafness.) Sculpture became . . . well, almost anything, even draping a landscape, a bridge, a building in fabric. (One sculptor in the late twentieth century scattered granular material on the floor of a bare room and declared it an "art-installation.") As for the theater, a play titled *The Vagina Monologues* consisted solely of a woman on stage talking about feminism. This didactic play, or onstage lecture, introduced the term and the concept of "victim art" to the American art scene. And, once-respectable universities like Harvard and Princeton hire professors like Cornel West to teach "protest art" for university credit in what purports to be higher education.

Musicians, sculptors, and dramatists who produce art like this have no interest in creating something of enduring social value. Immediate political consumption is their standard, though they invoke the idea of art to justify their performance. Anyone who rejects protest art as art is scorned as an intolerant, narrow-minded ignoramus. The late twentieth century made performance, or the self-conscious breaking of conventions, the equivalent of art. The more bizarre the iconoclasm, the better. The way in which the artist destroyed conventions was his style, and style—or rather the impact that a style could have—was the value of the performance.

In the 1990s among the works displayed at the New Museum of Contemporary Art in New York City was a painting showing penises inserted in a woman's eyes, nose, mouth, and ears. Another artwork on display was hundreds of varnished bars of soap, each having an obscene word painted on it; another, a large photograph in color of a man's genitals draped over the head of a doll. At New York's Whitney Museum, a puddle of vomit was presented as "mixed-media" art and titled "The Sweet and Pungent Smell of Success." In Washington, D.C., at the Museum of Natural History, performance artists in makeup and costume, inside a cage labeled "Undiscovered Aborigines," spoke gibberish and feebly swayed when docents (as per instruction) encouraged museum visitors to ask them to dance and tell stories. These performance artists, as they termed themselves, were, according to the museum's description of their performance, supposed to represent the effects of the West's "cultural imperialism" on non-Western peoples. A photograph of a crucifix immersed in the urine of an artist has also been displayed; and this

artist denied that he had intended any insult to Christianity. (Benders typi-
cally proclaim their innocence when accused of wrongdoing.) Protest art
could also be an American flag on the floor of a museum that visitors are
invited to step on or a sheep carcass cut longitudinally in two.[9] All of the
above passed for art in the late twentieth century, and museum-goers solemnly paid to see it because museum directors exhibited it as such.

Protest art is political exhibitionism. Such art is motivated by hostility to
Western civilization and is restrained only by the limits of the artist's ability
to imagine what will shock and demean the values of anyone who reveres
that civilization. The rejection of convention represents more than an
attempt to be original. It has the political purpose of subverting the existing
culture.

The first big art movement in the United States after the Second World
War was Abstract Expressionism, and Jackson Pollock (1912–1956) was its
biggest name. His paintings expressed the spirit of the iconoclasm that would
become more and more pronounced as the second half of the twentieth century wore on. One art historian has praised the "tangled, tormented lines
and lack of central focus" of Pollock's paintings as "revolutionary attempts
to liberate himself and American culture from the constraints of traditional
art-making and postwar consensus." This same art historian describes the
general subject-matter of Pollock and his fellow Abstract Expressionists as
"personal expression and social alienation."[10] Abstract Expressionists seldom
represented the human form. If they did represent something that even
vaguely suggested the human form, it was sure to be jagged, contorted, dis-
jointed, unnaturally colored.

There were many schools of avant-garde art besides Abstract Expressionism in the postwar period of the second half of the twentieth century. A few
of the schools or movements originated in the Southwest, on the West Coast,
or in the District of Columbia. But for the most part they were centered, like
Abstract Expressionism, in New York City, the reputed "art capital of the
world" in the decades following World War II. To name some of these
schools and movements, there was assemblage art, black art, body art, con-
ceptual art, earthworks, feminist art (including Guerrilla Girls), the figura-
tive school, Fluxus art, found art, funk art, happenings, installation art, the
light and space movement, minimalism, neo-Dada, neo-expressionism, neo-
geo, op art, outside art, pop art, postminimalism, postmodernism, psyche-
delic art, video art, the Washington school, and word art. The shelf life of
avant-garde art before it got stale was brief. To have impact a style had to be
new. Potential art patrons, museum directors, and art critics in the postwar

period required constant innovation to keep them interested. And in the late twentieth century, the vacuous, value-free adjective *interesting* became the all-purpose term of praise in art talk.

The media used in this ephemeral art were also nontraditional. Besides paint and canvas, avant-garde artists worked in excrement, urine, neon, video, shards of glass, yarn, fur, blocks of molded lipstick, chocolate, soap, chicken bones, bottle caps (and other refuse), light, space, and dirt, among other things. Traditional distinctions between painting and sculpture, art and gadgetry, political propaganda and landscaping, theater, or commercial art dissolved in the necessity of having an "interesting" style. In the post–World War II period, montage, collage, and mixed-media became standard practices among artists, just as cross-disciplinary studies became the rage among academics. Old categories of thought were among the things that had to be broken. And the old standards for judging the worth of art (Is it beautiful? Will it stand the test of time?) were cast aside. Art was deliberately created with the intent of being repulsive. One New York art critic in the 1960s, Clement Greenberg, even created an often-quoted maxim to justify the deliberate production of ugliness: "All profoundly original art looks ugly at first."[11]

Postwar artists like Jackson Pollock and Andy Warhol who were supposedly alienated from American society nonetheless depended on that society for their livelihood. They brokered their artworks through art dealers, gallery owners, professional art critics, and museum directors to any collector who wanted to establish their credentials for "cutting edge," sophisticated modernity by purchasing an avant-garde work of art that challenged conventional standards of art. But there were not enough wealthy individuals, corporations, and foundations to support every iconoclastic artist seeking support. Another source of funding was required. Hence the idea was put forth in the 1960s to establish an endowment for the arts that would tap the federal treasury to carry on the revolutionary work of protest art. After all, it was disingenuously argued, did not European countries such as France make money available to artists? Did America want to be known in the world as a backward, unsophisticated country that did not support the arts?

And so in 1965, Congress made American taxpayers the patrons of artworks that all but a tiny handful of them would have found repulsive had they known what their taxes were paying for. That same year, Congress also established a parallel foundation to support the humanities. Those who knew the roster of projects that the National Endowment for the Humanities (NEH) and the National Endowment for the Arts (NEA) were funding tried to inform Congress and the taxpayers of the situation. A former head of the NEH during Ronald Reagan's presidency, for instance, testified in 1995 that it was "time to do away with the Endowment, time to turn handling of the humanities—and the arts as well—back to the private sector." In Lynne V. Cheney's opinion, the expenditure of billions of dollars on the humanities and the arts since the 1960s had accomplished very little other than to make them "the servant" of what she politely called "social and political transformation." Among the arts projects she knew of that had been subsidized by the NEA were Joel-Peter Witkin's photograph of severed human limbs and an infant's corpse arranged amid prawns, grapes, and pomegranates as in an old-fashioned still-life painting of food; Andres Serrano's graphic photographs of corpses in a city morgue; and Ron Athey's art performance in which he sliced designs in the flesh of a fellow performer and two assistants wove needles through his scalp and put twenty-four hypodermic needles in his arm, after which he punctured the assistants' cheeks with very thin steel needles. (Yes, public money has been expended on such sadomasochism pretending to be art.) And professors of humanities at some of America's leading institutions of higher learning have defended art of this sort. Professor H. D. Buchloh of the Massachusetts Institute of Technology (MIT), for instance, laid down the following comprehensive dictum regarding anything-can-be-called-art art: "The central tool which bourgeois hegemonic culture (that is, white, male, Western culture) has traditionally used to exclude or marginalize all other cultural practices is the abstract concept of 'quality.'"[12]

The theory that the right to freedom of artistic expression justifies whatever anyone declares to be art is equivalent to the moral relativism that is so prominent a feature of the counter-culture movement. For moral relativism, too, embraces the idea that each individual has the right to decide what is right regardless of the traditional conventions and standards of decency in a society. The moral and cultural relativists (with the support of a good many academic "humanists") are attempting to prod Americans down the road to self-destruction by imposing their new definition of freedom. They have failed to move most middle-class Americans, but their tempting idea of liberation seems to have separated millions of young Americans in the last two generations from the values of their parents' and grandparents' culture.

The biggest art event of the counter-culture movement in the 1960s was a mammoth outdoor extravaganza held on a farm near the town of Woodstock in upstate New York that attracted an estimated 400,000 young people from all over the United States. This was a three-day orgy of drunken liberation, "getting stoned" on drugs, fornicating (sometimes in the midst of a crowd), and "letting it all hang out." This massive party was something entirely new under the American sun. It got a lot of young Americans over their middle-class "inhibitions." The self-proclaimed "pot head" and "Commie" Jerry Rubin who advocated having wild fun as a surefire way to transform "Amerika" was very clear about the purpose of such hedonism: "We will build our culture, and destroy capitalist, Christian culture."[13]

Uninhibited language, like uninhibited art, represents a significant bending of an essential element of America's democratic culture, that is, self-restraint. In a democratic society when self-restraint becomes bent, its deformity can destroy that society because democratic societies depend on the self-restraint of their citizens. In recent decades, a lack of self-restraint has even been evident in the decisions of the highest court in the United States, which no longer curbs lewdness and pornography. Repeatedly since the 1960s, the Supreme Court of the United States has ruled that to enforce long-established community standards in regard to lewd speech or pornography would be a blow to freedom of speech. In 1971, for example, the Court granted First Amendment free-speech protection to a man who entered a courtroom wearing a jacket emblazoned with an imperative statement telling any male who read it to go have sexual intercourse with himself. In rendering this decision, the highest court in the land was completely unmoved by the argument that a community's idea of decorum provides a sufficient standard for declaring such clothing impermissible in a courtroom. In overturning the man's conviction by a lower court, the majority of the judges on the Supreme Court in their unaccountable wisdom posed the question, "How is one to distinguish this [word] from any other offensive word?" and answered the question by declaring, "One man's vulgarity is another's lyric." (By this same logic, one knowledgeable student of the Supreme Court has remarked, one could justify armed robbery by asserting that one man's armed robbery is another man's "just redistribution of wealth.") Perhaps public nudity will be the next free speech the Supreme Court will sanction. After all, what one man views as nudity another man might see as an exercise of his right to choose whether to wear clothes.

And what is one to make of the Supreme Court's rulings in 1972 reversing lower-court verdicts in the following three cases: a man found guilty of disorderly conduct, breach of the peace, and obscene language (in addressing a school board meeting at which some forty children were present) for repeatedly using the adjective *motherf—ing* to describe the school's teachers and board, the town, and the United States; a verdict against a woman who shouted the same expletive at police who were arresting her son; and a finding of wrongdoing by a man for speaking words like that at a meeting in a university chapel? To put it mildly, such actions reflect the Supreme Court's "loss of will to maintain conventional moral standards." By thus refusing to allow punishment "for the same obscene and assaultive speech that was tolerated by supine university faculties and administrators in the late 1960s and early 1970s," the Supreme Court has legitimized such language and allowed it to become a behavior authorized by law.[14]

In *United States v. Playboy Entertaining Group, Inc.*, the Supreme Court found a federal law prohibiting sexually-oriented programming on cable television at times when children might be able to view it to be an unconstitutional infringement of free speech. The Court's bending of freedom of speech in this case included the following lofty rhetoric: "It is through speech that our convictions and beliefs are influenced, expressed, and tested. It is through speech that we bring those beliefs to bear on Government and society. It is through speech that our personalities are formed and expressed."[15] All well and good. But the speech in question was female masturbation. It had been the intent of the law passed by Congress to lessen the chances of children viewing such speech on television. How does televised female masturbation become a means of influencing, expressing, and testing (to quote the Court) "our convictions and beliefs"? How does the sight of female masturbation bring "those beliefs to bear on Government and society"? And how is personality "formed and expressed" through seeing female masturbation as a form of "speech"? This sort of judicial reasoning is as abstract as a Jackson Pollock painting and just as alienated as Pollock reputedly was from the norms of American society. Even though the justices of the Supreme Court have sworn to uphold the Constitution, which is supposed to serve the interests of American society, they have not been doing that in cases like the above.

Decisions like these by the Supreme Court have been largely responsible for what has been called today's "suffocating vulgarity of popular culture." The Court did not create the vulgarity. Base instincts are part of human nature. But it has traditionally been one of the functions of law to restrain such instincts.[16] The Supreme Court's rulings in recent decades have consistently defeated attempts to defend community standards of decency. They have allowed the idea of free speech to be so bent out of shape that uninhibited individuals can now violate the social decorum of whole communities in the name of freedom of speech. When restraints on pornography and obscene language are put in place by communities, state legislatures, or Congress and then nullified by the Supreme Court, base instincts and abstract rights rule the day.

The bending that has inflicted the most damage on American culture in the last four decades, however, has been in regard to freedom of religion. Anyone who understands American culture understands that belief in God is at the heart of the culture and is kept alive from generation to generation by freedom of religion. In other cultures, religion may not occupy a central position, but in American culture it does. The democratic principle of equal freedom and the republicanism of American government are both based on the belief that God has made human beings equals by endowing them, as his children, with an equal birthright to life, liberty, and the pursuit of happiness. The counter-culture movement opposes belief in God and equality based on that belief. It is committed to class rights and a totally secular politics that is hostile to religion.

As the U.S. Constitution was being debated in 1787 and 1788, several state constitutional conventions insisted, as a condition for their consent, that a set of amendments be added to the Constitution immediately after its ratification to protect the states from any infringement by the proposed federal government of the rights they and their citizens already enjoyed. And the first freedom protected in those first ten amendments to the Constitution (the Bill of Rights ratified in 1791) was religious freedom. This First Amendment to the Constitution reads: "Congress shall make no law respecting an establishment of religion, or prohibiting the free exercise thereof; or abridging the freedom of speech, or of the press, or the right of the people to peaceably assemble, and to petition the Government for a redress of grievances."

The importance of religion in American culture is reflected in the order of the liberties the First Amendment protects: freedom of religion, freedom of speech, freedom of the press, freedom of assembly, and freedom of petition. They were ordered in this way, it appears, because of the frequency of their exercise in the daily lives of most Americans. Freedom of religion was given priority as the freedom most often exercised by most Americans in their day-to-day lives. (Annual polls conducted in the United States from 1982 to 1993 regarding religion indicate that on average, even today, 55 percent of Americans pray daily, and only 2 percent say they never pray. That data corresponds closely with more recently gathered information in a UNESCO poll of international attitudes toward religion that found that 58 percent of Americans say God is "very important" to them, while only 19 percent of Britons responded in that way and only 13 percent of Frenchmen.[17]) Because the freedom to criticize government would also have to be protected, though its exercise would probably not be an everyday occurrence in the lives of most Americans, it was given second position after religious freedom. Since the freedom to express ideas in print would be exercised on a day-to-day basis only by writers and publishers, freedom of the press came third. And since attending an assembly of persons or signing a petition to government to redress a grievance would be a rather uncommon occurrence in the daily lives of most Americans, freedom of assembly and freedom of petition were given fourth and fifth positions.

Besides the priority given to freedom of religion, one also notices something else in studying the First Amendment: freedom of religion is the only one of the five First Amendment freedoms to have *two clauses* devoted to it. Why was that? Why was the free exercise clause insufficient? Why did the establishment clause have to be added?

There is a specific answer to this question. When the First Amendment became part of the Constitution in 1791, half the states of the United States—seven of the fourteen—had religious establishments. The establishment clause protected the religious establishments in New Hampshire, Massachusetts, Connecticut, New Jersey, Maryland, Delaware, and South Carolina from federal interference. That is why the establishment clause has the peculiar wording: "Congress shall make no law *respecting* an establishment of religion." (The meaning given in Webster's 1828 dictionary for the word *respecting* is: "Regarding; having regard to; relating to." And the example for the verb *respect* given by Webster is political, like its usage in the First Amendment: "The treaty particularly *respects* our commerce.") The establishment clause therefore was *not only* a prohibition against Congress establishing a religion. (That had already been provided for in Article VI of the Constitution, before the Bill of Rights was written, in the provision in its third paragraph, stating that "no religious Test shall ever be required as a qualification to any Office or public Trust under the United States.") The First Amendment was primarily, as its wording indicates, a prohibition on Congress in regard to the religious establishments in the states that had religious establishments when the amendment was ratified in 1791.

Thomas Jefferson expressed this understanding of the First Amendment's pair of religious clauses when he declared: "In matters of religion, I have considered its free exercise is placed by the Constitution independent of the powers of the general government."[18] That was Jefferson's most public definitive statement on the separation of church and state. In his judgment the First Amendment made religious practices entirely a matter for the states to decide. He stated this conviction in his Second Inaugural Address as president in 1805, several years after his often-quoted letter of January 1, 1802, to the Danbury Baptist Association in his first term as president, refusing the association's request to proclaim a national day of prayer. It was in that 1802 letter that Jefferson likened the First Amendment to "a wall of separation between church and State."[19] The capital-S *state* he referred to in this metaphor was *the federal government*. We can be quite certain that that was his meaning because when Jefferson was governor of Virginia he did proclaim a day of prayer for that state. He had no problem as a governor of a state in making a religious proclamation. Thomas Jefferson clearly understood, and declared publicly in his Second Inaugural Address as president, that the first religious clause in the First Amendment protected the states of the United States from federal trespass in all matters of religion, *even in the existence of an establishment of religion in the state*. That was the point of his famous metaphor of the wall. For a wall is something to keep interlopers and trespassers out.

An establishment of religion can take more than one form. But whatever form it takes, it always has two definitive features. First, there is always a law announcing the establishment and naming the religion being established. Second, the law states the government's exclusive preference for the named religion and extends to it some benefit that is only in the power of government to bestow, a benefit that is withheld from all other religions and persons of no religion. (The most common benefits are support from public money and the exclusive right of members of the established religion to vote and to hold public office.) These are the distinguishing features of every religious establishment. If no establishment law has been passed exclusively conferring on the religion named in the law some governmental benefit, then no establishment exists. No exclusive benefit, no establishment. Allowing expressions of religious belief on state property does not constitute an establishment of religion.

At the time the First Amendment was submitted to the states for ratification and incorporated into the Constitution, Massachusetts and Connecticut had laws establishing the Congregational Church. (These were the only strong establishments in the sense that only Massachusetts and Connecticut restricted the right to vote and hold office to members of a single church.) The establishment laws in New Hampshire, New Jersey, and South Carolina, established "the Protestant faith"; the establishment laws of Delaware and Maryland, where there were many Roman Catholics, favored "the Christian faith." All seven of these states bestowed on the religions they had established by law support from public funds that other religions were excluded from receiving.

All religious establishments in the United States ceased in 1833 when Massachusetts, the last state in the Union to have a religious establishment, rescinded its establishment law as New Hampshire, Connecticut, New Jersey, Delaware, Maryland, and South Carolina had already done. So for the better part of a century and three-quarters now, the establishment clause has been obsolete because there has been no religious establishment in any state for it to protect.

Besides the fact that the establishment clause is an obsolete provision of the Constitution (i.e., it protects a constitutional right no state has exercised for 173 years), a further matter should also be emphasized. And that is that neither religious clause in the First Amendment was written to give the federal government authority over religious practices in the states. Indeed, all six of the clauses in the First Amendment, including these two, restricted federal power. *Restricting federal power was the whole point and purpose of the Bill of Rights*, of which the First Amendment is the leading article. Given the multitude and diversity of churches in the United States, the states (not the federal government) were the only sensible repositories of civil authority over religious matters. The religious clauses in the First Amendment to the Constitution acknowledge that practical reality by prohibiting any federal trespass on religious practices in the states. If South Carolina, Maryland, Delaware, New Jersey, Connecticut, Massachusetts, and New Hampshire, acting through their elected legislatures, wanted to have an established religion, the establishment clause of the First Amendment protected their right to do so. The establishment clause was a special stipulation for the protection of religious freedom in the states.

Nonetheless, the establishment clause in the First Amendment has been bent during the past forty years into an instrument giving the federal government authority over religious practices in the states. This has been done despite the glaring fact that both of the religious clauses in the First Amendment were designed to coordinately serve the purpose of protecting religious freedom in the states from federal government regulation.

Since the 1960s, an irrational fear that might be called "theophobia" has been created by benders of the Constitution, and it now grips the public mind, and even the thinking of most Supreme Court justices. This fear would have Americans believe that any expression of belief in God that is condoned by an agency or official of a state government, such as a public school principal, is an establishment of religion. Under the coloration of *protecting* religious freedom from the nonexistent threat of making a religious establishment, the counter-culture movement has bent the American cultural belief in religious freedom into a policy of suppressing the public expression of belief in God. Benders of religious freedom have used theophobia to claim that the *sight* of a student silently praying to God in a public school is an establishment of religion if officials of the school have approved the practice. And the Supreme Court in 1985 agreed with that argument (*Wallace v. Jaffree*), thereby making even silent prayer unconstitutional in public schools. Because of such rulings, some public school principals have become so fearful of the counter-culture's redefinition of the separation of church and state that they have even banned use of the word *Christmas* from the schools they supervise! Theophobia has affected so many judges, lawyers, teachers, school administrators, school board members, university professors, journalists, media pundits, elected and appointed officials, and bureaucrats that millions of ordinary Americans now no longer regard religious freedom as including tolerance of public expressions of belief in God. It is significant in this regard that when communists took over the government of Russia, the People's Commissar for Foreign Affairs said, in denying that religion was being suppressed by the Communist Party, "After the separation of church and state was realized in Russia, religion has been regarded here as a private affair."[20]

The bending of the First Amendment's establishment clause into an instrument to confine the exercise of religious freedom to private places began in 1962 with the Supreme Court decision in *Engel v. Vitale* (370 U.S. 421) that declared prayer in public schools unconstitutional. *Engel v. Vitale* concerned a religious exercise in the public schools of the state of New York. The state's board of education had approved *voluntary* recitation of a prayer at the beginning of each school day as part of the "moral instruction" of students in the system. This was the prayer: "Almighty God, we acknowledge our dependence upon Thee, and we beg Thy blessings upon us, our parents, our teachers, and our country."

Lawyers for the plaintiff in *Engel v. Vitale* conceded that the prayer was nondenominational and that it simply expressed a belief in God and his providence. But, they said, that was irrelevant. What was relevant was that an agency of the state of New York (its board of education) had approved the prayer. That made it an establishment of religion, and the First Amendment, according to them, prohibited an establishment of religion in a state. A majority of justices on the Supreme Court agreed with this blatant contradiction of the explicit, historical purpose of the establishment clause and ruled that voluntary recitation in a public school of the prayer "Almighty God, we acknowledge our dependence upon Thee, and we beg Thy blessings upon us, our parents, our teachers, and our country" was in violation of the Constitution.

Quite apart from the Supreme Court's denial of the historical fact that the establishment clause had been included in the First Amendment to protect the religious establishments in seven states of the Union from federal interference, the Court's decision in *Engel v. Vitale* raises a more serious question. Is it judicious to use one clause in the Constitution to curtail another clause? Was the establishment clause included in the First Amendment in order to be at odds with the free exercise clause? No. They were coordinate, harmonious features of a constitutional protection of religious freedom in the states.

Furthermore, nothing in the Constitution warrants either Congress or the federal judiciary in banning a public expression of religious belief because that expression may offend someone. In any large society, what pleases the conscience of one citizen or group of citizens is bound to displease the conscience of some other citizen or group of citizens. To permit in public only expressions of religious belief that are offensive to no one is to prohibit all public exercises of religious belief, because there are no universally inoffensive religious beliefs. Who would claim that the only permissible political speech is that which offends no one? To argue that expression of religious beliefs must be limited to private gatherings of like-minded persons in churches, the home, and private schools so that no one will be offended by the public expression of religious beliefs practically nullifies freedom of religion as a civil liberty. That represents a double standard because the exercise of no other First Amendment freedom is restricted to private gatherings of like-minded persons.

No provision in the U.S. Constitution guarantees a citizen protection against having either their religious or their political sensibilities offended by the orderly expression of the political or religious beliefs of some other citizen. In the nature of things, no government is capable of providing *equal protection of feelings*. That truth is well illustrated in the *Engel v. Vitale* decision. By banning voluntary prayer in New York public schools, the Supreme Court made the plaintiffs in that case and their supporters feel good but offended the feelings of the citizens in the state who wanted their children to participate in a religious exercise affirming belief in God. The Court in this ruling was declaring the sensibilities of those parents and their supporters and the exercise of their religious rights under the free exercise clause of the First Amendment to be of lesser importance that the sensibilities of the plaintiffs.

When a cultural belief like religious freedom that is vital to a culture has been weakened by being bent in upon itself, the bending must be straightened out for the culture to survive. The people of the United States ought, therefore, to insist on amending the Constitution of the United States to distinguish "an establishment of religion" from "the free exercise of religion." The many injudicious applications of the obsolete establishment clause by the Supreme Court and other federal justices since 1962 indicates the need for a two-part amendment:

> Section 1. The free exercise of religion protected in the first article of amendment to the Constitution shall include religious references in a public document, inscription, pledge, motto, oath, song or ceremony, prayer at public events, and voluntary participation in religious exercises in public schools; and opportunities for the free exercise of religion may be provided by elected or lawfully appointed representatives of the people.
>
> Section 2. No state shall make a law establishing a religion as part of its government, support one religion to the exclusion of others, or require any religious test as a qualification to vote, hold office, or receive any other benefit under its government.

Section 2 of this amendment would apply to the states the prohibition against making a religious establishment that Article VI, Paragraph 3 of the Constitution applied to the federal government by forbidding the states from linking a person's religious beliefs or affiliation (or lack thereof) to receipt of a government benefit. And it would furthermore constitutionally recognize the fact that there have been no religious establishments in the United States for the better part of two centuries (i.e., since 1833), and constitutionally it would forbid that there should ever be any.

None of the religious exercises in the states that the Supreme Court has struck down as unconstitutional conferred any exclusive government benefit on any group of citizens. The public school students in New York, for instance, who voluntarily recited the prayer "Almighty God, we acknowledge our dependence upon Thee, and we beg Thy blessings upon us, our parents, our teachers, and our country" received no benefit whatever from the state for doing so, nor did their parents. But, it must be remembered, the receipt of a benefit that it is only within the power of a government to confer and that only practitioners of a named religion receive is one of the defining characteristics of a religious establishment.

Section 1 of this proposed amendment would also serve more than one salutary purpose. Besides allowing state and local authorities to authorize voluntary religious exercises in public schools as part of the moral education of American youth, it would reassert the people's right to worship God in public as well as in private places. It would affirm that expressing belief in God is a civil right that, like freedom of speech, freedom of the press, freedom of assembly, and freedom of petition, can be exercised both publicly and privately. And it would give constitutional protection to recitation of the Pledge of Allegiance, which affirms God's existence; the national anthem with its words "in God is our trust"; the motto In God We Trust that Congress has established by law as the official motto of the United States and has put on U.S. currency; congressional resolutions and presidential proclamations that may have occasion to mention God; the references to God in various state mottoes; inscriptions on public monuments with religious references in them; the traditional prayers at presidential inaugurations; the prayers that have been delivered at the beginning of the daily sessions of the U.S. Senate and House of Representatives for more than two centuries now by chaplains in the pay of Congress; and the prayers that were once common at public school graduation ceremonies and athletic games across the country. Section 1 would also allow the display on public property of reproductions of such precious documents as the Ten Commandments and the Declaration of Independence, both of which affirm Americans' belief in God and are among the most momentous and culturally important writings in the history of Western civilization.

Three conditions must be met to ensure religious freedom and a true separation of church and state: (1) the protection of the free exercise of religion in public as well as private places, a freedom not provided by the separation of church and state in nations with communist governments; (2) the provision of equal status under the law for every religious institution; and (3) the separation of government benefits from religious affiliation. Restricting expressions of belief in God to private places is *not* a separation of church and state. It is a severe diminishment of the free exercise of religion. It is bending religious freedom, an essential component of American culture, into a curtailment of religious freedom.

CHAPTER SEVEN

Bending Education

Several general trends in American society following the Second World War formed the backdrop for the counter-culture movement's radical changes to public education in the United States. First of all, it should be noted that to stimulate people to consume more in the postwar period, advertisers of consumer goods began playing up the idea that anything new was better. Another relevant trend in postwar America was an increasing demand for entertainment. Perhaps this remarkable trend had something to do with the introduction of television, which in the 1950s spread to the humblest homes in America. It might also have been an effect of the growing affluence of the postwar years. Or it may have been a result of the fear, so incessantly expressed in the media in the 1950s, 1960s, and 1970s, of the possibility of nuclear war, which engendered a feeling of let's have fun today because tomorrow we may be annihilated. In any case, there was a noticeable growth in mass entertainment in the second half of the twentieth century.

Experts with doctorates in education theory played upon the idea of novelty as progress and the demand for entertainment to sell the American public on a new curriculum for their public schools. Their new concept of education was that it should be stimulating; it should be entertaining; it should be innovative; and most of all, it should not be boring.

By the 1970s, innovations in education were sweeping the country. And the establishment of a federal Department of Education encouraged innovation in education by making available funding for "curriculum development." Among the special features of the new curriculum were interdisciplinary studies, multimedia instruction, interactive learning, and new concepts of pedagogy. The use of television, film, and more recently, online learning was a particularly striking feature of the new curriculum, which especially favored technological innovation. Officials at the U.S. Department of Education even claimed that television in the classroom cultivates "high-order thinking skills." These experts also claimed that "learning increases when information is presented in a dramatic setting, and television can do this better than any other medium." Neil Postman in *Amusing Ourselves to Death* refers to these assertions in his analysis of the new curriculum. He notes that the use of television in classrooms has given students the feeling "that learning is a form of entertainment or, more precisely, that anything worth learning can take the form of an entertainment, and ought to."[1] Despite the claims of officials at the Department of Education, Postman reports that an independent survey of some 2,800 published studies on the influence of television, including its effect on cognitive processing, revealed no evidence that learning increased when information was presented in a dramatic format. Nonetheless, multimedia classrooms were novel, and innovation was felt to be a sure sign of progress.

In addition to the technological innovations that gave the new curriculum its aura of progress, radically new educational methods, and ideas about the desired content of instruction in the public schools were also introduced and approved by the same certified experts in education. In particular, they approved for the new curriculum such innovative ideas as New Math, Whole Language, Process Writing, and "multiculturalism." (See Richard Bernstein's appraisal of multiculturalism as "a movement of the left emerging from the counterculture of the 1960s" in *Dictatorship of Virtue: How the Battle Over Multiculturalism Is Reshaping Our Schools, Our Country, Our Lives*.[2]) Process Writing was a typical idea of the changes that were made to the curriculum. In this theory of how to teach English composition, "Students form small groups—one earth-mother teacher at City College [of New York] calls it 'making hoops'—to read aloud and comment on each other's writing, while the teacher surveys the scene benignly."[3] The theory of Process Writing is that students will teach each other to write. According to this notion, good English is a mistaken concept. There is no competent authority for saying what is or is not good English. No one's opinion is better than anyone else's. The students know as much as their teacher about what is right for them. Learning rules of grammar and other principles of clear writing is boring. What is important is to involve students in *the process of writing*.

Starting in the 1960s, theories like Process Writing have become the hallmark of improved education. (Process Writing is now being used even in university level composition courses.) In the new curriculum, the more novel a concept was the better. And the idea that education should be entertaining applied no less to teachers than it did to students. Teachers were encouraged to rely on television, film, and video for classroom instruction and to organize dramatic role-playing exercises in their classes to stimulate students to become involved in expressing their emotions and opinions. Teachers were never to "put down," that is, correct a student who might be unintelligible in expressing himself or who might say something while expressing himself that the teacher knows to be plainly an error of fact or logic, or just flat-out dumb. Such moments were to be handled with the most delicate care so as not to make students ever feel that they had been wrong about something. The new, "interactive" concept of education made teacher and student equal partners in "the educational process." Teachers were told to employ teaching strategies that would be agreeable to their students. They should not be judgmental or authoritarian. Classroom discussion in which the opinions of students counted as much as their teacher's were the preferred pedagogy. Being "judgmental" and "authoritarian" was old-fashioned and hurtful to students. Authority was to be questioned (except the authority of the management of the new curriculum). This radically egalitarian theory of the proper relationship between student and teacher (sometimes involving students calling a teacher by his or her first name) put the interests and the ideas of callow students on a par with their adult teachers.

Giving students a voice in deciding what should go on in a classroom was part of the much broader concept—self-esteem—that has provided the structure of the new curriculum. The old curriculum expected students to acquire knowledge and skills worthy of esteem. The doctrine of self-esteem is quite different. Self-esteem is not something earned through achievement. It is a state of mind, a way of regarding one's self. This concept requires teachers from kindergarten through high school to praise students for whatever minimal effort they make, or even if none is made. In other words, students were to be continually treated from first grade through high school as if they were young children in perpetual need of unconditional approval from their teachers. They were not to have any peremptory demand made of them to live up to a teacher's or their society's standards.

The old curriculum permitted acknowledging God, and thereby it communicated to public school students that they were God's creations. Even though religion was not being taught as a subject prior to the banishment of prayer from public schools by the U.S. Supreme Court, students learned from the simple religious exercises that were allowed that God existed and that human beings have equal worth in God's sight. This humbling truth gave them respect for themselves and others as God's creations. It gave self-esteem a transcendent origin that had nothing to do with whether one was academically accomplished or not. That respect for one's self and others, including one's teachers, classmates, and parents, was the great religion-based lesson of democracy. In the new, secular pedagogy, however, students are merely told they are "special." They are not given any reason for being special except that everyone is entitled to feel good about themselves.

Students are now promoted to the next higher grade simply because they "deserve to have" an education. This means in practice an almost automatic certification of them as passable students, quite apart from any failure on their part to attain a higher level of knowledge and skills worthy of promotion. In the last three decades of the twentieth century, a secular concept of self-esteem became the controlling principle of public schooling in America and replaced a religiously-based concept of self-esteem and self-esteem deriving from acquiring knowledge and skills, as the paramount goal and standard of success in public education.

This new, supposedly better, emotional standard has necessarily meant a lowering of intellectual standards, which in some school districts have now practically been thrown out. The idea of having demanding academic goals and standards of knowledge and skills is now considered to be "inappropriate" and "unfair," according to the certified education theorists, because students who fail to live up to such standards suffer a loss of their self-esteem. No one should be made to feel, the experts say, that they have failed to live up to a rigid, arbitrary, or authoritarian standard. And how can that be avoided if students who do not pass a course are held back from going on to the next higher grade in school? Everyone should succeed. In this way of thinking, competition is counterproductive. Competition is said to demean those who do not come out on top.

The doctrine that the main mission of public schools is to cultivate self-esteem in the young disregards the truth that enduring self-esteem is created either by religious faith or by real achievement. In the old curriculum if no one failed, then no one succeeded. That was the controlling idea of education before the 1960s. The idea since then has been that if everyone succeeds, then no one fails, and to be certain that everyone succeeds, expectations have been lowered. In the new curriculum, the concept of objective right and wrong, and of a truth that does not depend on feeling or personal opinion, applies only to the most extreme behavior. Apart from physical assault, murder, or the most abysmal ignorance, in the new curriculum hardly anything is considered wrong. The current curriculum construes both morality and knowledge as the "right to choose."

It ought to be obvious to anyone who gives the matter even a moment's thought that teaching self-esteem cannot provide moral guidance or lead to respect for others, because self-esteem concerns only one person. Teaching self-esteem fosters the attitude, "I deserve to be esteemed by others." It does not oblige a student, who is thus encouraged to center his life on his own feelings, to be respectful of others.

The old curriculum thought of education as something students past the age of eleven or twelve had to "get." The new pedagogy insists that students be "given" an education. The old idea of education was also quite unsuited to the new curriculum's insistence that learning had to be entertaining. Since the 1960s, having the right teaching method or "educational technology" has been the crucial consideration. Otherwise, education can not be entertaining. Consequently, in training teachers today, courses on theories of education, teaching methods, and education as a process are more important than a teacher's knowledge of a subject. (In 1982, 17 percent of public schoolteachers had a master's degree in the subject they taught; now, only 5 percent do.[4]) The new emphasis on process, methodology, and theory has been rationalized by the notion that knowledge of a subject is not as important as "teaching the whole child" and the idea of "learning to learn."

Another sign of the severe erosion of academic standards in the new curriculum for public education has been the proliferation of "special education" classes. Such classes practically abolish competition among students and thus (supposedly) foster self-esteem. The idea of a common basic education is now as outmoded an idea as the concept of an education as being about acquiring knowledge and skills. Under the idea of special-ed classes, the brightest students are segregated into advanced placement courses so that average students do not have to compete with them. (Because the theorists of the new curriculum have authorized this segregation, however, it seems not to qualify as elitism.) Students of ordinary ability have been further subdivided into various special education classes so that they can "feel comfortable" and "unthreatened" by any expectation to achieve. These further segregations, however, also have the effect of making the nonelite students feel that they are in some way deficient and in need of special help.

On the face of it, such segregation would seem to contradict the theory of self-esteem and contribute to low self-esteem. In noticing this contradiction, one naturally wonders if the new curriculum has truly been designed for the purpose of enhancing the self-esteem of students, or whether it is only claimed to do that, while its real goal is the destruction of the old system of education and the culture that the old system represented. Certainly by the end of the twentieth century, special education classes and even special schools (in some of which English is not the language of instruction) enrolled a majority of students in some school districts. Fewer and fewer ordinary classes teaching basic, traditional subjects are now in evidence in the United States.

The new curriculum and its special-ed courses allow, with few exceptions, students who are in advanced placement courses to receive the highest possible grade, most students of average ability an above-average grade, and the poorest run-of-the-mill students an average grade. (The most radical of the new curriculum proponents, of course, would like to do away with grading altogether on the grounds that it is a vestige of the benighted, judgmental past.) This "grade inflation," as the phenomenon has come to be called by its critics, has also had the effect of weakening academic standards. And students have readily understood what was happening. They saw that grades were being devalued and that a general separation of evaluation from performance was occurring. Consequently, they have lost respect for honest work.

Academic dishonesty invalidates the whole idea of getting an education, but under the new curriculum it hardly matters since the purpose of education is to "give" students an education. And since one of the most important new concepts of the new curriculum is that both morality and knowledge are ultimately matters of choice, cheating has become rampant. (One remembers in this connection that the 1962 Supreme Court ruling on school prayer expelled God from public schools, and with that expulsion eliminated the most compelling reason for honesty: belief in a transcendent authority for distinguishing right from wrong.) One poll conducted in 1995 revealed that four out of every five high-school students admit they have cheated. There have always been cheaters, of course, and there always will be. But four out of five American students cheating is unprecedented. It is an alarming development. Moreover, this dishonesty in American public schools under the new curriculum is occurring among students with high academic ability and from functional families as much as among students of supposedly lesser academic potential from so-called disadvantaged and dysfunctional family backgrounds. A poll of *over 3,000 top high-school juniors and seniors* found that 78 percent of them had cheated, and 89 percent of these superior students said cheating was common in their schools. According to the founding director of the Center for the Advancement of Ethics at Boston University, "Moral standards have become so eroded that many children can no longer tell right from wrong." And indeed, surveys indicate that there is no general sense of guilt about cheating among today's students. They think of it as insurance for the inflated grades (another form of dishonesty) that are being given them. In the article from which this information has been taken, Daniel R. Levine has concluded that "A big part of why cheating has become so common is that it is rarely challenged or punished by school authorities."[5]

And teachers who do punish cheaters have been criticized for taking a stand. During the 2001–2002 academic year, for instance, a biology teacher in a public high school in Kansas discovered that thirty-eight of her students had plagiarized from the Internet on their semester projects, and she gave the plagiarists zero credit. The school board received so many complaints about this penalty from the parents of the teenagers that the board asked the teacher to give the students partial credit for their dishonest work and to reduce the weight of the semester project from the announced 50 percent to 30 percent of the semester grade. These parents in America's heartland evidently wanted their children's biology teacher to be nonjudgmental and to give their offspring grades that they did not earn. Christina Pelton, the teacher in question, resigned from her job rather than submit to the school board's request, because if she complied she would no longer have any authority over her students. They would know, she said, that "if they didn't like anything in my classroom from here on out, they can just go to the school board and complain." The newspaper report of this incident also quoted the founder of the Josephson Institute of Ethics, who said: "This kind of thing is happening every day around the country, where people with integrity are not being backed by their organization."[6]

One of the worst aspects of this attempt to make education entertaining is that kids get from the new curriculum and the new pedagogy the mistaken impression that school is divorced from real life, and that whatever they do or do not do in school will have no real-life consequences for them. The disconnect that has been created between school work and a student's promotion from one grade to the next has resulted in a lowering of both academic standards and achievement (as measured by standardized tests). And cheating is now not the only thing that has become common in public schools; so too have vandalism, littering, graffiti, and violence. These developments have no antecedent in the pre-1960 curriculum. They are new developments correlating with the post-1960s curriculum.

Just as the theory of special education has compromised the idea of a basic, common education, the concept of multiculturalism has devalued patriotism in America's public schools. By the 1980s and 1990s, public school students were no longer being taught that their country's history and the civilization that it is part of have any special value. Instead, they were being taught that all cultures are equally valuable (even though the diversity of these cultures makes it impossible for the student to base his or her life on the beliefs of every culture). Old-fashioned love of country and pride in American beliefs and America-the-Beautiful, I-pledge-allegiance-to-the-flag love of America have been discouraged. According to the doctrine of multiculturalism, pride in America and its history is "chauvinistic." In the new curriculum, American history is studied as much to condemn the United States for its imperialism, oppression, racism, genocide, sexism, homophobia, greed, social injustice, and environmental destruction as it is for any other reason. The aspect of the new curriculum that is called multiculturalism has been in many instances little more than a pretext for teaching anti-Americanism.

No educational theory such as teaching self-esteem, however, can alter the reality that knowledge and skills are necessary for making students into self-supporting members of a developed modern society. The consequences of the policy of making self-esteem rather than knowledge and skills the paramount goal of education have been quite real and are far from trivial. After three decades (1970–2000) of teaching self-esteem, the results are evident. Now so few young adults in America are either interested in or academically prepared to pursue higher education in demanding fields like engineering, mathematics, science, and medicine that graduate and undergraduate programs in these subjects at many American universities depend for their viability on students from outside the United States. At some American universities, programs in these crucial areas of modern research and technology now enroll a preponderance of foreign students.

This decline in the number of American science and engineering students has led to a severe shortage of available workers in vital high-tech sectors of the economy, such as the aerospace industry, in which America has heretofore always been the world leader. Entrepreneurs in advanced technologies now must lobby Congress to pass immigration laws that will allow them to recruit enough foreign-educated personnel to make it possible for them to stay in business. Many employers report difficulties in finding enough Americans with the necessary skills, knowledge, and disciplined habits of thought to be economically competitive in high-tech endeavors in today's world.[7]

A newspaper report in 2003 on the seriousness of this problem with regard to the National Aeronautics and Space Administration (NASA) points out that "The math and science performance of U.S. 12th graders continues to rank near the bottom internationally"; that fewer and fewer young Americans are taking engineering and science degrees at American universities;

and that prior to the 1970s there were enough qualified American graduates of institutions of higher learning in the United States to fill the needs of the aerospace industry.[8] Dr. Robert C. Richardson, chairman of the National Science Board and winner of a Nobel prize in physics, candidly summed up the state of science education in the United States in a 2004 interview with the *New York Times* in these terms:

> We have to face facts. We've got a serious scientific manpower problem, and it's been developing since the 1970's. We used to be third in the world, behind Japan and Finland, in the percentage of our students who became scientists and engineers. Now we're 23rd. For 30 years, we've made do by importing a large portion of our scientists. Smart, motivated people from places like China and India studied and settled in the United States. Today, about half of our graduating engineers are foreign-born.[9]

John H. Marburger III, director of the U.S. Office of Science and Technology Policy in 2004, made the same point when asked whether concern about the quality of American science education is valid.

> The real concern is that we're not preparing enough young people in the K-12 years for them to fulfill their aspirations to become scientists when they get to college. We're losing too big a fraction of the young people who aspire to be scientists and engineers within the first two years of college when they hit those tough courses. In most cases, the reason people drop out is because their quantitative skills just aren't up to it. That's one of the reasons that the [Bush] administration has tried to focus on the quality of math and science teaching in the early grades.[10]

How much longer can American university programs in science and engineering afford to rely on students from abroad to remain viable is a question that affects U.S. national security. Once they have earned their science and engineering degrees at American universities, many of the foreign students return to their native countries. And American law bars those who do stay in the United States but do not become citizens from taking science and engineering jobs that involve the most sensitive national security matters. So there is now a chronic shortage of highly qualified people in those areas.

A healthy democratic society, prosperous modern economy, and high standards of living cannot be maintained unless there is an ample supply of knowledgeable, skilled workers with honest, self-disciplining work habits. That should be self-evident. Public education in the United States once served those basic needs. It no longer does. The new curriculum, which has as its goal the teaching of self-esteem, has the opposite effect, and deprives students who most need to get a solid education to be self-supporting of the chance of advancing in life. According to the National Assessment of Educational Progress, *one out of three* white fourth-graders and *two out of three* black and Latino fourth-graders are *functionally illiterate*.[11]

To grant high-school diplomas to young Americans regardless of whether they actually have basic skills in English and math leads inevitably to damage to their self-esteem when they discover that in the modern world even low-paying jobs require some ability to read and a functional knowledge of arithmetic. The resentment that tens of millions of young Americans—black, brown, white, it makes no difference—naturally suffer in discovering that they cannot compete in the modern world creates a fertile breeding ground for despair and self-destructive behavior. (In 1999, suicide was the eighth leading cause of death in the United States with thirty thousand Americans taking their own lives—far more than the nineteen thousand murders in the country that year.[12]) *The Black-White Test Score Gap*, a collection of twelve essays on the question of whether racism or a lack of knowledge and skills causes the income disparities between white and black Americans, concludes that the latter causes the gap.[13] A lack of skills and knowledge needed to be self-supporting is also a contributing factor in criminal behavior.

In other words, the counter-culture's novel conception of education as entertainment has been a formula for social, economic, and political disaster. Moreover, because that concept of education is based on low expectations and is seldom challenging, it almost never leads to a sense of accomplishment and is often stupifyingly boring. And it is seldom even truly entertaining. In these respects, the new curriculum is basically like television. Perhaps instead of looking at television's influence on education, we ought to be examining the ways in which the public school curriculum has been deliberately restructured to be like television. Certainly, the new curriculum seems to have no clear, well-thought-out sequence that progressively challenges students from one grade level to the next by requiring them to build upon earlier mastery of knowledge and skills in order to achieve ever higher levels of competence. The new curriculum's peculiar combination of feeble intellectual content, invertebrate structure, and extreme redundancy has made public schooling in America today a tiresome pastime for both students and teachers. These are also characteristics of television programming today.

Since the novel pedagogy of the new curriculum was implemented, American students have come to regard their schooling as a pastime rather than a necessity. They have become academically flaccid. They, and their parents, have been sold the twin concepts that competition is bad for self-esteem and that entertaining stimulation is necessary to one's being "given" an education. Parents are, as parents, naturally disposed to believe the best about their children. Few of them take the trouble to obtain direct knowledge of the curriculum and methods of instruction used in their children's schools, and most parents are quite willing to accept as legitimate the generally inflated grades that their children bring home from schools. They readily conclude from these inflated grades that their children are learning what and as they should. The public relations experts of the new, unionized educational establishment complete the process of persuading parents that all is well in the American public school system, except for the special cases of what are referred to as "inner-city schools." The public is told by the education experts that the problems in those schools have little to do with curriculum or educational policies and everything to do with social and economic conditions outside the public schools. (It is useful to note here another important development since the 1960s: unionization of primary and secondary public school teachers, which occurred in the United States in the 1970s. This greatly diminished the power of school boards and school administrators to judge teacher competence and define standards for job retention, and transferred it to the unions.)

Professors at large state universities know from experience that a large percentage of today's high-school graduates in America are not up to college-level work because they graduate from high school with poor language skills in reading and writing, weak knowledge of mathematics, and poor work habits. They know that college admission standards have been lowered in recent decades to take that reality into account. Three-fourths of American college teachers were reporting in the mid-1990s that their students lacked basic skills and rudimentary knowledge. And perhaps as many as 40 percent of entering college students now require remedial help in reading and writing; more than that need it in math.[14]

Students in American middle and secondary schools are too often intellectually passive in school and at home. They flop down in front of the televisions their parents have bought for them, and before they graduate from high school they watch as many as sixteen thousand hours of what purports to be entertainment. They also spend endless hours playing mindless computer games—thus converting this supposed tool for education (the computer) into little more than a vertical electronic game machine. They gorge themselves on the colorful, incessantly advertised junk food that progress has also made available to them, and wait out the years of their adolescence until their turn comes around to "make progress." They become flabby both physically and intellectually. And not surprisingly, some American adolescents become tired of vacuous TV programming and crash-bam video games and seek entertainment in other forms that are even less productive of intellectual development and wholesome knowledge than television and video games. They seek the stimulation of "adult entertainment": taking drugs, consuming pornography, drinking heavily, and "being sexually active." A comprehensive study in the late 1990s by the National Campaign to Prevent Teen Pregnancy showed that one out of five 12-, 13-, and 14-year-olds was having sexual intercourse and that one out of seven sexually experienced 14-year-old girls had been pregnant. This report was a synthesis of seven studies conducted in the late 1990s.[15]

Many (probably most) proponents of the new, nonjudgmental, radically egalitarian curriculum dismiss such behavior as nothing new or particularly disturbing, and regard it as a normal part of growing up. That attitude raises some basic questions. First of all, are the new sex education courses that entered the curriculum of public schools in the 1970s and are now in place throughout the land the effect or the cause of the unprecedented sexual activities of American adolescents in the last two generations? Certainly, before the introduction of courses in public schools featuring the idea of how to have safe sex, there were not the levels of sexual activity, venereal disease, and pregnancy among American adolescents that there presently are. Forty years ago, for adults to tell teenagers that sexual activity was wrong and to encourage teenagers to abstain from sexual intercourse was deemed sound counsel. Now it is "inappropriate." According to the new educational doctrines, adolescents should be free to make their own choices regarding "sexuality." The new curriculum is designed to encourage students to examine "a range of choices." This curriculum withholds moral guidance from young Americans at an age when they most need it and could derive the most benefit from it.

It is a false claim that there has always been as much sexual license in the lives of middle-class American teenagers as there is today. It is also a mistake to think that what adults tell adolescents can have little or no effect on their behavior. Before sex education became a standard part of public schooling in America, it would have been impossible to find a picture in a senior yearbook in any high school in America of a graduating senior holding the infant she gave birth to out of wedlock during her high-school years. For school authorities to have condoned a picture of that sort in a yearbook would have been a shameless, scandalous contradiction of something that still had great importance in the 1950s: community standards of decency. By the 1990s, after decades of the new curriculum, there are now so many unwed teenage mothers in some school districts that special classes have been set up for them. According to the Kaiser Family Foundation survey of teenage sexual behavior and attitudes, one in five American teens has had sex before age fifteen; and before they graduate from high school, two out of three American teens has had sex.[16]

The counter-culture movement, which is hostile to the family, the fundamental building block of Western civilization, would have everyone believe that the sexual urges produced by hormones in pubescent bodies will have their way no matter what students are taught about premarital abstention and self-restraint. But social expectations play a major role in determining human behavior. Human beings of all ages and of every social class are quick to perceive what those around them, especially those in authority, expect of them and the behavior they will tolerate. The sexual activity that is now rampant among American teenagers, in comparison to several decades ago, was brought about through willful disregard of that fact. When intellectual ignorance became "no big deal" under a new curriculum that placed a premium on teaching self-esteem instead of skills and knowledge, what had previously been considered immoral conduct also became "no big deal." In schools that deserve to be called schools, however, intellectual and moral expectations are inseparable, because when intellectual and moral standards are not mutually valued and equally enforced, meaningful learning cannot take place. For a student older than twelve to get an education, the first requirement is self-discipline, just as knowledge of the subject matter is the foremost requirement for a teacher who teaches grades 7–12.

Getting an education is work. It requires diligent, conscious effort. And the standards of conduct that both moral and academic learning require must be firm, clear, and consistently adhered to for good results. Learning is not entertainment. Neither is it a matter of one opinion being as good as another.

Being impolite to teachers was once unthinkable in American public schools and was inevitably punished on the rare occasions when it did occur. Now a teacher is sometimes cursed by a student in front of his or her class and even on occasion slammed up against a blackboard by a burly male teenager. And there have been instances of a school administrator pleading with an assaulted teacher not to "make trouble" by reporting the incident to the civil authorities. Other crimes besides assault are common enough in some schools today to require patrols of uniformed police officers to prevent and deal with outbreaks of violence on their grounds and in their buildings. Screening for drugs and concealed weapons has become routine in many school districts. But there are no mechanical or chemical detectors or police officers that can keep out of our public schools the policies that encourage the attitude of complete self-centeredness (i.e., self-esteem) that leads to the lack of respect for authority that precipitates such assaults.

A far graver symptom of the lax intellectual and moral atmosphere that is now too common in public schools in America are those extremely rare incidents in which teenage boys (even subteen boys) have gone on murderous rampages, shooting and killing their teachers, school administrators, and fellow students. These are the worst result of a growing disrespect since the 1960s for our heritage of Judeo-Christian morality that teaches the sacred origins of human life and belief in God and the human soul. Today's flaccid, entertainment-oriented curriculum of self-esteem is producing self-centered, antisocial, self-destructive behaviors.

School shootings do not mostly occur in poor or inner-city school districts, nor are the shooters necessarily from so-called disadvantaged or dysfunctional families. School shootings happen in all sorts of American communities, from wealthy suburbs and ordinary neighborhoods to impoverished communities, and the adolescents who commit these awful acts of extreme violence usually come from families that are not remarkably different from most families today. These horrific events are among the things that never occurred in American schools until the late twentieth century. Along with sex education and the suppression of references to God, they are part of the new educational landscape created by the counter-culture curriculum that since the 1960s has commandeered American public schools. It is significant that murders never occur in parochial and private schools where prayer and other expressions of belief in God are still permitted.

The new curriculum has been enormously expensive to implement. Between 1950 and 1970, spending in America on public schooling more than doubled, from a nationwide average of $413 to $955 per student in constant 1970 dollars; by the year 2000 it had risen (again in 1970 dollars) to $1,656 per student ($7,392 in current dollars).[17] This quadrupling in the cost of public education nationwide between 1950 and the year 2000 paid for a huge increase in certified experts on education to apply the new educational theories and to supervise the implementation of new educational policies and curriculum. It also paid for a nationwide reduction in the size of classes (which required hiring more teachers) and for a substantial escalation in the salaries and benefits to administrators and teachers.[18] (The average salary for public school teachers nationwide is now above $44,000 for a nine-month school year.)

But while the cost of per-student education, after adjusting for inflation, has quadrupled since 1950, there has been no corresponding increase in academic performance by students in the nation's schools as measured by standardized tests of their knowledge and skills. Quite the opposite has happened. Academic achievement has declined. Scores for college-bound high-school seniors on standardized tests have been mainly downward since the 1970s, and SAT scores today remain below what they were in 1960.

Between 1958 and 1964, when the old curriculum was still in place and science and math were being emphasized because of America's competition with the Soviet Union to be the first to put a man on the moon, American public education improved. First graders through ninth graders performed at nearly five months above their grade-level norms in reading and math. Then, as the counter-culture movement gathered momentum in the mid-1960s and made its influence felt on institutional and public policy in the late 1960s and early 1970s, the improving trend was reversed. Between 1964 and 1973, the average achievement of students enrolled in elementary schools fell to nearly six months below norm,[19] and it has trended down ever since, despite a campaign by teachers' unions and the certified education experts to make standardized tests easier. And as the scores on standardized tests have declined, there has also been a campaign on the part of education theorists, school administrators, and teachers' unions to criticize the concept of standardized testing.

Considering the quadrupling of public school funding since 1950, public education in the United States ought to have improved a great deal if the amount of money spent per pupil was the primary requirement for improving educational results—which it is not. U.S. students now consistently score near the bottom on international tests compared to students from Japan, South Korea, the Netherlands, Sweden, Germany, France, and Great Britain whose per-student expenditures are on average *one-third less* than the average U.S. per-pupil spending on public education.[20] On the Third International Math and Science Study in 1998, for example, American twelfth-graders placed sixteenth in science and nineteenth in math among twenty-one economically developed nations.[21]

The failure of American education to produce students with academic skills and knowledge that would justify the quadrupling of funding for public schools in the last half of the twentieth century has not, however, caused the educationists who created the failed new system to concede the fact of that failure or to alter their thinking. Those who have bent (in the name of progress) the old curriculum and its values into the new curriculum continue to insist that the changes do indeed represent progress. They insist that the minds of American public school students must be "opened" to "change" and new ways of thinking and behavior. Nor has their supporters' faith in those theories diminished (though it might be noted that many educationists and their supporters send their children to private schools rather than have them attend the public schools that their ideology has created). Those who support the current system dismiss, often indignantly, the complaints of anyone who questions it. They characterize criticism of the system—in the words of one true believer—as a "philistine" defense of "high culture" and a "reactionary" advocacy of "cultural privilege." The justification of the new curriculum by those on the Left is that in the modern world there are "too many things to know and too many ways of knowing" to warrant a common, basic public school education: "A genuine education today must consist of providing people with the skills to engage and enter the enormous number of worlds—aesthetic, intellectual, technological, scientific—that will increasingly be open to them."[22] To be blunt, that is a nice-sounding lie.

The evidence is abundant for anyone willing to look at it. The great majority of students enrolled in American public schools today are *not* having the demanding worlds of science and technology opened to them. The doors to those worlds are in fact being closed to them. Many students in the system are not getting the basic literacy skills required for even low-paying jobs that offer some glimmer of possible advancement. Young adults without basic skills and knowledge, self-discipline, and honest work habits are being willy-nilly forced into the stressful worlds of chronic unemployment and underemployment. The education favored by the Left is *not* an education that leads to competitive competence. Students in far too many instances today get a multicultural education for failure—a granular, namby-pamby education rather than the solid knowledge and developed skills that they need to be self-supporting citizens and that their country needs them to get to maintain America's economic competitiveness in the world market.

By offering so-called disadvantaged students self-esteem instead of the skills and knowledge that would allow them to earn their way in the world and improve their lives through their own efforts, today's public school curriculum in America is fostering a permanent underclass. The counter-culture movement believes in victimization and class struggle. And education in America today delivers the sort of education that practically guarantees a goodly supply of the victims that the counter-culture movement needs to justify its accusation that America is a land of oppression rather than a land of opportunity.

The new education's watchwords are *self-esteem, diversity, open-mindedness, multiculturalism, process, communication, choice*. But on what is the self-esteem based? Just *telling* kids they are "special," that they're "OK," is not enough. And "openness" to *what*? To "diversity" and multiculturalism? And how is choice possible for the many graduates of American high schools who lack basic literacy? How can communication take place when disciplined skills in reasoning and composition have not been acquired?

Here is a sample of English submitted as a writing sample in making *an application for college admission* by a student who was "given" an education in an American public school in the 1990s. The topic on which this aspiring college student was asked to write was "Do you think the personal life of a political candidate . . . should be considered a factor in determining his or her ability to do the job?"

> We are living in a world that's getting worse everyday. And what we are doing nothing, just complaining about the other person life. We should stop because if we don't stop by looking on every candidate lifestyle and focus more on how, we could make it better. We all gonna die of, hungry, because we wouldn't have nothing to eat and no place to life.
>
> People tends to make mistake in life. We all are humans. That's why we should never judge a person for the cover of a book. People change in life, most of them tends to learn from their mistake. We live in a world that we should learn to forgive and forget everyone mistake and move forward.[23]

The chief significance of this appalling essay written by an American high-school student in the 1990s is this: the writer believed he was ready for college. It demonstrates what an education for self-esteem produces: sincere, deluded incompetents, who have been encouraged to think they deserve to go to college. (It also shows that one of the main messages of the new curriculum—don't make moral judgments—is indeed being learned by students in today's public schools.)

Any veteran teacher at a state university or personnel director of a company that employs large numbers of people could tell you that many American high-school graduates today have only the barest proficiency in reading and writing and that their skills in critical reasoning are extremely weak. (After twelve years in American public schools, some high-school graduates are so illiterate they cannot even read and fill out a job application.) Professors who taught at good state universities forty years ago could also tell you that students in upper-division courses for English majors then were regularly assigned and had the skills to write twenty-five-page term papers for their literature courses, papers that required research and had formal bibliographies and footnotes. That was before the counter-culture movement transformed America's educational policies and established a new curriculum supposedly designed to make students feel good about themselves. The results of this new curriculum could perhaps be succinctly summarized as Less Education for More Money. Now, after thirty years of the new curriculum in American primary and secondary schools, undergraduate English majors at American institutions of higher learning are incapable of routinely writing twenty-five-page research papers. They lack the necessary skills and intellectual discipline to do it. And a considerable portion of the resources of every state university now goes toward remedial teaching of undergraduates who have been admitted to college without actually being prepared for college-level work. Even in graduate-level programs of departments of English at some state universities in the late twentieth century, the requirement to write a dissertation for the doctorate degree has been replaced by a requirement such as this: "The dissertation for [graduate] students with [undergraduate] English majors may take the form of three extended essays."[24] Three extended essays is roughly the amount of writing an undergraduate English major forty years ago would have done in two semesters of course work.

Defenders of the new curriculum protest that the public schools of America are being unfairly criticized. One of the more prominent recent apologists for the new curriculum and its pedagogical theories is David C. Berliner, the author (with Bruce J. Biddle) of *The Manufactured Crisis: Myths, Fraud, and the Attack on America's Public Schools*. It is the contention of the authors of this work that "attacks" on public schools (as they term criticism of present-day American public schooling) are the result of a "right-wing conspiracy" of "conservatives" who are politically interested in discrediting the achievements of progressive education. (This point of view will seem natural to anyone who believes that truth depends on the politics of a speaker or writer and that every utterance must have a political motive and purpose.) The public education system now in place, the authors of this book contend, is not only not as bad as its supposedly politically-motivated critics allege but is actually a "miracle" (Berliner's and Biddle's term) of achievement.

First of all, Berliner and Biddle find fault with the principal test that has been used over the last four decades to measure the effectiveness of public education in America. The Scholastic Aptitude Test is flawed, they say. They concede that SAT scores have declined but say they have not declined significantly and complain that noneducationists do not know how to properly evaluate test scores. They therefore devote the second chapter of *The Manufactured Crisis* to analyzing what they say are "myths" about public education in the United States.

> We begin with the SAT story. To be sure, *aggregate* total SAT scores obtained by the nation's high school seniors fell between about 1963 and 1975. Moreover, that decline came about because aggregate scores fell for both parts of the SAT—the parts that measure, respectively, verbal and mathematical achievement.

This would seem to be plain enough: scores on both parts of the SAT fell, therefore the overall score fell—minus 2 and minus 2 equal minus 4. But Berliner and Biddle see problems with these facts because the SAT measures only verbal and math skills, and the miracle of the new curriculum lies in other areas. Secondly, they find fault with the weight that conservatives give the SAT results because, they claim, large numbers of students from disadvantaged homes began taking the SAT in the late 1960s and early 1970s and this, they say, was responsible for lowering the national averages of the scores.[25] Advocates of the new curriculum routinely charge that critics of their policies do not take into account the minority students who are now taking the SAT—a peculiar way to defend an educational policy that was supposed to help all students, particularly so-called minority students. The downward trend in test scores has lasted now, with minor fluctuations, for thirty-five years. One would have thought that at some point the allegedly superior educational policies, pedagogical techniques, and ample funding of the new curriculum and its theories of education would have provided students from households that were not academically-oriented with the skills and knowledge being measured on the test. Moreover, Charles Murray and R. J. Herrnstein in "What's Really Behind the SAT-Score Decline?" point out that "The surge in the proportion of high school students taking the SAT did not occur in the late 1960s, as is commonly supposed, but in the 1950s and early 1960s," and therefore could not have been the cause of the decline in scores that became apparent in the late 1960s.[26]

The defense that Berliner and Biddle make of the poor educational results of the new curriculum and pedagogy is curious. They blame American culture. Until American culture is radically changed and the social handicaps of the disadvantaged are remedied by a change of culture that eliminates racism and poverty, education in American cannot be expected to be what it should be. The failure of the radically changed public education of the past four decades is thus explained as a failure of American culture. This reasoning claims that the public school system, which is supposed to overcome racial stereotyping and help persons get out of poverty, cannot do that until poverty and racism have been eradicated in the United States. Historically in America, education has been regarded as a way for individuals to improve their individual lives. In the thinking of the counter-culture movement, however, individuals (as John Dewey said in the 1930s) can do nothing until a new social organization for American—that is, a new culture—has been engineered.

David Berliner, in a three-page epitome of his defense of current educational doctrine that was written in 1996 for a pro-and-con debate on the state of American public education, reiterated his complaint that the scores on the SAT are not being properly evaluated.

> The conservative critics also say the average scores dropped 90 points between the early sixties and the mid-seventies, and that certainly scared a lot of Americans. However, those were not raw points but "scaled" points. Think of it this way: When a hockey team gets four goals, it gets a score of 4; when a football team makes four goals, it may get a score of 28, but it only scores four times. So the SAT didn't really go down 90 points, it dropped about seven raw score items, a loss of 5 percent over more than 30 years. That's not nearly as scary as a 90-point drop, and it seems unlikely that America has been ruined because of this small drop in correct answers to multiple-choice test items.[27]

This of course is blowing smoke. A decline is a decline is a decline whether it's called a 5 percent decline or a 90-point decline, just as a defeat in hockey is the same as a defeat in football even though the two sports are scored quite differently. Likewise, a quadrupling of funding for public schools is a quadrupling of funding, and such a lavish increase in resources ought to have produced some increase in the testable skills and knowledge of students instead of a decline, however small or large that decline may be said to have been.

Berliner, his fellow educationists, and their left-wing supporters who defend today's counterproductive public school system in America deny that any crisis exists. Yet they offer reasons to account for what they say does not exist. There is no national crisis in public education, they say, but this is what has caused it. At least, that seems to be their reasoning. The only thing they are consistent and clear about is that they are not responsible for any deficiency in the public schools. Berliner concludes his succinct summary of his views with this typical sentiment:

There is indeed a crisis of achievement in some of our schools. But the conservative critics of the nation's public schools wrongly have pointed the finger at America's educators. The nation's school problems are rooted in the culture of America. And there is no little irony in the fact that the cultural problems are worsened by the very economic and social policies espoused by . . . the extreme right.[28]

There you have it, in a nutshell. In the debate over public education in America, leftists like David Berliner believe, when all is said and done, that any deficiency in public schools in America is, as he says, the fault of "the culture of America." Until American culture is corrected, public education in the United States cannot be what it should be. In considering this assertion that American culture is to blame for the crisis in American public education, one ought to remember that it was not American culture that came up with such novel concepts as Whole Language and Process Writing, not to mention the policy of teaching self-esteem instead of knowledge and skills. Theorists with doctorates in education like David C. Berliner did that.

The End of Homework by Etta Kralovec and John Buell declares that public schools in the United States should be used to challenge "received wisdom" and attempt to "redress social inequities."[29] The authors of this intriguing book, like David Berliner, also say that the cause of the problems in American education lies in American culture.

We as reformers must ask parents a further question: Are you really happy in careers that consume most of your lives outside the home and in [homework] regimens within the home that control much of your interaction with your children? If the answer is no, isn't there some rationale for striving both individually and as part of a larger movement to limit both work and homework? We believe that at least some parents are becoming more receptive to these questions, and we propose that to the extent that more relaxation could be achieved around the kitchen table, citizens would feel less of a need to support narrow and punitive forms of discipline for workers and other community members who do not meet their every expectation and standard. . . . Homework issues cannot be neatly separated from such seemingly unrelated themes as workplaces and the global economy. . . . As long as our corporate economy remains unjust and undemocratic, these pressures will [persist]. . . . Failing progress in other areas, we fear that the pressure to impose more work on our children will continue to grow within our educational and political systems.

Earlier in their book, this pair of progressive thinkers, who regard public education as a tool for change, propose that the Social Security system should be extended to "our citizens in childhood as well as old age" through federal legislation establishing a nationwide system of government-run child care centers.

Professor Berliner's opponent in the 1996 symposium on the question "Is the so-called educational crisis a myth created by conservatives?" was Laurence Steinberg, a professor of psychology. Professor Steinberg cited data indicating that the percentage of students performing "at the top levels" on the National Assessment of Educational Progress (NAEP is a different standardized test than the SAT, and is also in nationwide use) is "shockingly low, especially considering that the definition of excellence on these tests is exceedingly liberal."[30] Fewer than *2 percent* of juniors in American high schools, Steinberg pointed out, "earned top marks on the [NAEP] writing assignment, where the highest proficiency level was characterized simply by 'coherent' writing that 'tended to contain supportive details and discussion that contributed to the effectiveness of the response.'" (Such a standard resembles being satisfied with someone who *tends* to tell the truth or *tends* not to steal.) In one part of his remarks, Professor Steinberg could not restrain himself and became somewhat sarcastic:

> Educational-conspiracy theorists, like David C. Berliner, need to explain why the view that American education is in trouble is held not only by conservative commentators . . . but by Albert Shanker, president of the American Federation of Teachers, who has little to gain by undermining confidence in public schools and is too wise to be taken in by a manufactured crisis. They also need to explain the complicity of a 23-year-old cashier at my local convenience store, who keeps pretending not to know how to make change without the use of an electronic cash register, or my undergraduate students, who, to undermine my faith in American high schools, cannily fill their essays with spelling and grammatical mistakes that reasonably educated eighth-graders in other countries wouldn't make.

The home-schooling movement, which has grown immensely in the past twenty years, would have to be considered part of the alleged right-wing, conservative attack on public schools because millions of American parents have taken their children out of the schools their taxes pay for and are now educating them at home at an additional expenditure of money and an enormous investment of time. Other parents in the past three decades who could ill-afford the financial burden have spent upwards of ten thousand dollars a year (and in some cases more) to send a child to a private school rather than have him or her attend public schools as they are presently constituted. And the more recently inaugurated charter school movement is yet a third major indictment of the present public school system. It too indicates the growing dissatisfaction among parents in all classes in American society with the noneducation their children are being "given."

Those who deny that the present policies in education are failures often claim that not enough money has yet been spent on public education in the United States to do the job of improving it. How then do schools in the United States run by churches, which enforce high moral and academic standards and allow belief in God to act as an influence in classroom instruction, operate at a much lower cost-per-student than public schools and produce graduates who on average outscore public school students on standardized tests? Could it be that the moral values and standards that a teacher in a parochial school is allowed to enforce are more important than the per-student amount of money being expended on K-12 education in public schools? In addressing that question, it will not do to say that religious schools are selective in admitting students and that they do not have to educate disadvantaged students as public schools must. Private parochial schools *do* admit and educate disadvantaged students in large numbers, many of whom come from families that do not even belong to the church sponsoring the parochial school, and who attend it on scholarships provided by public-minded, private donors of scholarships to parochial schools.

If insufficient funding were in fact the reason why America's public schools are not doing as well as taxpayers have a right to expect them to be doing, and if more money is indeed needed to rectify the situation, how is it that in the year 2000 New York State spent $10,957 per student and South Dakota spent $6,037 ($1,355 below the national average), yet South Dakota students outscored New York students on the SAT by 95 points in the verbal portion of the test and by 80 points in math skills? And how are we to regard the fact that the state of Mississippi spent $5,356 per student while the District of Columbia spent more than twice that amount of money ($11, 935 per student), yet Mississippi students outscored D.C. students on the SAT by 54 points in verbal skills and 63 points in math?[31]

Money is *not* the problem. The problem is attitudes, goals, policies, and expectations. *Spending more money does not guarantee a better educational result.* What is wrong with public primary and secondary education in America lies in nonmaterial factors. Teacher certification laws that require substantial knowledge of academic subjects, high intellectual and moral standards for students, sound curriculum policies, and rigorous teacher training are more fundamental considerations than the amount of money expended on salaries, buildings, and technologies. The willingness of school administrators and parents to back up the authority of classroom teachers when those teachers discipline unruly students and give failing grades for failing performances is also crucial to achieving higher levels of achievement. Most important of all is having teachers in the classroom who are more dedicated to and knowledgeable about the subjects they teach than they are dedicated to and knowledgeable about educational theory. These are the primary—the vital—considerations in helping students "get" a solid basic education.

Twenty-some years ago, in 1983, a presidential commission of distinguished Americans from various fields of endeavor and varied political backgrounds investigated the state of public education in the United States. The report they issued was appropriately titled "A Nation at Risk." Perhaps the most striking statement in the report was this: "If an unfriendly power had attempted to impose on America the mediocre education performance that exists today, we might well have viewed it as an act of war."[32] In other words, had the Soviet Union during the Cold War been given the chance to design the set of educational policies that would devastate American public schools and hence weaken the United States, it could not have done a more effective job than has been done.

Schools and universities have become the battleground in the culture war on which the counter-culture movement has scored its most spectacular gains by selling the idea that self-esteem is what students lack.

In its purest forms, ignorance can sometimes be charming, as when a student writes: "The sun never set on the British Empire because the British Empire was in the East and the sun sets in the West." But in a democratic society with a republican form of government and a high-tech economy, ignorance is anything but funny. It is detrimental to the body politic and the general welfare of society. Healthy democracies and their economic productivity in today's world depend on their citizens' ability to think critically, make knowledgeable judgments, and effectively perform demanding tasks with honesty and dependability. That truth applies more forcefully now than it ever did in the past. If America is to remain faithful to the highest ideals of her historical culture, then American public schools must desist from social engineering. Furthermore, the schools' educational expectations for children from so-called disadvantaged families must be the same as those for children of upper-class families if the former are to have an equal chance to improve their lives and pursue a better future for themselves.

The assumption that all young Americans have a capacity for improvement and can improve when achievement and improvement are expected of them is a sign of true democracy, and of true equality. That is the way to repair, preserve, and fulfill a belief of American culture that has been greatly damaged by the new curriculum and the counter-culture movement, namely, the belief that every person's success improves society.

CHAPTER EIGHT

Instrumental Government

The counter-culture's ideology of political correctness now dominates the thinking of many influential Americans (journalists and judges for instance) and enough important institutions in America (such as the universities and public schools) to justify calling it a new Establishment. The boast of the counter-culture activist Jerry Rubin in the title of his book *We Are Everywhere* may have been a hyperbole in the 1970s, intended to give his fellow radicals in revolt against the Establishment an encouraging sense of belonging to a mass movement, but today sympathizers with the active promoters of the counter-culture's ideology are truly everywhere in positions of influence in institutions that shape the opinions and behavior of Americans. And public schools, in adopting course material based on the counter-culture's revisionist history of America as a land of oppression, as well as universities in creating programs of study devoted to so-called minorities (such as women, who make up more than half the population of the United States), have been highly effective in eroding the beliefs and principles of American culture.

Other signs of the damage that has been done to the cultural unity of American society are noted by Alfred H. Kelly, Winfred A. Harbison, and Herman Belz, authors of a scholarly study of the history of the Constitution of the United States, *The American Constitution: Its Origins and Development*. In the concluding paragraphs of this work, they remark on the "litigation explosion" of the 1960s and 1970s and the fragmentation of American society during those decades into groups driven by "ideologically based single-issue politics."[1] These were interrelated consequences of the counter-culture movement's assault on American culture, and they were symptomatic of the movement's effective promotion of unbridled individualism, victimization, and an animus against "corporate America." This kind of litigation, known as class-action lawsuits, particularly reflected the growing class consciousness that undermined the American cultural belief that society is a collection of individuals (not classes) and that each person is responsible for his own well-being.

Other beliefs of American culture, especially those concerning the purpose of government, have also been affected by the counter-culture movement. American culture believes that God has endowed each human being with the freedom to pursue happiness, and that governments exist to protect this God-given freedom. The counter-culture, in opposition to those beliefs, preaches the need for liberation from oppressive conditions and the need to use government as an instrument of liberation. In the counter-culture's completely secular (i.e., atheistic) and socialistic view of man, happiness is not an individual pursuit. Rather it is the responsibility of society. And because the state can regulate the creation and distribution of wealth and pass positive laws to compel correct social organization and behavior, it must be used for those supposedly liberating purposes.

The American philosopher John Dewey (1859–1952) set forth the idea of instrumental government in three lectures delivered at the University of Virginia at the end of his long career in academia. In these discourses, which were published in 1935 under the title *Liberalism and Social Action*, he traced the evolution of liberalism and called for its transformation to adapt it to the new social and economic environment of the twentieth century. He regarded the doctrine of natural law that lies at the heart of American culture as too rigid and out of touch with modern conditions, although he acknowledged it had played a part in what he termed "early liberalism." Dewey correctly pointed out that natural law, which is inseparable from belief in God, is the concept that there are "rights inherent in individuals independent of social organization." He also pointed out, again quite rightly, that

> The whole temper of this philosophy [of natural law] is individualistic in the sense in which individualism is opposed to organized social action. It held to the primacy of the individual over the state not only in time but in moral authority. It defined the individual in terms of liberties of thought and action already possessed by him in some mysterious ready-made fashion [i.e., belief in rights bestowed on human beings by God], and which it was the sole business of the state to safeguard.[2]

Dewey did not think that belief in natural law offered anything of use to men living in a scientific age.

Dewey likewise accurately observed that in the doctrine of natural law, reason is "an inherent endowment of the individual." But he preferred to think of reason or intelligence (he used the terms interchangeably) as a social construct, a certain kind of organization in society. Intelligence to him was collective. By way of illustrating this view of intelligence, he cited the improvements to health and productivity wrought by twentieth-century science. These achievements were not the work of individuals. Rather, Dewey argued, they were the result of a community of scientists employing the same methodology and collaborating with each other in a collective fashion. Dewey proposed that every human problem should be approached in a scientific way and scientific research should be applied to the organization of society. That would be intelligent. To refrain from applying science to every human problem would be unintelligent. To Dewey's way of thinking, human nature was not a practically unchangeable thing but something susceptible to benevolent, scientific manipulation and controlled improvement. Science had liberated man from chronic scarcities of material goods and had created a wholly new prospect of limitless material abundance. Man, Dewey said in the 1930s, because of science, lived in a radically altered social and economic environment. Abundant productivity was the new fact of life in the twentieth century. It was time to apply science to every aspect of human existence in order to effect a comprehensive, systematic improvement in the human condition. The society of the future should be scientifically structured.

With his rejection of old ideas—natural law, early liberalism, and capitalism—which were in his judgment deficient in intelligence, Dewey foreshadowed fundamental aspects of the counter-culture movement of the 1960s with its emphasis on change and the replacement of American cultural beliefs.

"Only by participating in the common intelligence and sharing in the common purpose as it works for the common good," Dewey grandly proclaimed in *Liberalism and Social Action*, "can individual human beings realize their true individualities and become truly free."[3] This was the central idea of his call for a new kind of society. It was a radical redefinition of freedom and a sharp departure from American culture because it looked upon individuals as having their true individuality, worth, and freedom *only as participants in a correctly organized social enterprise.*

In anticipation of the concept of freedom that was going to be accepted by many young Americans in the 1960s, Dewey in the 1930s said, "Liberty in the concrete signifies release from the impact of particular oppressive forces; emancipation from something once taken as a normal part of human life but

now experienced as bondage."[4] This was the 1960s idea of freedom as liberation. And the new age that Dewey argued for would, like the 1960s, put
"freed intelligence" (i.e., liberated thinkers) at the helm of "social action."[5]
"[T]he problem of democracy," he said, was "not solved, hardly more than
externally touched, by the establishment of universal suffrage and representative government."

What had to be fixed was nothing less than "the problem of that form of
social organization, extending to all the areas and ways of living, in which
the powers of individuals shall not be merely released from mechanical external constraint but shall be fed, sustained and *directed*"[6] (emphasis added).
The particular temper of the counter-culture movement of the 1960s is
encapsulated in that remark. And in this: "[T]he notion that there is some
inherent opposition between emotion and intelligence is a relic of the
notion of mind that grew up before the experimental method of science had
emerged. For the latter method signifies the union of ideas with action, a
union that is intimate; and action generates and supports emotion."[7] Dewey
anticipated the revolutionary spirit of the 1960s that called upon young
Americans to embrace new ideas with a passion that would move them to
action.

If an idea was correct, then it should be taken to its logical extremes. That
seemed to be Dewey's point, just as it was the point of the radical activists of
the 1960s. The counter-culture movement urged that the way to discover
correct ideas was to reject the inherited social order and its culture and open
one's mind to bold experimentation energized by emotion. That was John
Dewey's call to action as well. Thus in the 1930s was the intellectual ground
prepared in America to receive the revolutionary seeds of radical activism
that would be sown in the 1960s, seeds that have brought forth the bitter
harvest of today's political correctness.

Instrumental government is necessarily big government. To implement a
grandiose vision like Dewey's of the total organization of society, government
has to be big. The counter-culture movement did not, however, have to
invent instrumental government. That was done in the 1930s. The activists
of the 1960s opposed the U.S. government because it was being used for ends
they disapproved of, not because it was too big and too powerful. The instiga-
tors of the counter-culture movement in the 1960s were anti-Establishment
because the government of the United States was trying to prevent the takeover of South Vietnam by communist North Vietnam. American capitalism
and American government were the enemy of the movement because they
represented an establishment that was guilty of "war-mongering" and "impe-

rialism" (i.e., militarily opposition to the spread of communism). Protests against the existing Establishment and the Vietnam War were therefore minimal qualifications for participating in the movement. Getting middle-class American youths to "drop out" of American society weakened the enemy. Refusing to register for the draft was one way to drop out; so was joining a back-to-nature, nonprofit commune or adopting a lifestyle of promiscuity, shoplifting, panhandling, and drug use. Such "liberated," anti-American behavior was applauded by the movement as an alternative to settling down to a steady 9-to-5 job, a faithful marriage, and the raising of children.

The counter-culture has made headway in the United States by representing itself as a protest on behalf of the weak and aggrieved against those in power. But now that it has become a new Establishment of politically correct managers of influence, it faces the problem of maintaining the notion that it speaks for people who are still disenfranchised and "marginalized" after forty years of progressive social legislation and policy making on their behalf. Were it to lose its credibility as a movement to right wrongs, the appeal that constitutes its primary power would vanish. Hence it must continually claim that little or no progress has been made to correct the injustices of pre-1960s America. Richard Bernstein in his book *Dictatorship of Virtue* comments on this particular problem that the counter-culture's successes have created: the problem of how "power holders conceal their strength."

> How do they dominate the discourse while pretending to be the meek and beleaguered force of rebellion? Multiculturalism, in turning inside out many of the goals of the great civil rights movement of the 1960s, provided a means. It left the new power holders with an establishment to do battle against, the establishment of Eurocentric, racist, white male hegemony, and doing so allowed them to cloak themselves in the mantle of the good fight, the moral struggle, the progressive crusade. By dressing themselves in the finery of virtue, multiculturalists gained the power to intimidate and to limit the range of views that are acceptable in our society, even while pretending that they had no power and therefore could neither intimidate nor coerce.[8]

If, because there are no longer gross social injustices to redress, the perception fades that the counter-culture movement represents the virtue of defending oppressed classes of society, the movement will experience serious difficulties in maintaining itself and sustaining its grip on power in America. It must continuously invent new injustices and exaggerate everything that is not yet (and never will be) perfectly just. Its demands must become increasingly at odds with common sense and the existing culture. That is the difficult situation in which the counter-culture movement currently seems to find itself.

To understand the threat instrumental government poses for American culture, it is necessary to review what caused this kind of government to arise in America in the 1930s and to comment on the cultural history of government in America.

The history of government in the United States has revolved around two cultural beliefs: the least government possible is best, and a written constitution is essential to government. Each of the three successive proposals for a national government in American history—presented in 1754, 1781, and finally in 1787—has been based on these beliefs. The first of these three constitutions was put forward during colonial times by Benjamin Franklin. The main purpose of the constitution that he wrote in 1754 was to create "one general government" that would give the thirteen English-speaking colonies in America some unity, thus increasing their strength for mutual defense and allowing them to consult on other matters of common concern. Franklin proposed a unicameral legislature of elected representatives from each colony and required ratification by the colonial legislatures for his plan to take effect. Clearly, belief in the need for a written constitution that would have the consent of those who would live under its authority was already in an advanced stage of enculturation by 1754. The Albany Plan as it was called (Franklin presented his proposal for a unified government to a conference of colonial delegates meeting in that city) failed to win the consent of the thirteen colonial assemblies because it was regarded as giving the king of England too many new prerogatives. The British king was opposed to it because he thought it conceded too much authority to his colonies in America.

The second constitution for a national government, the Articles of Confederation and Perpetual Union, was prepared by the Second Continental Congress during the American Revolution and ratified in 1781. But the Articles of Confederation lasted only seven years after its ratification because it failed to give enough authority to the national government to ensure a viable union and an effective national defense. Under its provisions, each state had one vote in a unicameral legislature, and a super-majority of three-fourths of the states was needed to pass any bill of national consequence. This was states' rights taken to an unworkable extreme.

The third constitutional proposal, the Constitution of the United States, written in 1787, has proved enduring. It is the constitution the nation has lived under ever since its ratification in 1788. Through the creation of a bicameral legislature and a series of other brilliant compromises, it resolved the problem of how to achieve a just representation in a national government of states having unequal populations. It also created a better balance between the national government's authority and the authority of each constituent state and thereby formed "a more perfect Union." (Americans were the first people in world history to have a constitution written by their elected representatives and submitted to further specially elected assemblies for ratification. That is one of the foremost facts of the cultural history of the United States of America and should not be overlooked in any assessment of American culture.)

Each of these three written constitutions—the Albany Plan, the Articles of Confederation and Perpetual Union, and the Constitution of the United States—addressed the same question: how little government is possible for a viable union of states? Each one expressed in its own way, in regard to the circumstances at the time it was written, the American cultural belief that the best government is the least government possible.

Political parties naturally sprang up around the different answers that were given by different interest groups in American society to the question of how little government was practical in regard to particular concerns. The general answer before 1860 and the Civil War, however, was that the amount of government needed was only the amount necessary to protect the God-given rights of Americans and to maintain a common defense, interstate justice, and the general welfare of society as a whole.

During the 1930s, a different question was formulated: how much *bigger* can the federal government be? And the answer that began to be given then was: much, much bigger. Why did this change take place? It happened because of a series of crises. It was not the thinking of a particular political party or the growth of the American population that moved American society in the direction of big, instrumental government. Rather, it was the exigencies of this series of national crises.

With the survival of the nation at stake during the Civil War (1861–1865), the federal government had to assume extraordinary powers, including a forced draft of men to serve in the armed forces of the nation, something that had never before happened in American history. During the twelve years of reconstructing the Union after the war (1865–1877), federal military forces controlled the eleven secessionist states that had been in rebellion. As a stipulation for ending their military occupation and being readmitted to the Union and having their representation in Congress restored, they were forced to ratify the three amendments to the Constitution implementing the abolition of slavery and the granting of citizenship to the former slaves. Two of these changes to the Constitution, however—the Fourteenth and Fifteenth Amendments—altered the relationship between the federal government and the states of the Union by making federal citizenship superior to state citizenship. This was to be the main constitutional legacy of the Civil War. But even so, even in the aftermath of the great upheaval in government that the Civil War represented, the federal government did not become the overbearing behemoth that it was to become during the middle decades of the twentieth century. And this war did not tremendously diminish states' rights the way they were to be diminished in the twentieth century. It certainly did not politicize the Constitution and make it an instrument for social engineering. The relatively slight effect that the Civil War had on the size of the federal government may be judged by the fact that half a year after the war ended the U.S. Attorney General's office still employed only ten clerks.[9]

The next crisis to affect government in the United States was America's entry into the First World War in April of 1917. This did greatly expand the size of the federal government. The war required a multiplication of federal bureaus and commissions to rapidly mobilize the nation's manpower, coordinate its productive capacity, and thereby enable America to fight its first major war overseas. This expansion of the normal powers of the government did not, however, outlast the war. When World War I ended in November 1918, the size of the federal government, which had increased tremendously during America's twenty months of participation in the war, shrank back to nearly what it had been before the war. There was, as was aptly said at the time, "a return to normalcy," and the military forces that had been marshaled during the war were soon demobilized, as they always had been after every war in American history.

Eleven years later, however, during a time of peace, a third crisis befell the nation. This crisis established the idea of instrumental government that John Dewey called for, and this new concept of government has endured since then.

The crisis of the Great Depression struck the nation like a thunderbolt in October of 1929. The collapse of the stock market and many banks threatened to destroy the nation's capitalist economy, which was and still is deeply rooted in America's individualistic culture. Seeking a solution to this crisis, which was so different from a war, seemed to warrant in the thinking of many American leaders and a great portion of the public, sweeping and more than temporary changes to the governmental institutions of America. Most importantly, this crisis justified, they thought, setting aside the Constitution in favor of governmental activism.

The Great Depression of the 1930s affected all of Western civilization, not just the United States. But the high rate of unemployment that it caused in America (unemployment reaching the unprecedented range of 25–30 percent of American workers) amounted to a crisis of culture because America has always been a country whose primary cultural belief is that everyone must work. The attempts to redress this economic crisis, which was also a cultural crisis, brought about a profound alteration in the federal government's relation to the American people and to the states in the Union. Furthermore, the augmentations of federal power that took place during the 1930s on account of the Great Depression were not looked upon as expedients, like those adopted for the duration of a war, whose justification would end when the war ended. Rather, they were regarded not only as concessions of authority to the federal government in a time of grave crisis but also as concessions of indefinite duration. And more importantly, this increase in federal authority, even though it affected the balance of constitutional powers, was made without any amendments to the Constitution.

The scope of this increase in federal authority and responsibility was enormous. In 1933, during the first one hundred days in office of the president who had been elected to do something about the Depression, more "far-reaching and direction-altering legislation" was passed in the single special session of Congress that had been convened by President Franklin Delano Roosevelt and was conducted under his political control than in any other four-month period in American history, including times of war.[10]

President Roosevelt was determined to do whatever it took to alleviate the severity of the economic distress of the American people, Constitution or no Constitution. His determination became clear in his threat to the Supreme Court to increase the number of justices on the Court from nine to fifteen if it persisted in opposing his expansion of executive authority as unconstitutional. Constitutional practice had given Congress the power to specify how many justices should serve on the Supreme Court. And President Roosevelt's threat to "pack the Court" with his political allies by nominating half a dozen additional justices and having them confirmed by the Senate where his political party held 72 out of 96 seats (80 percent in the House of Representatives were Democrats) had plausibility. Under this kind of formidable political pressure, the Court backed down and stopped opposing as unconstitutional the president's expansion of the powers of the executive branch. In thus becoming subordinate to Franklin Roosevelt's political program, the highest court in the land became an instrument of executive branch policies. It was politicized. And because of the politicization of the Supreme Court in the 1930s, the federal judiciary was later available to the activists of the counter-culture movement. Indeed, the federal court system, along with the public schools of America, has been one of the principal instruments applied to changing the belief-behaviors of American culture. Some constitutional scholars even refer to "government by judiciary."

The landslide of votes in 1932 that elected Franklin Roosevelt to his first term of office as president and the second landslide in 1936 that confirmed his popularity gave him—he and his supporters said—a "mandate" to experiment with government in order to find a solution to the crisis of the Great Depression. That idea, that a president with a large vote has a mandate, translated into the proposition that he and his political party had been empowered by the voters to read the Constitution in any way that suited their political policies, or to ignore it altogether. One of the greatest wits of the period, H. L. Mencken, published a mock constitution in the June 1937 issue of *The American Mercury* satirizing that view of the executive branch of the federal government. His mockery began with this preamble: "We, the people of the United States, in order to form a more perfect union, establish social justice, draw the fangs of privilege, effect the redistribution of property, remove the burden of liberty from ourselves and our posterity, and insure the continuance of the New Deal, do ordain and establish this Constitution."

Besides President Roosevelt's threat to "pack the Court," his attitude toward government and the Constitution was also evident in his decision to ignore a very important constitutional custom, albeit not a provision of the Constitution. This constitutional practice was as old as the presidency itself. It had been established by the first American to fill the office of president under the Constitution. Having twice been unanimously elected to the presidency by the Electoral College—no other president has ever been elected even once by an unanimous vote of the Electoral College—George Washington would certainly have been elected again had he chosen to run for a third term. But after two terms he stepped down from office, and every two-term president after Washington followed his example. Franklin Roosevelt's decision to seek a third term broke with this unique and wholesome political custom of voluntary self-restraint in the exercise of executive power in the federal government. In choosing to run for a third term, he reinforced the dangerous idea that politics ought to take precedence over constitutional practice. (The Twenty-second Amendment to the Constitution, passed in

1951, made two-term presidencies a constitutional limitation on executive power.)

In the 1930s, Franklin Roosevelt erased the distinction between politics and constitutionality, between the idea of government as the protection of the people's God-given, unalienable rights and the idea of government as an instrument to effect social change. One constitutional historian has noted that during Franklin Roosevelt's presidency constitutional law was "assimilated to politics," and judicial decisions became "justified by the social justice they embodied."[11] The American cultural belief that the least government possible is best was largely replaced in the 1930s by the idea that maximum government is best and that every branch of the federal government, including the federal judiciary, must be an instrument for social justice.

A new governmental tradition—John Dewey's idea of government as organized "social action" that aimed at bringing about a supposedly more intelligent organization of society—took center stage as the federal government assumed the role of being responsible for the well-being or "social security" of every American. This new concept, that the purpose of the federal government was to assure the well-being of Americans, justified a broad new claim by the executive branch and its partisan collaborators in the legislative and judicial branches. Whereas the original intent of the framers of the Constitution had been to create a federal government whose powers were carefully delineated and limited vis-à-vis the states, Roosevelt's administration claimed to have whatever powers were necessary to carry out his political program. Critics of the New Deal (like the wag who sneered at the New Deal slogan A Chicken in Every Pot by adding the words "and a finger in every pie") were dismissed as out-of-touch with contemporary conditions. They were regarded as defenders of atavistic ideas, persons who refused to see the wonderful future that instrumental government could deliver. In their disregard of that promise, they were looked upon as unintelligent.

Roosevelt's New Deal in the 1930s established what critics of it rightly perceived as "[social] security without personal responsibility."[12] There was more at stake, however, than just the American cultural principle of individual responsibility and the cultural belief that the least government possible is best. Another belief of American culture was also in play, namely that human beings will abuse power when they have it. That belief manifested itself in the Constitution's systematic checks on power that are meant to keep any one man or organized interest from acquiring tyrannical power. The founding fathers knew, as one of the wisest critics of the New Deal said, that "the highest humanitarian motives to do good, as the [government] official sees the good, does not alter the dangers of concentrated executive power."[13] This was not unintelligent, partisan criticism. This was, and is, the common sense of American culture and of the checks and balances that that culture has structured into the Constitution.

Ironically, the New Deal's programs in the 1930s did not solve the crisis of the Great Depression any more than the War on Poverty and the Great Society programs of the 1960s and 1970s succeeded in eradicating poverty in America. It was the advent of another crisis in Western civilization that revived the American economy and put Americans back to work. This crisis was precipitated by Nazi Germany's invasions of neighboring countries as part of the plan of Adolf Hitler and his National Socialists to establish an empire in Europe to be called the Third Reich. And President Roosevelt, in response to pleas for military aid from Great Britain and the Soviet Union to meet this menace, inaugurated the first large-scale production of military supplies in U.S. history during peacetime. It was that expansion of production in agriculture, mining, and manufacturing to meet the needs of America's future allies, who were already at war with Nazi Germany,[14] and the buildup of America's armed forces in case America had to go to war, that ended the Great Depression in the United States. Milton Friedman and Anna Jacobson Schwartz in *A Monetary History of the United States, 1867–1960*,[15] and more recently David Kennedy in *Freedom From Fear*,[16] document that it was not the New Deal but peacetime military production that lifted the American economy out of the Great Depression. They also show that New Deal policies and programs sometimes actually worsened the economic conditions they were supposed to alleviate.

For Americans, World War II (December 1941–August 1945) was two wars—both of unprecedented magnitude—waged simultaneously on opposite sides of the globe. One was among the far-flung archipelagos of the Western Pacific and the other on the North Atlantic, in North Africa, and on the European mainland. The scope of these land, sea, and air wars dwarfed U.S. overseas military operations in Belgium and eastern France in 1918 during World War I. In World War II, America became the granary and arsenal of the Western democracies and provided their principal naval, air, and land forces material support in the fight against the fascist regimes of Italy, Japan, and Germany. Thus did the United States of America preserve freedom and democracy in Western civilization.

To coordinate efforts of this kind both in and outside the Western Hemisphere—efforts that saw sixteen million American men and women put on the uniform of the armed forces of the United States and many times that number mobilized on "the home front" as workers in the production of war material—required the biggest, most regulatory national government in American history. Every aspect of public life was subjected to federal control for the duration of the war, including wages, prices, and the production and distribution of goods for civilian consumption. Such basic items as sugar, clothing, shoes, and gasoline were strictly rationed. Industry, farming, state governments, universities, the media, and other institutions received directives from Washington on coordinating production, developing research, keeping information from the enemy, and controlling criticism of the war effort. At the federal government's insistent urging, Americans invested their savings in government bonds to finance the war. Children were mobilized to collect scrap (metal, rubber, and paper) for the war effort, and even their meager holdings of pennies, nickels, and dimes were solicited to buy U.S. bonds. In short, the life of the nation was focused on just one task: winning the war. And the federal government necessarily organized this whole-hearted, patriotic dedication of the American people to that single-minded effort.

Only a few years of uneasy peace (1945–1948) ensued between the end of World War II and the beginning of the next crisis for the American people, which augmented the power of the federal government still more: the Cold War with the Soviet Union. This crisis was precipitated by a foreign enemy with strong military forces, an enemy motivated by an ideology totally opposed to American culture. And the misery of the Great Depression of the 1930s in America had given a certain plausibility and attractiveness to Soviet theories about central planning, the elimination of private property, and government control of all social and economic matters. Franklin Roosevelt's acceptance of the idea of instrumental government was in line with some of that thinking, though it stopped well short of abolishing private property and capitalism, as had been done in the Soviet Union.

The USSR claimed to have an economy and a government based on science, and in the United States there were believers not only in an application of Marxian "science" but in the kind of applied social science that John Dewey advocated. Both types of American socialists wanted a world in which, as Dewey had said in *Liberalism and Social Action*, Americans would realize "their true individualities and become truly free" by participating in "the common intelligence and [sharing] in the common purpose as it works for the common good." What this meant was the replacing of the old culture with a new one that would be scientific. Socialists of Dewey's stripe and socialists of the Leninist-Stalinist kind disagreed on the methods that were allowable in reorganizing society on scientific principles. Dewey and liberals like him disavowed the systematic punishment and killing of political opponents that Lenin and Stalin thought were justified. But both kinds of socialists wanted a comprehensive new arrangement of social, political, and economic matters. Had the U.S. foreign policy of containing the USSR within its postwar so-called sphere of influence failed, and had the Soviet Union's intention of creating a communist culture throughout Europe, Africa, Asia, and the Americas succeeded, the way would have been cleared for such an unrestrained, allegedly scientific reorganization of society.

Let us illustrate some of the characteristic inanities of big government as it currently exists in the United States, inanities that ought to give every thoughtful American pause, whichever political party they may belong to. Item: In the last decade of the twentieth century while Congress subsidized the growing of tobacco, the U.S. Department of Health, Education and Welfare and other federal agencies expended millions of dollars on advertising the bad health effects of tobacco products, and the U.S. Department of Justice prosecuted manufacturers of these unhealthy products. Item: In 1993, there were 150 separate federal job-training and employment programs.[17] Item: In the last decade of the twentieth century, over 40 percent of federal "entitlement" aid was going to persons with incomes of between $30,000 and $200,000 a year.[18] Item: At the beginning of the twentieth century, there was one agricultural bureaucrat in the federal government for every 1,667 farmers, but by 1990 that ratio had become one agricultural bureaucrat to every 35 farmers, despite the fact that the number of farmers had *decreased to less than half of what it had been in 1900.*[19]

Recent budgets of the federal government are in the *trillions* of dollars. (If one dollar bought one mile of space travel, a trillion dollars would buy 2,083,333 round trips to the moon.) Such budgets are so astronomical that no one can accurately know, account for, or control where all the money goes in any fiscal year. In the 1993 budget, for instance, $246 billion was allocated for "other services" *for which no specific appropriation was voted by Congress.*[20] The waste in the federal government due to sloppy accounting practices, undetected embezzlement, uncollected federal taxes, and nonessential spending cannot be accurately calculated but probably is in the hundreds of billions of dollars annually. Yet every year speeches are made in Congress that Americans are not paying enough taxes or that some segment of American society is not paying its fair share. Given the federal government's colossal wastefulness, one wonders what a fair share of such wastefulness would be.

Here is a sample of the sort of things the federal government has funded in recent years: the preservation of a Trenton, New Jersey, sewer as a historical monument; a study of the sex life of the Japanese quail; the building of a museum to the memory of Franklin Roosevelt's secretary of state; the purchase of President McKinley's mother-in-law's house; a study of the history of the feud between the Hatfields and the McCoys; an investigation of why people fall in love; a study of how to avoid falling spacecraft; a project to teach college students how to watch television; an access ramp to a privately owned stadium in Milwaukee; the construction of a Hawaiian canoe; a study of the komungo (a Korean musical instrument); the reconstruction of an old railroad yard in Scranton, Pennsylvania; a study of why people don't ride bicycles to work; a replica in Indiana of Egypt's Great Pyramid; a demonstration project on building wooden bridges; installation of a toilet for mountain climbers on top of Mt. McKinley (at a cost of $800,000); the construction of a million-dollar Seafood Consumer Center; an inquiry into the gas emissions produced by cow flatulence; the construction of a bike path in Macomb County, Georgia; and a study of whether pigeons follow human economic laws.[21] The list could be extended manyfold. Hundreds upon hundreds of thousands of projects like these have received federal funding. And of course each of them had merit in the eyes of its proposer. But should the people of the United States of America pay for such projects? Or should their proponents rather seek local-government funding, state-government funding, or private donations to finance them, or even perhaps pay for them out of their own pockets? A "special interest group" once meant an organization like a labor union or a business corporation that represented some economically important segment of American society whose activities affected many thousands, perhaps millions of Americans. Now the idea of a special interest seems to be whatever someone can dream up and get federal money to fund. Even "the homeless" have self-appointed lobbyists in Washington actively begging millions of federal tax dollars (what might be called budgetary panhandling).

These expenditures that consume trillions of dollars in federal taxes and federal borrowing against the good name and credit of the hardworking people of the United States are a direct result of the concept of instrumental government. The increase in the number of departments in the executive branch in the last half-century attests to the growth of this kind of government since the end of World War II. In 1950 there were nine executive branch departments in the federal government; today there are fifteen. And these fifteen departments have among them 164 large subunits. In the year

2000 there were 1,500 persons working directly for the president of the United States on his personal staff. And according to U.S. Office of Personnel Management figures published in *The World Almanac and Book of Facts 2003*,[22] the total number of persons employed by the federal government in 2003 (excluding men and women serving in the military) was approaching 3 million, 2.6 million of those in the executive branch.

The present size of the executive branch of the federal government is but one sign, however, of the effect that the reconception of government as an instrument to ensure the happiness and well-being of Americans has had on the checks and balances originally built into the Constitution of the United States.

Another indicator is Congress's habit of passing a type of legislation known as "omnibus bills." These federal laws are loaded with appropriations called "pork," which is federal money allocated to nonessential projects that particular legislators want to fund in order to win favor with their constituencies. Not even the most conscientious congressman (or his staff) can read and study everything in an omnibus bill. (Senators and representatives sometimes receive these monster bills just days before the scheduled vote on them.) The passage of such bills makes a mockery of the legislative process because it is fraudulent for Congress to claim to be a legislative body when its members cannot know what is in every bill they pass.

Omnibus bills also compromise the president's veto power granted to him by Article I, Section 7, Paragraph 3 of the Constitution. They confront him with the dilemma of either withholding his constitutionally required assent to a needed piece of legislation that has been loaded with pork or signing the bill into law, pork and all.

The separation of powers that the Constitution specifies among the three branches of the federal government has also been skewed by the president's encroachment on Congress's legislative powers. The first section of the first article in the Constitution states unequivocally and categorically: "All legislative Powers herein granted shall be vested in a Congress of the United States, which shall consist of a Senate and a House of Representatives." But it has become common practice for presidents to issue executive orders having the authority of federal law. The first president of the United States in the twentieth century, Theodore Roosevelt, a young patrician do-gooder, issued more executive orders during his tenure in the White House (1901–1909) than all previous presidents combined. And the increase in this practice has gained for the executive branch of the federal government legislative powers that it was never intended to have under the Constitution.

Influenced by the idea of instrumental government, political factions in the Congress have also been guilty of practices that amount to an unconstitutional usurpation of authority. Rules adopted by the U.S. Senate and the House of Representatives for conducting their business, which Article I, Section 5, Paragraph 2 of the Constitution authorizes them to write, have given senior congressmen, particularly the chairmen of important committees, power to keep proposed legislation from being voted on by the people's representatives. Under the rules of the Senate, it is even possible for a determined minority in that chamber of Congress to keep a majority of senators from exercising their constitutionally mandated responsibility to either give or withhold their approval of the judges the president nominates to the federal court system, as Article II, Section 2, Paragraph 2 of the Constitution requires. In this way also the Constitution's wise system of checks and balances, whose purpose was to forestall undemocratic concentrations of power in the hands of a few, is dangerously unbalanced.

In the post–World War II period of American history, government by judiciary is an even greater malpractice of federal authority. What this means is that federal judges, particularly justices of the Supreme Court from whose verdicts no appeal is constitutionally possible, create rights not specified in the Constitution. They also nullify as unconstitutional laws enacted either directly by a majority of voters in a state through referendums or by their elected representatives in their state legislatures or in Congress—in the latter case with the approval of the president of the United States. Declaring a statute unconstitutional was almost unheard-of before the middle of the twentieth century and was always based on some recognized constitutional principle. Now that judicial decisions creating rights and nullifying statutes are becoming comparatively frequent, the reasons that judges give for their decisions are becoming more and more bizarre and airy. In 1965, for instance, the U.S. Supreme Court found that "penumbras formed by emanations" from the Bill of Rights constituted a "right to privacy" (*Griswold v. Connecticut* 381 U.S. 479). Since *penumbra* means a dimly lit outline, one hardly knows what to make of such reasoning. To say the least that could be said about it, penumbras do not furnish an illuminating basis for law in a democratic society like the United States with a population in the hundreds of millions. In such a large, diverse society, maintaining a healthy respect for law requires that the reasoning by which the highest level of judicial verdicts are arrived at should seem sensible to the people who are to obey them, especially when the judicial decision may be repugnant to a majority of citizens.

Basing judicial decisions on a murky concept like "penumbras formed by emanations" is not good jurisprudence.

The most egregious offenses of instrumental government against the Constitution and the republican form of government it structures, however, have been in regard to states' rights. Since the idea of instrumental government became entrenched in Washington, all three branches of the federal government have shamelessly asserted a nearly tyrannical federal power over state governments. In fundamental contradiction of the Union established in the Constitution of the United States, the fifty states have become in recent decades little more than administrative units of the federal government. That was not the relationship between the states and the national government envisioned in the Constitution. The Constitution consented to by the people in the original states of the Union and the people in each of the thirty-seven territories that subsequently became states was intended to limit the powers of the federal government to those enumerated in the Constitution. What the people in the states consented to was not a document that conferred on the federal government limitless implied powers. The Constitution has no meaning or intention if limiting the federal government is not its meaning and intention.

The Constitution exists for a reason, and the Tenth Amendment leaves no doubt as to what that reason is. "The powers not delegated to the United States by the Constitution nor prohibited by it to the States, are reserved to the States respectively, or to the people." That is the formative premise of the government of the United States: *to constitute a union of states that carefully proscribes the power of the central government.* (Belief in the necessity of having a written constitution goes back to the colonial era, when the people in each colony relied on their written charters to defend them against the imperious will of the British crown.) The purpose of the Constitution of the United States was to prevent federal tyranny over the states. The constitutive power of the people in their states, who initiated and consented to the Constitution of the United States because it was needful to their general welfare, remains supreme. (Article V of the Constitution, in providing for amendments, allows for adjustments required by unanticipated circumstances.) Nowhere in the U.S. Constitution is the power of the people in their states to amend the Constitution delegated to the judicial, the executive, or the legislative branch of the federal government. The Constitution was written by and for the people. They alone have the power to judge, through a super-majority of the states, acting under the provisions of Article V, through the elected representatives of the people in the states, whether the delegated powers enumerated and distributed in the Constitution should be altered.

Under the influence of the idea of instrumental, big government, the three branches of the federal government currently seem to operate on the mistaken notion that powers not specified in the Constitution as belonging to the states *belong to them*, rather than to the American people in their states as the Tenth Amendment clearly proclaims. Not only does this notion contradict the fundamental principle explicitly articulated in the Tenth Amendment and implied in the American cultural belief in the necessity of having a written Constitution, it also violates the principle that the federal government is dependent on the people in the states for its powers. The very existence of the Constitution proclaims that the federal government is the creation of the people in the states; and the state governments collectively, as the originating representatives of the people, remain superior to it. The authority of the people in their states cannot be usurped by the federal government any more than the political powers enumerated and distributed in the Constitution can transcend the power of God, the creator of man and nature, whom the beliefs of American culture acknowledge.

Instrumental government regards the Constitution as meaning whatever it has to mean in order to make it a useful instrument for carrying out a political program or enforcing an idea that happens to be the politically correct fashion of the moment. But the Constitution was not written to be the instrument of a political program. Nor does it belong to one generation of the American people more than another. It belongs to all of the generations of Americans who have ever lived, the generations alive today, and the unborn generations who will (it may be hoped) live in the future under its authority.

During World War II America had a single, clear goal: the unconditional surrender of fascist Germany, Japan, and Italy. In America's Cold War with the Soviet Union, victory was more complicated than the straightforward objectives of a strictly military conflict. True, the Cold War required the use and the threat of the use of military force to contain aggression by communist regimes and insurgents intent on gaining military control over more territory. But it also involved a need to prevent the internal subversion and takeover of the governments of noncommunist countries. It further required combating brazen lies. Foremost among these was the stupendous falsehood that the United States wanted to rule the world, while the USSR, a "nation" as large as the British Empire at the height of its imperial expansion, wanted only to defend the rights of the world's suffering peoples and liberate them from tyranny. In other words, with a stunning disregard of the truth, the propaganda emanating from Moscow during the Cold War reversed the respective histories and post–World War II roles of the United States and the Soviet Union.

The counter-culture movement that began to make itself felt in the 1960s has heaped on the United States the same accusations that were put forward during the Cold War in the propaganda of the Soviet Union. Certainly the accusation that the present-day form of the counter-culture movement levels against American culture—that it wants to impose its beliefs on every-one—is as bogus as the lies told by the CPSU about the United States during the Cold War. The truth of the matter is that the beliefs of American culture have been under constant assault and on the defensive since the 1960s. It is pure propaganda to claim that anyone is trying to impose the cultural beliefs that before 1960 were already in place in American society. It is patently the counter-culture movement that has been, and is, trying to impose on American society its ideas of correct thought and behavior.

Besides its extraordinarily long duration (1949–1991), the Cold War with the Soviet Union had several other features that made it a different kind of crisis from any the American people had previously faced in their history: (1) it required on the part of the U.S. government covert operations and cooperation with foreign dictators and tyrants; (2) it required, for the first time in American history, immense armed forces in peacetime; (3) it included fighting the longest war in U.S. military history (the Vietnam War) without a declaration of war by Congress as required by Article I, Section 8, Paragraph 11 of the Constitution; and (4) it resulted in a good many young, middle-class Americans being convinced by Soviet Cold War propaganda that American culture is oppressive and imperialistic, which created for the first time in U.S. history an anti-American consciousness among a considerable portion of the American middle class. All four of these aspects of the Cold War were without precedent in U.S. history and were detrimental to the health of America's democratic society and its culture. But the creation of a counter-culture movement (the fourth item) was the most damaging.

A hodgepodge of groups—some small and short-lived, others large and more continuous—have comprised the counter-culture movement; and each has contributed to a piecemeal rejection and general distortion and weakening of American cultural beliefs. There have been on the one hand a multitude of local, single-issue action groups like the ephemeral Nuclear Free State in Tucson, Arizona, in the late 1970s and early 1980s, and thousands of other short-lived action groups during the 1990s and the present decade.

On the other hand, there have been old, nationwide, dues-paying "liberal" organizations like the American Civil Liberties Union (the ACLU was founded in 1920); self-proclaimed revolutionary organizations like the National Organization of Women (NOW); co-opted, supposedly apolitical institutions like the World Council of Churches and the YWCA; and established philanthropic and professional organizations like the Ford Foundation and the Modern Language Association (MLA) whose leaders want to walk in the aura of standing for world peace, social justice, and liberation. And at times in the last four decades, the federal judiciary has seemed to take more interest in being politically correct than in upholding the Constitution. What has held this sprawling movement together has been the rejection of American culture that its disparate constituencies have engaged in with varying degrees of passion. Opposition to some or all of American culture has been the common denominator that has given the movement its unity and purpose; one has only to believe that America stands for this or that categorical oppression to be a soldier in the culture war.

It may be safely assumed that the Soviet Union had little attraction for the great majority of the middle-class, idealistic American young people who became part of the counter-culture movement in the 1960s or whose patriotism was neutralized by its propaganda. The same would be true of the next generation that came of age in the 1980s and joined in the culture war. Nevertheless, those Americans who have been convinced that the United States is an imperialistic, corporate monstrosity that stands for nothing but greed and racism have served the ends of America's worst enemies.

The counter-culture movement has stirred up many issues—the separation of church and state, group entitlements, educating for self-esteem, social justice, a living Constitution, moral relativism, tolerance of "anything goes" sex, environmental rights vs. private property rights, absolute and unqualified abortion rights, same-sex marriage, and many others—and it has appropriated, redefined, and used for its own purposes broader issues like racism, greed, and "gender bias." Yet, despite the extraordinary challenges and crises of the Great Depression, followed by World War II, the Cold War, and a domestic culture war that has now lasted for two generations, the center of American culture still holds. The American people have met every challenge thus far.

CHAPTER NINE

Strict Materialism

American culture, like every culture in the history of mankind, contains beliefs that presume the existence of a reality that transcends the powers of nature and human beings. In American culture these beliefs express a faith in the creator of the universe to whom Abraham and Jesus Christ prayed. The specific beliefs are:

> God created nature and human beings.
> God gave men the same birthrights.
> God created a law of right and wrong.
> Doing what is right is necessary for happiness.

The first pair of these beliefs is vital to the principle of equal freedom that the Declaration of Independence proclaimed in its most ringing phrase, "all men are created equal," and which has been and is the distinguishing principle of social and political relations in America's democratic society. The second pair of beliefs provides the cultural basis for morality in American society. The four of them together are the foundation on which rest social unity, law, and political order in the United States.

The idea that impersonal matter and energy are the only components of everything that exists, including man—in other words the idea that there is no creator—began to be an article of faith among Western intellectuals during the century in which the United States of America declared its independence. That doctrine of strict materialism was part of a larger intellectual movement in the eighteenth century (the Enlightenment) whose European leaders in most cases espoused a secular faith in science, education, and government as the only means of human redemption. However, the English-speaking colonies in North America that became the United States of America in 1776 had been spared the religious wars that wracked Europe in the seventeenth century, wars that had provoked a strong reaction against religion among European intellectuals. Americans were a Christian people whose trials and tribulations in colonizing a Stone Age wilderness had strengthened, not weakened their belief in the God of Abraham and Jesus to whom they had in their tribulations so often called upon in prayer. To be sure, Americans knew of the Enlightenment (Benjamin Franklin was one of its internationally renowned figures). But both the American people and their leaders in the eighteenth century believed in the God who created nature, man, and what the Declaration of Independence called "the Laws of Nature." Americans believed in immutable physical laws that God had created and immutable moral laws that he had also ordained. And Franklin and the other leaders of the American Revolution believed that in the nature of things nations as well as men had to heed God's moral laws.

Because of the constant anti-American propaganda of the Soviet Union during the Cold War, rejection of America and its culture was "in the air" following the Second World War. The doctrine of strict materialism, however, has been pervasive in Western civilization since the eighteenth century. The Enlightenment attracted adherents by claiming to represent an outlook superior to (i.e., more enlightened than) Christian theology. The Enlightenment promised a brighter future for mankind by eliminating "the superstition of religion" generally. Enlightenment intellectuals regarded Christianity's belief in the fall of man and man's consequent need for God's redeeming grace as backward thinking. For European intellectuals in the eighteenth century, acceptance of the doctrine of strict materialism was a sign of progressive thinking. In the nineteenth century, Marxism emerged from the mindset of strict materialism, and in the twentieth century applied Marxism led to the gargantuan experiment called the Union of Soviet Socialist Republics, a disastrous failure that resulted in incalculable suffering and the deaths of many millions of human beings.

Soviet anti-American propaganda accused capitalists of being greedy and materialistic. But the most pernicious form of materialism is not the pursuit of profit. It is belief in the doctrine of strict materialism that explains everything, including man, in terms of material considerations. This doctrine is the Midas touch. It transforms all loveliness and goodness and every human virtue into mere matter. Under the Midas touch of strict materialism, a mother's tender care of her offspring becomes the impersonal drive of her genes to perpetuate themselves; the worth of a conscientious worker's labor in making or doing something for the benefit of himself and other human beings is reduced to mere economic measurements; and worshipping God becomes a ridiculous waste of time because the doctrine of strict materialism does not authorize belief in God. Strict materialism cancels free will. It denies the existence of the soul and transcendent goodness. It reduces human beings to the sum of their genes and the influence of their environment.

The steady rise of this doctrine in Western civilization during the last three centuries, like the rise of instrumental government in the United States since the 1930s, comprises a serious threat to American culture. Strict materialism, which teaches that matter and energy are the sole determinant realities in the universe, claims that everything, including human nature, must be seen only in terms of material considerations. Were this doctrine to be accepted by a majority of Americans, it would extinguish American culture's belief in freedom as a gift from God, in the equality of human beings as children of God, and in self-determination as a God-given right. The extinction of those beliefs would be the demise of America culture. Because the doctrine of strict materialism is intertwined with the rise of modern science, it is the most serious single threat to American culture. It, like instrumental government, is a major battlefront in the culture war in the United States. Because of its importance, the doctrine of strict materialism and its cultural effects must be separately considered in assaying the present condition of American culture.

The first thing to be considered is the connection between science and strict materialism. Science searches for truth about measurable natural phenomena and assumes that everything measurable is a manifestation of energy and matter; the essential idea of strict materialism is that nothing exists except energy and matter. Strict materialism and science thus share compatible outlooks.

The great discoveries of modern science and the many wonders of their applications have given science an immense, well-earned prestige in Western civilization. Since the mid-twentieth century, the improvements wrought by scientific knowledge in the conditions of human life have been without precedent. This material progress has been so pronounced and so beneficial that many Westerners now regard science with the same kind of reverence and submission to its authority that was once accorded the teachings of Christian theology. More and more in recent decades, anything claiming to have the imprimatur of science has generally been accepted as valid, and beliefs and ideas not endorsed by science have been regarded as dubious.

But however much we may admire the accomplishments of science, few thoughtful persons today would agree that every consequence of science has been of unequivocal benefit to mankind. Weapons of mass destruction, of course, would not have been possible without the application of knowledge gained through scientific investigations of nature. But besides this, in creating modern science Western civilization may have invented an intellectual tool that will in time destroy the basis of man's confidence in himself and his dignity by reducing him to the status of just another animal. Strict materialism eliminates belief in free will, the human soul, and the potential of individuals for self-determined happiness; and the assumptions of strict materialism are employed in doing science. Thus the achievements of science over the last two centuries have unintentionally strengthened the doctrine of strict materialism and unintentionally weakened the religious and moral foundations of Western civilization.

Besides noting the effect of science on the civilization to which American culture belongs, several other matters should also be noted. First of all, the inadequacy of science to analyze and satisfy the spiritual needs of human nature should be appreciated. Secondly, it should be understood that the method for discovering truth about nature that defines science relegates nonmaterial truths to a status of lesser importance even when they are not canceled. And thirdly, the application of the scientific method to matters that are not amenable to scientific investigation has given science an undeserved reputation for having the answer to every question of human concern. Science has become for some Westerners a kind of neo-pagan religion and worship of nature, a religion that reveres the scientific method not only as the means to discover truths about nature but as the solution to every human problem.

The term *scientism* was coined to distinguish this modern religion from science itself. Friedrich A. Hayek, the great Austrian-educated social philosopher and Nobel prize winner, a half-century ago in his book *The Counter-Revolution of Science: Studies on the Abuse of Reason*, defined scientism as "an attitude decidedly unscientific . . . since it involves a mechanical and uncritical application of habits of thought to fields different from those in which they have been formed."[1] But this habit of applying the scientific method to subjects that by their nature do not lend themselves to scientific study was established long before 1950. In an undated letter written in 1839 or soon thereafter, Charles Darwin's wife, Emma Darwin, wrote to her husband complaining of his scientism (though she didn't use that term): "May not the habit of scientific pursuits of believing nothing till it is proved, influence your mind too much in other things which cannot be proved in the same way, and which if true are likely to be above our comprehension."[2]

Scientism is a quite different matter from science. No real scientist would, I think, ever claim that the scientific method for discovering the truth about nature offers the only way to understand and solve every human problem. There is, as Emma Darwin rightly perceived, an inherent disjunction between the methodology that defines science and the truths of the human heart, truths including of course Western civilization's religious and moral heritage. Though quite a large proportion of scientists believe in God and the soul (the proportion held steady at 40 percent throughout the twentieth century[3]), science can only be practiced and scientific truth discovered by investigating measurable phenomena. To proclaim a truth to be scientific requires accumulating reliable data on a phenomenon, formulating a hypothesis based on that objective information, and then testing the validity of the hypothesis through controlled experiments to see if the same result is obtained each time. These are well-known scientific protocols. By applying them, faulty hypotheses can be discarded as untrue and true hypotheses can be demonstrated to be valid. The scientific methodology of data-hypothesis-experiment defines what it means to do science and to be a scientist, and it leads to the discovery of truths about the laws that govern measurable, physical phenomena. But God and the souls of human beings are immeasurable, immaterial phenomena. They are not part of the natural order. They are supernatural. God's will exists apart from the universe it created, and the human soul, which God has created, sets man somewhat apart from nature as well.

Furthermore, truths discovered by the methodology of science must be considered tentative or conditional (as any scientist worthy of the name will proudly tell you) because any discovery made in this way is subject to subsequent scrutiny when new data become available on which additional experiments can be based. The results of further experimentation may require modification or even the invalidation of a previous finding as more is learned from further observation, measurement, analysis, and testing. This principle of the tentativeness of scientific truth is one of the great beauties of science. But once scientists arrive at a consensus that a hypothesis has been scientifically tested and verified, it is acted on for practical purposes as if it were an ultimate truth, even though scientists know that subsequent data and experimentation could reveal that it is only partially true or even false. There is one exception to these admirable protocols. Doing science requires the assumption that the laws of nature that govern the operations of energy and matter are universally constant and operate without exception.

The assumptions and teachings of Christian theology, which have had a fundamental shaping influence on the cultures of Western civilization, are different in some respects from those of science. Like science, Christian theology teaches that the universe that God created is orderly. But it also teaches that the operation of God's will transcends the universe and is superior to its forces and nature and ultimately unknowable unless God wishes to reveal it. The ancient Jews, the people God first chose to reveal himself to and whose religion Christianity extended, believed God created the laws that govern nature but that he can for a purpose that suits his will suspend a physical law's specific operation without canceling its universal operation. To do otherwise would cause God's universe to fall into disorder. In other words, the glory of the creator is manifested in the workings of the universe he created but is not limited by that order which he has created. Unlike anything else in the universe, God's infinite power operates in both universal and particular ways. The almighty creator of the universe can make particular exceptions to a physical law he has created and can prevent such an exception from interfering with that law's general operations. God is not part of what he has created but is necessarily superior to it.

These religious teachings are at variance with doing science, a practice that is predicated on the assumption of a universe whose operations are of absolute, unvarying sameness throughout space and time. Scientists resolve the problem of God's discontinuity with nature by simply assuming, as they go about their work as scientists, that for all practical purposes in doing science God does not exist, even though it is impossible to prove this negative. Most scientists today (roughly 60 percent according to the long-term surveys of the scientific community cited above) go beyond the working assumption that God does not exist for the practical purpose of doing science and either believe categorically that he does not exist or that his existence is improbable. They adopt this atheistic position perhaps out of their love for uniformity and consistency. For some scientists, God's existence may possibly be offensive to their sense of the integrity of the work they do as scientists. However that may be, the majority of scientists (the 60 percent who embrace atheism instead of theism or agnosticism) forget when it comes to God the beauty of their discipline's principle of the tentativeness of scientific truth. They also refuse to accept the possibility that some things may be, as Emma Darwin told her husband, beyond the ability of the scientific method to discover. That possibility is not agreeable to scientism.

But the scientific method *is* limited in what it can discover. The universe, for instance, cannot be created over again to allow a modern-day scientist to observe how it actually began. In the creation story scientists tell, everything starts with the premise that in the beginning there was matter and energy in a singular state of compression, and that this matter and energy suddenly expanded, or went "bang," under singular conditions that had never existed before and that have not existed since that moment, which naturally came to be known as "the Big Bang." From that instant on everything, that is to say, the known universe, began an expansion that is still in process. So in the beginning there was matter and energy, scientists say, but it cannot be scientifically demonstrated how this energy and matter that went "bang" reached the unique state that preceded their expansion; nor can it be scientifically stated how matter and energy came to be present in the first place in order to go "bang." These questions lie outside the parameters of science's creation story. The Judeo-Christian creation story, on the other hand, starts with the premise that in the beginning there was God's transcendent, omnipotent, eternal will.

Some scientists, it appears, prefer not to think about the possibility of an infinitely powerful, willful, and eternal being antecedent to the universe's existence, a being whose power and reality are altogether different from and superior to the reality and potency evident in matter and energy. (In Judeo-Christian theology, this difference from the universe that he created is referred to as God's holiness, or ineffable otherness.) It appears to rankle the pride of quite a few scientists to think that there could be a reality apart from the one that the methodology of their profession applies to and has been so successful in investigating. Every claim of a miraculous event, such as the virgin birth of Christ or his resurrection from the dead, galls them because it contradicts the doctrine of strict materialism and represents a limitation on scientific methodology. Nonetheless, something caused the universe that we can observe and measure. And something happened in Jerusalem two thousand years ago to cause simple Jewish fishermen to know beyond doubt, and to act on their knowledge at the risk of their lives, that Jesus of Nazareth was the Christ. That Peter, James, John, and many other followers of Jesus came to believe with an absolute certainty that Jesus was the living Christ is clear from their fearless devotion to that belief after his crucifixion. For three days, they were in hiding, cowering in despair over their teacher's death and in fear of the authorities who had had him executed. Then, suddenly, they and hundreds of other followers of Jesus began to publicly proclaim him the Christ and were willing to suffer death rather than be quiet about this "good news." Such a sudden, complete conviction, like the sudden transformation of Paul from a zealous persecutor of Christians into one of the Christian church's great leaders, had to have a cause. So also, ever since science established that the universe had a beginning, it is self-evident that it must have had a cause. But science has no way of accounting for that cause.

Neither the creation of the estimated 100 billion galaxies in the universe and the energy and matter they represent, nor the inspiration that led to the creation of the Christian church, can be subjected to scientific testing. Both were unique events about which no reliable data can be obtained by direct observation. We have only effects and the inferences that may be drawn from them to rely on. The Christ cannot be repeatedly crucified and entombed under guard to see for the benefit of science whether and how he will rise from the dead. As with every miracle, the resurrection of Christ from the dead was an unrepeatable, unique event, whereas the scientific method applies only and entirely to regularly recurring events. Likewise, the creation of the universe was a unique, unrepeatable event.

It is the faith of strict materialists and those who worship science that miracles never happen. And it is easy for them to reason away a miracle. John Stuart Mill, the English philosopher, did so succinctly in 1843 in his *System of Logic Ratiocinative and Inductive*. This was his reasoning:

> If we do not already believe in supernatural agencies, no miracle can prove to us their existence. The miracle itself, considered merely as an extraordinary fact, may be satisfactorily certified by our senses or by testimony; but nothing can ever prove that it is a miracle: there is still another possible hypothesis, that of its being the result of some unknown natural cause: and this possibility cannot be so completely shut out, as to leave no alternative but that of admitting the existence and intervention of a being superior to nature.[4]

In other words, had John Stuart Mill seen a man walking on water, he would not thereby have been convinced that he had witnessed a miracle. He would simply have invoked his hypothesis of an "unknown natural cause" to claim that such an event was no proof of the existence of any "being superior to nature." But can that negative hypothesis—the claim that seeing a man walk on water would *not* prove the operation of a supernatural agency—be put to a scientific test? No, it cannot. The power of a man who could walk on water is beyond science to prove or disprove, because if a person existed who had that power it would be peculiar to him, since it is the common sense of mankind, and not just scientists, that walking on water is absolutely contrary to the laws of nature. (That, of course, is the definition of a miracle. It is an exception to the natural order.) And the hypothesis that walking on water would reveal a supernatural power peculiar to the walker cannot be so completely shut out (to use John Stuart Mill's own logic) as to leave no alternative but that of believing that every such event invariably has a natural explanation. In other words, belief in a strictly material world view requires as much faith as a world view that includes supernaturalism, since no mortal, not even a scientist, can claim to know every event that has ever happened or could happen in the universe. The methodology of science is based on an assumption about how the universe has operated since the miraculous creation event that scientists call the Big Bang, namely that everything that can be known from observation or inference represents only the unvarying operation of impersonal matter and energy.

By the middle of the nineteenth century, faith in strict materialism was widespread among European intellectuals. W. E. H. Lecky described this development in these terms on the first page of his *History of the Rise and Influence of the Spirit of Rationalism*:

> At present, nearly all educated men receive an account of a miracle taking place in their own day, with an absolute and even derisive incredulity which dispenses with all examination of the evidence. Although they may be entirely unable to give a satisfactory explanation of some phenomena that have taken place, they never on that account dream of ascribing them to supernatural agency, such an hypothesis being, as they believe, altogether beyond the range of reasonable discussion.[5]

One notices in both Lecky's diction in this passage and in his book's title the implication that belief in miracles is irrational. And since all religions ultimately come down to a belief in something superior to nature, there is the further implication in Lecky's words that no conclusions derived from some spiritual experience or from theology could possibly be true. This haughtiness, whether explicit or only implied, is characteristic of the teachings of strict materialism. Theists acknowledge the existence of matter and energy; strict materialists like Lecky and John Stuart Mill do not return the favor by conceding that something supernatural could exist.

According to strict materialism, miracles *cannot* occur; therefore, they do not occur. The same self-validating, unscientific opinion applies to God. Because his existence would contradict the postulates of strict materialism, God *cannot* exist and therefore does not exist, regardless of the findings of innumerable intelligent persons over thousands of years of time that God does exist. Theism asserts that a being can and does exist and events can and do occur that transcend the natural order of things. But to a strict materialist, belief in supernatural realities is irrational. It is a sign of delusion, mental deficiency, or ignorance.

The rejection of supernatural phenomena, on the grounds that they are not uniform recurrences, increased among intellectuals during the nineteenth and twentieth centuries. And because the doctrine of strict materialism has been strongly associated with science and its many benefits, faith in that concept has gained prestige while the authority of religion has declined.

English-speaking people in the late nineteenth century had a saying, "Civilization is soap." But the essence of civilization is not (or at least not mainly) a matter of cleanliness. Rather, it is the self-restraint induced by belief in a power that transcends man and nature, an almighty being who cares whether human beings act benevolently toward each other or use other human beings to satisfy the most selfish impulses of human nature. Without belief in a personal, caring creator, the only basis for morality that we have is human reason. And, as Benjamin Franklin wisely reminded us in his *Autobiography* more than two centuries ago, reason is too "convenient" a thing to be trusted completely, in that it allows us to rationalize whatever we may want to think or do. Reason certainly has its necessary (and one may add, God-ordained) role in deciding how we should act, but so too do conscience, spiritual experiences, and common sense. Any system of morality that starts with the premise that reason alone is a sufficient means for obtaining goodness is in for unpleasant surprises, as the twentieth-century history of the applications of Marxist reasoning amply demonstrates. One might well ask, did the behavior of civilized man become less violent, less immoral, and more self-restrained as the authority of religion declined in the twentieth century and the authority of science increased? Those who claim that man's salvation lies in embracing the doctrine of strict materialism and eliminating religion should be required to answer that question.

The marvelous discoveries of science over the past three centuries constitute irrefutable evidence that modern science is unrivaled in its ability to discover truths *within the limits of its interests*. But the human race has interests that are beyond our material existence, interests in ontology, teleology, cosmology, morality, and justice. (That was Mrs. Darwin's point in complaining to her husband about his scientism.) And these intellectual questions are every bit as vital to the survival and health of the human race as meeting the physical needs of human beings. Like any other intellectual discipline, science has limitations that are defined by its particular interests, procedures, and assumptions. The methodology of science for discovering truths about the world of matter and energy has been so eminently successful that every thoughtful person, and not just scientists, can and should take pride in science as a human invention. But no intellectual discipline, no matter how marvelous its achievements may be, is capable of explaining everything. As wonderful as science is as a means of discovering the truth about nature, we need not on that account cede to it final say in everything of vital concern to human beings. John Stuart Mill's hypothesis that there are no realities "superior to nature" is a statement of faith in strict materialism. It is untestable by the protocols of scientific methodology. Science as a religion (scientism) could destroy our humanity by reducing our conception of ourselves to that of beings that are merely and only a part of nature.

As the doctrine of strict materialism gained acceptance in Western civilization during the nineteenth and twentieth centuries, the methodology of science was misapplied to "soft" subjects in which value judgments, cultural viewpoints, opinion, and personal talents and interests are inherent. Such factors are not inherent to the impersonal, "hard" subjects of chemistry, physics, and astronomy, the areas of investigation in which the methodology of science was developed and came to define what it means to be a scientist. Soft subjects such as history, economics, psychology, politics, and sociology do not lend themselves to scientific study because they lack the uniformity and regularity that scientific investigation requires. Their laws—if indeed any can be formulated that deserve that designation—cannot be established through experiments that yield unvaryingly reliable results. (The first difficulty with regard to applying scientific methodology to a soft subject is that of obtaining precise, objective data on which to base testable hypotheses.) Nonetheless, over the last century and a half there has been a notable trend toward including soft subjects within the realm of scientific investigation. These alleged applications of scientific methodology have obviously been made in order that investigators of soft subjects might have the same prestige that investigators in the natural sciences have from the results of their study of hard subjects that are amenable to precise, objective measurement. This tendency reflects the worshipful modern attitude toward science as the be-all and end-all of truth.

If politics, history, social behavior, or economics could really be studied scientifically, then a political scientist would be able to forecast the outcome of every election every time, and the macro-predictions of a supposedly scientific historian like Karl Marx would turn out to be true. Furthermore, social scientists could resolve every social conflict, and psychologists could cure every one of their patients. If economics were really susceptible to scientific study, would not all risk-taking in investing be eliminated? Even processes that one might suppose were hard topics for study, like the technologies of metallurgy and glass-making, turn out to require at the highest level of production some art as well as science. The worst confusion of all results from treating subjects like medicine that have some aspects that are hard and others that are soft as if they were entirely hard subjects suitable for scientific study only.

To a doctrinaire strict materialist, mankind's free will is an illusion or, if not that, a grand irrelevance that ought never to be taken into serious account as something of primary importance to human behavior. When strict materialists study human beings and their behavior, they consider either environment, genetic inheritance, or some interaction of these factors to be of exclusive importance. Steven Pinker in *The Blank Slate* demonstrates that Marxists have believed exclusively in the influence of environment on man.[6] They deny the role of genes in Darwin's comprehensive hypothesis of natural selection, which holds that random genetic variations allow some organisms to better adapt to their environment and pass on more of their genes to the future and thus, gradually, to evolve into higher species. Marxists have been only partial Darwinists so far. Their politics has focused exclusively on the environment. Because they favor the masses over the aristocracy, they have believed in conditioning and have rejected the idea of genetic superiority achieved through selective breeding.

Yet, however much the universe inhabited by human beings includes the inescapable physical necessities we call laws of nature, the lives of actual human beings are determined fundamentally by religious, moral, personal, and cultural matters. The saying "Man does not live by bread alone" is absolutely true. Human conduct is not invariable; each person lives a unique individual life that is a testament to the reality of free will. That, in large measure, is what it means to be human. But in supposedly scientific studies of human beings, this paramount truth must be set aside. To engage in either social or political "science," one must basically disregard individuality and look at human beings only as if they were impersonal units of some general phenomenon that is statistically predictable.

American culture, however, has as one of its main components the belief in the capacity of human beings to exert their free will and to determine to a considerable degree, through the exercise of that free will, the outcome of their individual lives. That is why scientism and the doctrine of strict materialism imperil American culture.

The misapplications of the scientific method to human behavior that are now commonplace among intellectuals have led to the assertion that human beings do not differ from "other animals" in any way that would justify regarding them as having any sort of exceptional status in the natural world. In the past thirty years a great many articles and books have been published on anthropology, animal behavior, linguistics, biology, and similar subjects based on that view of man. These publications either directly or indirectly reject the Judeo-Christian teaching that man is God's special creation who, unlike any other creature on Earth, has been made in the image of God, which is to say that man is somewhat like his creator who is entirely discontinuous with the natural world.

This trend in Western civilization away from the Judeo-Christian view of man has been evidenced in many ways. Take the literary movement in Europe and the United States at the end of the nineteenth century and the beginning of the twentieth century called literary naturalism that described man as another animal in the natural order. Naturalistic American novels like Stephen Crane's *Maggie: A Girl of the Streets* (1893), Frank Norris's *McTeague* (1899), and Theodore Dreiser's *The Financier* (1914) portray human beings as driven by instincts in the same way as animals whose lives are determined by carnal needs, chance, environmental circumstances, and genes. In the same Darwinian vein, Desmond Morris in *The Naked Ape*, which became a best-seller in Britain and America in the 1960s, undertook what he called a "zoological" description of man. He claimed human beings differ from "the other apes" only in having a larger brain, larger male genitals, larger female breasts, upright posture, greater manual dexterity, and no pelt. Morris and the literary naturalists overlooked, however, one highly significant fact: no other species on Earth has ever written a book comparing its nature to that of other animals. Every book and article expressing the zoological view of man is a prima facie refutation of the thesis that there is nothing absolutely exceptional about human beings that distinguishes them from all other creatures.

By the end of the twentieth century, the process of reducing human beings to the zoological level of being just another animal was far advanced. The *New York Times* on June 17, 1999, for instance, reported as front page news that chimpanzees had been discovered to have culture. This meant that individual chimps had been observed to invent new ways of acquiring food, grooming, and feeding, that is, scrubbing food before consuming it, and their fellow chimps had been observed imitating these innovative behaviors. The chimpanzee culture reported on the front page of the *Times* even included a semblance of religion:

> Some of the cultural behaviors [of chimpanzees in the wild] have an almost religious sense to them. In six of the seven communities [that were observed], the chimpanzees performed a rain dance, a slow display at the start of rain. "You're in awe when you see this," said Pascal Gagneux of the University of California, San Diego, who spent two years in the Tai forests studying chimpanzees, but did not contribute to the current report. "The chimpanzees go into a quasi-trance, dancing even when they're alone, with no spectators, as if they were ritually celebrating the rainstorm.

The point of asserting that chimpanzees have culture, including religious sensibility, albeit their "rituals" may be in a quite rudimentary stage of evolution, could not be plainer: human beings are not justified in believing they are the only species on Earth that has culture. And, ten days after its report on chimp culture, the *New York Times* published an editorial explicitly scolding its readers for their "almost deific sense of difference from the animal creation." This prestigious newspaper's editorial writer proclaimed that the pride that humans take in their uniqueness shows a deplorable ignorance. He denounced human awareness of being different from other creatures as "a latent prejudice" that "obscures as much as it explains." (In contemplating this remarkable editorial, one cannot help but wonder how many chimpanzees were reading it on June 27, 1999, thereby proving the editorial's contention that it is mere prejudice to believe that man is in any way unique in comparison to other creatures.)

Similarly, the prize-winning American sociobiologist Edward O. Wilson seriously argued in his book *On Human Nature* in 1978 that the human tendency to make sacrifices for the good of other human beings is analogous to the behavior of the social insects. "Sharing the capacity for extreme sacrifice [as the social insects and man do] does not mean that the human mind and the 'mind' of an insect (if such exists) work alike. But it does mean that the impulse [of self-sacrifice] need not be ruled divine or otherwise transcendental, and we are justified in seeking a more conventional [i.e., material] explanation."[7] Wilson assumed that there are genes for selfish behavior and genes for altruistic behavior in the human genome, and noted that Darwin's hypothesis of natural selection encounters "a basic problem" in human altruism. Applying Darwin's theory of natural selection to human beings, those among the human race who sacrifice themselves for the good of others should over time have fewer and fewer descendants. And therefore, as Wilson noted, a "narrow interpretation of Darwinian selection" would predict that there would be "a tendency over many generations for selfish genes to increase in prevalence and for a population to become ever less capable of responding altruistically." But that had not happened in human populations. Wilson solved this dilemma for Darwinian theory by comparing human altruism to the behavior of "self-sacrificing and sterile termite soldiers" who defend the fertile termites of their communities so that those termites can procreate more of the genes they share with the termite soldiers. He called this behavior "kin selection," and said that the altruistic behaviors of human beings "closely resemble [the behaviors of] social insects."

This application of Darwinism to human beings—claiming that human beings are genetically driven by an instinct to perpetuate their genes either through their own procreation or that of their biological kin—overlooked some salient, commonly known facts about the behavior of human soldiers that are not evident in the behavior of termite soldiers. Human soldiers often spare the lives of their enemies on the battlefield by accepting their surrender and often give medical treatment to enemy wounded that they may survive. They usually repatriate their enemies after the cessation of hostilities, thus allowing enemy soldiers to live and possibly procreate future potential enemies. Wilson's scientism ignored these facts because the Darwinian model of life as a struggle for physical survival and procreation disregards any view of human beings that does not conform to it.

Among the many applications that the world has seen of alleged science to soft subjects, the work of three practitioners of scientism has had an especially significant impact on Western civilization. These three practitioners, two of whom I've already discussed in passing, are Sigmund Freud (d. 1939), Karl Marx (d. 1883), and Charles Darwin (d. 1882). Their combined cultural influence has been enormous through their supposedly scientific findings concerning subjects whose study involves value judgments as much as objective data. The careers of Freud, Marx, and Darwin both reflected and promoted the worship of science. Each had faith in scientific truth as the ultimate and only truth and claimed to practice the methodology of science. Each presented himself as a humanitarian motivated only by a disinterested devotion to truth and the service of mankind; yet each of them was strongly prejudiced against religion. (Darwin was the only one of the three who was at all discreet in expressing his atheism; Freud and Marx were notoriously scornful of religion.) And, each of them wanted to explain a phenomenon of fundamental interest to him—mental aberrations, class conflict, the existence of species—by means of historical analysis. They were putative scientists engaged in historical studies. As such, they faced a difficulty that besets all historical investigations, and that is the necessity of relying on supposition and value judgments to compensate for the lack of direct observation and complete data, history being preeminently a soft subject that cannot be studied scientifically.

Freud, in his analysis in human beings of the mental aberrations that he called "neuroses," traced their cause to a sexual episode in the early history of each person. He claimed to be able to cure his patients by making them aware of the meaning of the events in their past that had made them "neurotic." Marx studied class conflict in the history of civilization. He attributed its cause to private ownership of "the means of production" and predicted the inevitable seizure of private property by the masses and the creation of a worldwide communist culture. Darwin, in his history of Earth's biology, proclaimed that a process he called "natural selection" had produced every species of plant and animal that has ever lived.

Freud's allegedly scientific psychotherapy was discredited among clinical therapists decades ago, and the recent collapse of the USSR has conclusively exposed the fallacy of Marx's claims. The hypotheses of Freud and Marx have been tested in the real world of economic systems and mentally disturbed men and women and have been found wanting. Of these three allegedly scientific historians, Darwin alone still has a large (though now somewhat wavering) following among scientists.

In formulating his theory of natural selection, Darwin was fundamentally influenced by the remarkable modifications to species that animal breeders in England had achieved through *deliberate* selection. He thought the same kind of thing could happen in the wild through natural selection. According to Darwin, given enough time for random mutations to occur and to be naturally selected by means of adaptation to an environment in the ongoing struggle for food and sexual partners, "lower forms" of life could be transformed into new "higher forms" of life, as, for instance, a fish could be transformed into an amphibian. And who can say whether such transformations are impossible, given enough time and the right circumstances? Darwin's claims for natural selection may actually be valid for all we can know. But they cannot be conclusively proven to be scientific truth because they are untestable. They must remain hypothetical.

Nonetheless, the cultural influence of Freud, Marx, and Darwin has been incalculably great, and it persists to this day because of their claim to be scientific. Even Marx and Freud still have small followings of dedicated believers who revere their respective psychological and economic theories as scientifically validated hypotheses.

One historian of ideas, Paul Johnson, made this comment about Marx's scientism, and the same could be said of both Freud and Darwin:

> Marx was a child of his time, the mid-nineteenth century, and Marxism was a characteristic nineteenth-century philosophy in that it claimed to be scientific. "Scientific" was Marx's strongest expression of approval, which he habitually used to distinguish himself from his many enemies. He and his work were "scientific"; they were not. He felt he had found a scientific explanation of human behavior in history akin to Darwin's theory of evolution.[8]

In the heyday of Marxism in the decades following World War II when the USSR was one of the world's superpowers, Marx's disciples seem to have felt that they were sternly applying scientific truths to human societies for the good of mankind. The price of the Marxist experiments in scientism in Asia, Europe, and the Americas in the twentieth century has been close to 100 million deaths. And that toll is being added to even today as human beings in Cuba, Vietnam, North Korea, and China, where communist parties still govern, continue to be ruthlessly terrorized, imprisoned, and executed for their deviance from the correct, "scientific" truth of Marxism.

The doctrine of strict materialism, which was the matrix that formed the scientism practiced by Darwin, Marx, and Freud, cannot satisfy our uniquely human need for transcendent meaning. Man wants to know and to have far more than is necessary for mere physical survival and reproduction. Animals may be concerned only with survival and reproduction; not man. The story of Eden is a profoundly true story of human nature, of man's desire for knowledge and a willingness to make sacrifices to be loved. Even if everything were physically perfect for man (as it is in Eden), that would not suffice. For human beings, physical life is not the paramount issue. However much we may have confused the biblical Adam and Eve with mere representations of gender, their story truly represents two aspects of human nature: the will to be loved (Adam) and the will to have knowledge (Eve). Viewed in that way, they truly depict the first self-consciously-human beings. And they characterize in their loyalty to each other in affliction, and in their desire to know what God knows, attributes of human nature that have entailed countless generations of noble striving and suffering for human beings.

Man is of course an animal. No matter how much our feelings of civilized decorum, our polite habits of refined dining, or our immemorial customs of decency conceal the fact, human beings have the same kind of bodily necessities and physical attributes found in the animal kingdom. Our lungs, heart, digestive tract, blood, nervous system, reproductive organs, senses, and muscular-skeletal structure serve the same ends as comparable anatomical features in other mammals. But human beings are more than their animal part. Man has a soul as well as a body; and the imperatives of the human soul, though quite distinct from the imperatives of the human body, are as urgent and demanding as any physical need—and much more important to us as human beings.

Man has a combination of distinctive traits no animal has, a combination of six traits peculiar to him: (1) a freedom of reason and will that enables him to discern right from wrong conduct; (2) a need to choose between right and wrong; (3) a moral imagination that constantly seeks personal justification; (4) a consciousness from early in life of being mortal; (5) a compulsion to want to understand the universe; and (6) a need to know the creator of the universe. From the reciprocal operations of man's moral imagination, his ability to discern and choose between good and evil, and his need to know his creator have arisen human cultures, which have always contained a religious component. (Fundamentally, a culture is a set of justifying convictions about the right way to live that determines a people's habitual behavior.) Man's awareness of the inevitability of death begins when he is in the prime of bodily vigor and health. And it is then, in our earliest adulthood when we are becoming sexually mature and self-conscious, that we are most puzzled by our existence and yearn to know the meaning of it and to have an answer to the simple but important human question, Why was I born? This knowledge of mortality, which comes to every human being who lives beyond the age of puberty, is the fall from childhood's innocence and unawareness of death. From the subsequent search for a transcendent meaning, which man's universal awareness of his mortality prompts, have arisen his religions, philosophies, and science. The long history of this search for higher knowledge exceeds anything we need for survival and is perhaps the most prominent trait of the human race.

Religion does not ask whether human beings have a right to do something but whether human beings have an obligation to their creator to act in one way rather than another, guided by the moral laws God has created for man to live by. The great Christian apologist of the twentieth century C. S. Lewis (1898–1963) called this natural law "the way," or "the Tao," and traced its expression in the written moral codes of many civilizations through thousands of years (see appendix to Lewis's *The Abolition of Man*). These codes manifest moral prohibitions and injunctions that are nearly universal and that have distinguished human behavior in civilizations going back to the beginning of history. The nearly universal components of these ethical man-dates are beyond rational argument. (As C. S. Lewis says, "You cannot reach them as conclusions: they are premises."⁹) Who could give a rational reason for why it is wrong to have sexual intercourse with a child? Why is sexual intercourse with an animal shameful? Why is cannibalism abhorrent? Why is incest shameful? Why is it wrong to clone human beings? Why is it shame-ful to genetically combine traits from different species of animals to produced laboratory monsters such as a mouse with a human ear growing out of its back? Rational reasons—medical and hygienic reasons—may be offered as to why some of these acts should not be engaged in. But beyond any adverse physical consequences that might follow from them, each of these practices (pedophilia, bestiality, cannibalism, incest, cloning, and the deliberate cre-ation of laboratory monsters) is simply repugnant to our humanity and is held in contempt by all but a few human beings. Likewise, murder, lying, theft, terrorism, and disrespect to elders are also almost universally con-demned, while other behaviors—civility, caring for the weak and helpless, honesty, holiness, the pursuit of knowledge—are esteemed in nearly every society and culture.

Scientism completely ignores the Tao. This can be seen in the most full-blown articulation of scientism that I know of: Arthur C. Clarke's "The Obsolescence of Man," chapter 18 of his book *Profiles of the Future*, in which Clarke asserts: "The tools the ape-men invented caused them to evolve into their successor, Homo sapiens. The tool we have invented [the computer] is our successor. Biological evolution has given way to a far more rapid proc-ess—technological evolution. To put it bluntly and brutally, the machine is going to take over."¹⁰

Arthur C. Clarke was dissatisfied with the limitations of flesh. "With the eye, the ear, the nose—indeed, all the sense organs—evolution has per-formed a truly incredible job against fantastic odds. But it will not be good enough for the future; indeed, it is not good enough for the present."¹¹ He predicted the development of supercomputers and organs made in whole or in part with silicon and alloys that would not have to waste energy by contin-ually replacing organic cells as human tissue does and that could "detect radio waves or radioactivity" to facilitate space travel. (Clarke preferred androids and cyborgs to human beings.) In an appendix to his book *Profiles of the Future* (1963) titled "A Chart of the Future," he predicted "weather control" by 2010, "gravity control" by 2050, and by the year 2100 "immortality." (He demurely remarked in the head-note to this chart that "no present-day imagination can hope to look beyond the year 2100.") In other words, Arthur C. Clarke imagined men like himself in the future overcoming the limitations of mortal human life. He aspired to refashion man in an image that was to his liking: a half-organic, half-mechanical being that would be omniscient in knowledge by being plugged into supercomputers, able to freely travel in outer space, and omnipotent over death.

If, as a society, we should ever allow scientism to have its way and attempt the production of a superior race of designed beings, we will have surrendered the tradition of human culture and along with it our humanity. For when nothing is prohibited to science—when there is no forbidden knowledge, no moral limit to what science can undertake, no obedience to any imperative higher than science—then everything is permitted. It is as simple as that. Either there is a moral limit that science must heed or there is not.

Every human being has a stake in the biological future of the human race. And if proposals for a future based on scientism and strict materialism are made, the only power that could authorize their implementation in the United States of America would be the American people, acting through their elected representatives in an amendment to the Constitution. No appointed panel of certified experts or pundits in a democratic society like America's ought to be allowed to decide the biological future of the human race, no matter what assurances or promises they and those who appoint them may offer beforehand. Not even a normal federal law passed by a majority of Congress and signed by the president of the United States and approved by the U.S. Supreme Court on appeal would be adequate to legitimize the most momentous step in the history of mankind. Only a supermajority of two-thirds of both houses of Congress and a supermajority of three-fourths of the fifty state legislatures, acting under the provisions for amendment of the Constitution of the United States, would sufficiently express the will of the American people on an issue as momentous for the human race as producing designer human beings.

The problem, in all likelihood, will be that no forthright proposal will ever be made that could be submitted to constitutional conventions in the fifty states. What is likely to happen is what has happened over and over again during the culture war in America since the 1960s. Those who reject the present culture will start with some existing value that everyone agrees on (in this case, preventing inheritable maladies and physical defects), and then bend that agreement as many times as necessary until full control over human reproduction has been obtained. Once the idea of manipulating the human genome to correct biological imperfections (of whatever kind) has been established, that logic will only be limited by its own premise and promises.

Scientism is the worship of science to the exclusion of any other truth, and it has been a teaching of scientism for most of the last century that man is only another animal and should scientifically breed himself. Darwin's untestable hypothesis of natural selection provides the scientific justification for contemplating such a deliberate re-creation of man. (In 1947, C. S. Lewis wisely pointed out that the idea that man has the power to make of himself whatever he pleases means, in effect, "the power of some men to make other men what *they* please."[12]) Scientism proposes to liberate mankind from Darwin's model of random mutability and gradual evolution (which he referred to as "descent with modification") and to replace his hypothesis of natural selection with a deliberate, accelerated scientific selection through genetic manipulation. But such manipulations would have to be inerrant. For any error that might be made in managing the genome could lead to irreversible horrors. When science makes man himself an object of scientific study and genetic engineering, that is nothing more or less than animal husbandry with a human face. And scientific control of human procreation, like animal breeding, would inevitably mean, when taken to its logical conclusion, the eventual abolition of individual reproductive freedom and the transfer of procreative responsibilities and child rearing to the state.

In 1932 Aldous Huxley, an anti-scientism grandson of Thomas Huxley, the chief promoter of Darwinism in nineteenth-century England, imagined such a world five centuries hence, in which scientism and strict materialism rule supreme. In his novel *Brave New World*, no one except the system controllers has any freedom to decide anything of social, political, economic, or cultural consequence. Strict materialism and hedonism have become the foundation for a new social order. State-run cloning factories mass produce and custom-make the castes mandated by the state, from mindless "Gamma Minus" menials to the super-intelligent, elite "World Controllers." After being "decanted" (born) in the cloning factories, the different classes of infants are placed in state-run nurseries and schools to condition them to love the functions they have been bred by the state to serve. School children are taught that natural procreation and individual child rearing are horrid practices from a primitive past. And the idea that "everyone belongs to everyone else" (rather than to God) is continually drilled into them to justify this society's abolition of marriage and addiction to promiscuity. Kindergartners are taught erotic games that sexually stimulate them, while postpubescent students are taught that it is bad manners to turn down a request to be a sex partner (after all, everyone belongs to everyone else). There is no love or tenderness in this society, only good manners and orgasm. Accidental pregnancies almost never occur because women in this scientistic society are taught that being viviparous is disgusting (*mother* has become a dirty word); and from the time they become sexually active, females carry on their person in a special belt a supply of anti-pregnancy pills. Both males and females have access to a nonaddictive drug developed by the state's scientists that produces instant euphoria whenever anyone feels bored or depressed. Science sees to it that everyone has a long life and lifelong vigor until a precipitous rush of senility at the end brings a quick, sedated death in a state-run hospice. To help pass the time in this mindless, soulless society until the moment of death, there is the entertainment of "the feelies," the society's cinema in which moviegoers receive a full sensory experience of whatever is projected on the screen.

In 1965 I taught Aldous Huxley's *Brave New World* to a university class of about forty American students. Only three or four of them agreed with me that there was something fundamentally wrong in the society Huxley described. And since the 1960s, trends in American society have moved steadily and with an increasing tempo toward the kind of society he imagined in 1932. Now, in the fourth generation since the publication of *Brave New World*, teaching sexual techniques has become a standard part of the public school curriculum, contraceptives are provided to students so that they can be sexually active with impunity, and mood-control drugs are being widely prescribed and dispensed. Pornography is now widely available via the Internet, magazines, television, and the movies; abortions in the United States now exceed one million annually; and every year brings renewed proposals for a national system of state-run child care centers and cradle-to-grave, state-run health care. Court decisions have even been handed down legalizing marriage as a union of any kind involving consent between persons, regardless of existing social norms and current cultural beliefs. And the proportion of children born into families in which both of their natural parents are present has plummeted since the 1960s.

Strict materialism and scientism when applied to human beings result in the idea that man is only another species of animal. Charles Darwin's view of human beings was based on that premise. Darwin's hypothesis of natural selection explains the traits of man and every other species of living being that has ever appeared on Earth as an unending series of adaptations to various environments through chance mutations that have "survival value" and are therefore selected as advantageous traits and passed on genetically. Time is of the essence—a very great deal of time indeed—to make Darwin's theory of natural selection at all plausible. For what Charles Darwin proposed was an explanation of how primitive, one-celled organisms had become the immensely vast proliferation of complex, multi-celled animals visible in the fossil record as well as in the millions of species alive today. Darwin was quite emphatic on this point. In his principal work, *The Origin of Species By Means of Natural Selection, or The Preservation of Favored Races in the Struggle for Life* (1859), which explained his grand hypothesis on speciation by means of natural selection, he asked: "Why should not Nature take a sudden leap from structure to structure?" And he answered his question by saying: "On the theory of natural selection, we can clearly understand why she should not; for natural selection acts only by taking advantage of slight successive variations; she can never take a great and sudden leap, but must advance by short and sure, though slow steps."[13] That is the way animal breeders alter a species: incrementally, gradually, through taking advantage of small variations in individual animals and selectively breeding for the desired traits over successive generations. Darwin assumed that the creation of new species through natural selection was possible, given random mutations, the apparent lapse of millions of years since the first one-celled organisms, and his idea that every organism that has ever lived on earth, including man, must adapt to its environment as it competes in "the struggle for life."

Some believers in Darwin's hypothesis of natural selection, by which simple organisms develop into complex organisms, have disagreed with his insistence that evolution, as he conceived of it a century and a half ago, had to be a slow, gradual process that worked incrementally to change creatures into new species. In 2002 the late Harvard paleontologist Stephen Jay Gould issued his finding that the fossil record does not confirm Darwin's supposition of intermediate, successive stages of linked, lineal change from one species to another, as the universal characteristic of the history of life on Earth. Gould's 1,400-page magnum opus, *The Structure of Evolutionary Theory*, reports an absence of evidence in the fossil record for Darwin's concept of incremental morphing of one species into another. Gould's lifelong study of ancient life forms in the fossil record (most of which have been unearthed since publication of Darwin's *Origin of Species*) indicated long periods of biological stability followed by the abrupt appearance of multitudes of creatures having many different kinds of body parts. He found no evidence in the rocks of intermediate forms corresponding to Darwin's idea of "slight successive variations." He was particularly impressed by the fact that before 600 million years ago, there were few multi-cellular creatures in the fossil record; then "suddenly" (in terms of geological time) an "explosion" of multi-celled life forms occurred. He gave the name "punctuated equilibrium" to the process indicated by the fossil evidence. Gould's findings have not been welcome to defenders of the hypothesis of natural selection expounded by Darwin almost a century and a half ago. One defender of Darwinian orthodoxy in his review-essay even criticized Gould's 1,400 pages of evidence and analysis as "selective" (!) and dismissed his magnum opus as nothing more than "idiosyncratic revisions of evolutionary theory."[14] Darwinians reject the principle of the tentativeness of scientific truth and deny that the scientific discoveries of the last 147 years have any qualifying relevance to the absolute and final truth laid down in 1859 in Darwin's formulation of his idea of natural selection.

Quite apart, however, from the paucity of universal evidence in the fossil record of successively linked variants in organisms on their way to becoming new species, Darwin's formulation of natural selection has other inherent weaknesses as well.

The behavior of human beings, for example, contradicts another key component of Darwinism: Darwin's idea of adaptation to an environment. Man does not behave according to that proposition. Human beings adapt their environment to suit them; they do not adapt to but rather create their environment. This is one of mankind's most prominent behaviors. It alone would be enough to distinguish man as an exceptional creature in the animal kingdom. Not only the scale and variety of the changes that man works on nature distinguish humans from other creatures, but man also works changes in his capacity to explore and know God's creation that no other species manifests. Man has no wings, yet flies. He has only two legs, yet travels over land at velocities far exceeding those of the swiftest four-legged animal. He has limited senses of hearing and sight compared to some creatures, yet listens to the sounds of whales swimming deep beneath the surface of the ocean and examines many kinds of entities invisible to the naked eye. By choice—not because he had to—he has populated many harsh climates and environments.

The versatility of knowledge and range of interests that distinguish the human species put humans in a class by themselves. Other species may have been on Earth longer or may be present in far greater numbers (ants, for instance), but survival is not the measure of man. Unlike any other species, human beings contemplate new horizons of knowledge. Man's philosophies, religions, and science are all manifestations and proofs of his exceptional nature.

These truths are elementary. They would not have to be mentioned were there not so many denials of them today by those who embrace strict materialism and assert that man has no traits that differ in kind from those of all other species. To point out that man shares 96 percent of his DNA with chimpanzees says nothing that explains mankind—it would say nothing even if the percentage were higher than that. If anything, this discovery rather shows that man is a great deal more than the sum of his DNA. And to say that the linguistic ability of a chimpanzee or a great ape is in any way comparable in kind to the language displayed in, say, Shakespeare's *Midsummer Night's Dream* or the Manhattan telephone directory is simply preposterous and without any sense except as it is intended to deny the uniqueness of human beings.

A third inherent difficulty with Darwin's history of the Earth's biology is that irreducibly complex biological processes have been discovered within living cells. (Cellular biology was a field of scientific study that did not come into existence until seventy years after Darwin's death.) These irreducibly complex processes within cells are elementary to survival. But each step in such sequences has survival benefit only as part of the process to which it belongs. How could such precise, irreducibly complex arrays of biochemical processes evolve through Darwin's hypothesis of natural selection since none of their components *by itself* has any survival value?

Mammals with blood systems, for instance, depend for survival on a sequence of nine biochemical steps to effect blood coagulation at the site of a wound. And without coagulation, death would result from even the most superficial cut or the tiniest internal lesion. There is more to the process of coagulation, however, than this. Once the process has been completed and the bleeding has been stopped, the process must be shut down. Otherwise, coagulation would continue until the entire blood supply solidified, which would in that way kill the animal that had been bleeding. Eleven additional enzymal steps occur in shutting down coagulation. This makes a total of *twenty* steps that must be taken in a precise sequence to accomplish the complex, coordinate processes of coagulation and anticoagulation. Darwin's hypothesis of natural selection requires that we believe that such irreducibly complex cellular sequences as coagulation and anticoagulation and others equally complicated and precise could evolve even though no single step in any of them has, *by itself*, any survival value. A scientist who has studied such complex processes in living cells has reached the following conclusion:

To a person who does not feel obliged to restrict his search to unintelligent causes, the straightforward conclusion is that many biochemical systems were designed. They were designed not by the laws of nature, not by chance and necessity; rather, they were *planned*. The designer knew what the systems would look like when they were completed, then took steps to bring the systems about. Life on earth at its most fundamental level, in its most critical components, is the product of intelligent activity.[15]

For a strict materialist, that conclusion by the biochemist Michael J. Behe is more threatening than any claim the paleontologist Stephen Jay Gould made about punctuated equilibrium because Behe has concluded that intelligent design is evident in cellular biology. To a strict materialist that smacks of the abominable idea of believing in the existence of a willful being of illimitable, supernatural powers who could create the ineffable number of atoms and awesome forces at work in the universe's estimated 100 billion galaxies. It suggests a creator of the laws that order everything that is.

Twelve years after Darwin published *The Origin of Species*, he made in his second major work, *The Descent of Man and Selection in Relation to Sex* (1871), the pronouncement that has authorized his disciples' view of man as only another species of animal. "Spiritual powers cannot be compared or classed by the naturalist," Darwin wrote in *The Descent of Man*, "but he may endeavor to show, as I have done, that the mental faculties of man and the lower animals do not differ in kind, although immensely in degree."[16] That dictum is not a scientific truth. It is a value judgment. Yet it is believed as a scientific truth because it supports the doctrine of strict materialism. Darwin denied that any "spiritual powers"—that is, supernatural powers—exist and held that there is nothing absolutely distinctive or mentally exceptional about *Homo sapiens*. Therefore, the activity of building a turbine to generate electricity must be regarded as no different in kind from a chimpanzee stripping the bark from a twig and using it to fish insects out of a hole because both activities represent the making of a tool for a purpose. Fantastic value judgments such as these are sincerely accepted as scientific truth by educated Westerners in faithful adherence to Darwinian scientism.

Certain moral consequences, of course, follow from faith in strict materialism and scientism. And the writings of Peter Singer, a professor at Princeton University in the recently created academic specialty "bioethics" (a term that signifies how far we have come as a society down the road to a scientistic society), afford a revealing insight into what these moral consequences are.

In one of his essays, Singer argues that the common belief among human beings that they are superior to animals is "as indefensible as the most blatant racism." (He coins the term *speciesism* to refer to this blatant racism.) And in making this judgment, he asserts that belonging to a particular species is "not in itself, morally significant." In this same essay (pointedly titled "Unsanctifying Human Life"), Peter Singer further declares that the "direct killing of a retarded infant" is "often justifiable" and candidly states that his purpose is to challenge "the doctrine of the sanctity of human life" and "conventional moral standards."[17]

For over twenty years now, Singer has advocated the liberation of animals from what he calls the "species-selfishness" of human beings that puts human interests above those of "non-human animals." (The term "non-human animals" is a standard part of his rhetoric, which he uses to pound home his zoological thesis that man is just another animal: the human animal.) Because of statements like the following, Singer has a well-deserved reputation of leadership in the "animal liberation movement."

> There is no ethical basis for elevating membership of one particular species into a morally crucial characteristic. From an ethical point of view, we all stand on an equal footing—whether we stand on two feet, or four, or none at all. This is the crux of the philosophy of the animal liberation movement. . . . The more we learn of some non-human animals, particularly chimpanzees but also many other species, the less able are we to defend the claim that we humans are unique because we are the only one capable of reasoning, or of autonomous action, or of the use of language, or because we possess a sense of justice.[18]

Singer is adamant that animals have the same moral status and rights as human beings. His zoological egalitarianism even leads him to declare that animals are persons. In so saying, he removes any moral compunction (at least theoretically) against having sexual intercourse with or marrying a person who happens to be, say, a sheep. For if a sheep and a human are both persons and seeing any ethical difference between them is nothing but blatant racial prejudice, then why oughtn't such persons marry?

Professor Singer's view of human beings is fundamentally the same as a farmer's regard for his animals: utility. And in the introduction to a recent collection of essays, Singer has stated the inescapable conclusion of his bioethics: "I do not think that the fact that the human is a member of the species *Homo Sapiens* is *in itself* a reason for regarding his or her life as being of greater value than that of a member of a different species."[19] Thus, if a human baby has some biological defect, that baby for Singer has a lesser "ethical" value than a biologically normal pig, monkey, dog, or horse and may be put down for the same reason that a defective, incurably sick, or gravely wounded animal would be killed. Naturally, Professor Singer is a relentless advocate of abortion, whether it be in utero or the murderous natal "procedure" (as it is euphemistically referred to) of partial-birth abortion.

In his essay "Darwin for the Left" Singer laments the demise of the Soviet Union, and begins the essay with the declaration "The Left needs a new paradigm." Singer then observes that "The collapse of communism and the abandonment by democratic socialist parties of the traditional socialist aim of public ownership have deprived the Left of the goals it cherished over the two centuries in which it grew to a position of great political power and intellectual influence." As both a devout Darwinian and a dedicated socialist, he urges: "It is time for the Left to take seriously the fact that we have evolved from other animals. . . . It is time to develop a Darwinian Left."[20] That a leftist of Peter Singer's caliber should make this proposal suggests that strict materialism has suffered a major intellectual setback in the collapse of the USSR and that it is in need of emergency bolstering. If Singer's advice is heeded, and the Left does completely embrace Darwinism, it will be a utopian match: the wedding of Karl Marx's scientism with the scientism of Charles Darwin.

What the bioethics of this Princeton professor really comes down to is a rationale for treating human beings as if they were only animals. It is not the liberation of animals from human oppression that Professor truly aims at in his writings so much as it is the liberation of the human animal from the moral constraints of the Judeo-Christian heritage and the replacement of that heritage by the doctrines of strict materialism and scientism.

The rationale for a culture based on scientism and strict materialism, in which man would be just another species of animal, is being promoted as a sign of progress and intelligence. But is it intelligent to repeat the mantra "You can't stop progress" (meaning the application of science to every aspect of human life), or to believe that science should be completely free of any moral prohibition and entirely unhindered in doing whatever some scientist may conceive of doing and be able to do? We forfeit our humanity in that case, when everything is permitted. And if human beings truly aspire to no goal higher than mere utility and carnal satisfaction, our lives amount to nothing more than birth, copulation, and death, and we are then truly no better or worse than animals.

This generation, like no other generation in American history, is being called upon to say, on faith, whether God is, and whether a divinely ordained moral guide exists and must be heeded. Either there is such a fundamental transcendent law, or there is not. The choice offered by the present moment of cultural peril in the United States is that stark.

CHAPTER TEN

Will American Culture Be Replaced?

Will the counter-culture movement replace with a designed, politically cor-rect culture American culture's belief in practical improvement? Has the movement's ideology of victimization and liberation already irreparably bro-ken American culture's belief in responsible individuals and equal freedom? Have the counter-culture's assaults on American culture by bending Ameri-can beliefs, creating animosity between biological classes, redefining patrio-tism as anti-Americanism, policing language, banning religion from public places, and assaulting community standards of decency so debilitated the principles of American culture that its decline is at an irreversible stage?

No one can give certain answers to these questions. American culture has not been replaced but is on its way to being replaced, and will be replaced should the present trends continue. It can, however, be said with a great deal of assurance that cultures are exceedingly resilient and enduring. No people will change for slight or transient reasons the convictions that have been expressed through the behavior of many continuous generations of their cul-tural ancestors. And it must never be forgotten that a love of freedom does seem to be an enduring, universal trait of human beings. The circumstances under which a culture could be replaced by an ideology would probably be either a cataclysmic catastrophe, a rapid series of crises, or more than three generations (sixty years) of consistent, deliberate attacks. None of these con-ditions has yet come to pass in the United States, though counter-culture adherents have been active for more than two generations now (forty years) in trying to subvert, destroy, and replace American culture.

Truth-telling—the only foundation on which a democratic society and a republican form of government can hope to long endure—has suffered a great deal as a consequence of the counter-culture's politicization of many

important institutions of American life. Words have been distorted for political purposes, and have even had their meanings reversed. We have neglected
to educate our children and called this neglect "teaching self-esteem." We
have assailed the worth of American culture and called this attack "multiculturalism." We have abused the American system of political checks and balances and called this abuse "politics as usual." We have allowed ideology to
dominate our lives and called it "liberation." We are killing more than one
million human beings in utero each year and calling it "choice." We are pol-
luting our society with pornography and profanity and calling this pollution
"freedom of speech." We have substituted biological traits for the merit of
achievement and called the substitution "diversity." We have committed hei-
nous crimes and referred to them as "mistakes." (In the mid-1990s in Tucson,
Arizona, an eighteen-year-old man was found guilty of beating, raping, and
setting fire to a woman, and as he stood before a judge after his conviction
asking for clemency, he referred to his brutal assaults as "a simple mistake,"
which he said he had made because he had had "a rough life." Cody Wil-
liams belonged to the second generation to grow up in America under the
influence of the counter-culture movement's ideology of victimization.[1]) We
have repeatedly rewarded illegal immigrants with U.S. residence and said we
were only exercising "compassion." We have prohibited mention of God in
public schools and called the prohibition "freedom of religion." We have
refused to take personal responsibility for our lives, and we call this refusal
"social justice." We have permitted the highest elected officer and chief mag-
istrate of the United States, sworn to uphold and faithfully execute the law,
to lie under oath before a federal grand jury and have refused to remove him
from office for his perjury, calling his felony "a personal matter." We have
repeatedly changed the content of the Constitution of the United States
without amendment and called this corrupt practice "interpretation." At the
same time, we have refused to consider wholesome amendments to the Constitution because, we say, they would "burden" the Constitution. We have
believed that blind chance has created human beings, and we say that it is
"science." We have allowed minorities to impose their will on the majority
and called the imposition "democracy." We have reviled our country and
called this "patriotism." We have abandoned common sense and foolishly
prided ourselves on our "enlightenment." We have mocked morality, marriage, and love and called it "sophistication."

Despite what the counter-culture may call things, the catastrophic massa-
cre of American civilians in New York City, Washington, D.C., and in western Pennsylvania near Pittsburgh on September 11, 2001, and the reaction

of the Left to those massacres reveal with great clarity the counter-culture's anti-American thinking.

Anti-Americanism is a quite different matter from criticism of the United States and the policies of an administration in office. What the counter-culture movement says about America is not criticism of policies. It is rejection of the culture that embodies the historical beliefs of Americans. In the political outlook of the counter-culture, everything the United States has ever done and all it stands for and is now doing is blameworthy.

While the general public reacted to the appalling slaughter on September 11, 2001 not only with grief but with heartfelt expressions of love for their country and the resolve to thwart further attacks, Americans who reject American culture reacted in an entirely different way. Supervisors in a noticeable number of workplaces, schools, and universities throughout the United States forbade displays of the American flag and other manifestations of patriotism, portraying such gestures as insensitive and calling for understanding the Islamic terrorists who had just killed thousands of Americans. Although these heartless attacks on American civilians on American soil were acts of war far worse that the surprise attack on the military facilities at Pearl Harbor on December 7, 1941, that propelled America into World War II, counter-culture activists and their sympathizers saw the events of September 11 from a quite different perspective. They organized meetings, signed petitions, marched in the streets, took out full-page ads in newspapers, gave interviews on television, wrote letters to newspaper editors, and published magazine pieces—all for the purpose of elaborating the terrorists' point of view and putting responsibility for the attacks on the United States. They tried to make it appear that there would have been no slaughter of American civilians had the United States not been allegedly guilty of centuries of imperialism, corporate greed, and racism.

On September 11 at the University of New Mexico, history professor Richard A. Berthold told his class: "Anyone who can blow up the Pentagon has my vote." That was protected free speech. But administrators at Orange Coast College in California suspended political science professor Kenneth Hearlson, who told his class in reference to the terrorists' attacks: "I want to see the Arab world stand up and say, 'This is wrong.'" Professor Hearlson's statement was considered insensitive, and he had to be punished. At San Diego State University, when an Ethiopian student dutifully reported to university authorities having heard Arabic-speaking students praising Osama bin Laden for killing thousands of Americans, he was put "on warning." In New York City, where the worst of the three massacres occurred, the president of ABC News, David Westin, told newscasters they were not to wear American-flag lapel pins on camera because that would be "taking sides." And within three days of the attacks of September 11, leftists were marching shoulder-to-shoulder on the streets of Washington, D.C., with printed signs that said such things as "No Further U.S. Violence," as if the United States had attacked itself.[2] Indeed, almost immediately after the attacks, conspiracy theories popped up all over America claiming just that—that the president of the United States, the CIA, or some other agency of the federal government, had carried out the slaughter on September 11, 2001, as a ploy to strengthen the power of the administration in office.

Before the month of September ended, Professor Paul Kennedy of Yale University had gone on record to say that American culture had provoked the hatred behind the September 11 attacks; and to illustrate his superior judgment and intelligence, he said: "Suppose that there existed today a powerful, unified Arab-Muslim state that stretched from Algeria to Turkey and Arabia. In those conditions, would not many Americans steadily grow to loathe that colossus?"

At Brown University, professors were issued guidelines on how to discuss the attacks with their students by having them focus on why their country was hated.

At the makeshift memorial where the twin towers of the World Trade Center once stood, someone left a note in parody of the American Pledge of Allegiance: "I pledge allegiance to the human race and to the love for which it stands."

At Haverford College outside Philadelphia, an emeritus professor rhetorically asked why America was the most violent nation on earth and declared in regard to the massacres in New York, Washington, and western Pennsylvania: "We are complicit."[3]

And of course from the point of view of the counter-culture and its sympathizers, America *is* responsible for every social, economic, and political ill in the world. America stands convicted of every wrong that must be put right. Pledging allegiance to internationalism is good; patriotic love for America is bad.

An article in the leftist journal *The Nation* one month after the September 11 attacks contained the observation that for the U.S. government to retaliate for those attacks by fighting a war on terrorism would "reinforce the worst elements in our own society—the flag-wavers, and bigots and militarists." Another writer for *The Nation* called the United States "the world's leading 'rogue state'" and accused the United States of having "taken the lives of literally hundreds of thousands, if not millions, of innocents, most of them children." Professor Noam Chomsky, ever since the Vietnam War a prolific, unrelenting publicist for the counter-culture movement, echoed that sentiment and denounced America for "the death of maybe a million civilians in Iraq and maybe half a million children." Michael Moore, an indefatigable leftist filmmaker, pointed to America's "taxpayer funded terrorism." Barbara Kingsolver, writing in the *San Francisco Chronicle* on September 26, indignantly declared that "the American flag stands for intimidation, censorship, violence, bigotry, sexism, homophobia, and shoving the Constitution through the paper shredder. Who are we calling terrorists here?" This was one week after Amos Brown at a memorial service in San Francisco for those who had been killed on 9/11 linked the terrorism to the American government's refusal to sign the Kyoto Treaty on global warming and its failure to send representatives to an international conference on racism. The editor of *Tikkun* magazine, in turn, criticized "the way that we are living, organizing our society, and treating each other," and said that the inability of Americans "to feel the pain of others" in a poverty-stricken world was the same as "the pathology that shapes the minds of these terrorists." Norman Mailer, the novelist and a prominent anti–Vietnam War protester of the 1960s, urged his fellow Americans to contemplate "why so many people feel a revulsion toward the U.S." The poet Robin Morgan let it be known that the attacks on New York City and Washington, D.C., were motivated by "despair over not being heard." Robert Scheer of the *Los Angeles Times* praised his fellow leftists for not "blindly" accepting the American government's actions in the days following the terrorist attacks. Professor Eric Foner of Columbia University was in some doubt as to which was more frightening: "the horror that engulfed New York City or the apocalyptic rhetoric emanating daily from the [George Bush] White House." And in Berkeley, California, where the free speech movement had launched the counter-culture movement in the 1960s, the city council prohibited flying the American flag at fire stations lest the sight of it provoke some selfless patriots of Berkeley to try to take it down and thereby come into physical conflict with the firemen.[4] These reactions of the American Left are reminiscent of similar reactions in 1979 to the Soviet Union's invasion of Afghanistan. Then, instead of denouncing the invasion, American leftists took *the United States* to task for trying to organize economic sanctions against the Soviet Union![5]

Anti-Americanism reveals itself in four ways: (1) the totality of its condemnation of the United States, (2) its magnification of the smallest wrongdoing by a representative of the United States or an ally of the United States,

(3) its invention of offenses supposedly attributable to the United States (e.g., Chomsky's claim of the deaths of "maybe a million civilians in Iraq and maybe half a million children"), and (4) its indifference to offenses committed by countries, organizations, or persons hostile to the United States. Like so much about the counter-culture movement, this anti-Americanism manifests a double standard.

Former U.S. president William Clinton reflected the point of view of the Left in regard to the slaughter on September 11 by making it appear that injustices in American history in the seventeenth, eighteenth, and nineteenth centuries had caused acts of war by Islamic terrorists in the twentieth century. In commenting on the September 11 massacres before an audience at Georgetown University, he said:

> Here in the United States, we were founded as a nation that practiced slavery, and slaves quite frequently were killed even though they were innocent. This country once looked the other way when a significant number of Native Americans were dispossessed and killed to get their land and their mineral rights or because they were thought of as less than fully human. And we are still paying the price today.[6]

As far as the ideology of the counter-culture movement goes, on September 11, 2001 the American people got what was to be expected after its centuries of racism. It was payback time for the sins of America's past. Germans, Japanese, Russians, Chinese, Arabs, and every other people whose histories contain some sort of atrocity may be forgiven, and new generations of those peoples may be permitted to "move on" (as the Left is fond of urging people to do whenever one of their own is discovered in some dereliction), but the American people are accountable in perpetuity for any real or alleged sins of their cultural ancestors. They will only be redeemed of their collective, perpetual guilt when the counter-culture movement brings peace to the United States by purging this land of oppression of its social injustice.

And yet tens of millions of ordinary people from around the world have come to America, and many more would evidently like to come, in hopes of finding freedom and a better way of life for themselves and their children. On the other hand, few American leftists have emigrated from the United States to find refuge and a freer way of life in another country. As evil and oppressive as American leftists claim the United States and its history is, the United States is nonetheless their chosen country. The place they revile and reject as the land of oppression is where they prefer to live.

The anti-Americanism of the counter-culture movement made headway among the American middle class in the 1960s through the Left's opposition to America's involvement in the Vietnam War. The movement may have its demise, however, in its opposition to the war on terrorism. Only in the twisted logic of anti-Americanism can there be any doubt about the necessity of waging and winning this war, regardless of the difficulties and the sacrifices that it will surely entail, perhaps for many years to come. The peril is all too real. And it is not out there in some faraway place in Asia or Europe. It is here. It is in the American homeland.

There are good reasons for believing the counter-culture movement's attempt to replace American culture will end in failure. For one thing, more and more Americans seem to be getting fed up with the counter-culture's language policing, its hypocritical double standards, its mocking of ordinary morality, its antagonism toward Christianity, and its willingness to excuse Islamic terrorists, tyrants like Fidel Castro, and monsters like Saddam Hussein for no reason except their welcome hostility to the United States.

A free man does not hate other men for having a different opinion than his, nor want to suppress that difference of opinion. Only men enslaved to an ideology have that mentality. And more and more, the counter-culture movement is revealing itself for what it is, a repressive, hate-filled political movement actively hostile to the beliefs of American culture. In contemplating the future of the United States, Americans ought to bear in mind what a wise woman of great loveliness of character once said: "Things based on hate don't last."[7]

There is yet another reason for believing that the project to replace American culture cannot succeed, and that is the history of the Soviet Union. The preamble of the 1977 Constitution of the USSR declared that "the building of a classless communist society" was "the supreme goal of the Soviet state." But the only accomplishment the CPSU could lay claim to in 1977, after sixty years of social engineering, was this: "In the USSR a developed socialist society has been built." Even if it had created a communist culture, the Communist Party in the Soviet Union could not have claimed that it had done so, because to have announced that would have, according to Marxist theory, meant that there was no more need for the party. The revolution must be perpetual. Otherwise, if perfection is achieved, the vanguard that leads the struggle for social justice serves no purpose. In the United States, people are tired of social engineering. They want to remind the counter-culture activists (if only they would listen) that, although perfect social justice will never be achieved in America or anywhere else, slavery was abolished in 1865 and the demeaning Jim Crow laws of the past have all been revoked. The perfection that the counter-culture aims at will not be achieved until the thoughts of every American on every subject of importance are exactly the same, which is a goal never to be attained. Like the revolution the CPSU headed, the revolution the counter-culture activists in America represent is perpetual. But Americans want to live their individual lives, not a life of endless revolution. Furthermore, it is contrary to the immigrant mentality of American culture to harp on the past, as the counter-culture does.

There is a further lesson to be learned from the history of the Soviet Union. The USSR collapsed at the beginning of the fourth generation after its founding in 1922. That is significant when one recognizes the totality of the power the CPSU exercised. The CPSU dictated control of education, the arts, the criminal justice system, religion, internal and foreign travel, book publishing, the press, television, military promotions, civilian honors and rewards, prices and wages, the activities of associations and institutions, admission to universities, economic planning and production, finance, and government at every level of Soviet society. Yet despite all of that, the CPSU—the most powerful proponent in the twentieth century of the idea of engineering a perfect, designed culture based on a politically correct, allegedly scientific ideology—now lies in "the dust bin of history." The explanation of why the Soviet Union collapsed is of course complicated. But it may be that the fourth generation of Communist Party leaders in the USSR in too many cases simply tired of doing what had to be done to keep the revolution going, and no longer wanted to go on violating their own humanity and that of their fellow man. Their human interests may finally have taken precedent over their politically correct interests because in the long run man does not live by politics alone. In considering who might be thanked for the collapse of the Soviet Union, we should certainly not overlook the American statesmen who created and steadfastly applied the policy of containing communism after World War II. And we should be properly appreciative of the courage of Ronald Reagan, Margaret Thatcher, Pope John Paul II, Aleksandr Solzhenitsyn, Andrei Sakharov, Lech Walesa, and other freedom-loving leaders, as well as millions of ordinary patriots in Central and Eastern Europe in the 1950s, 1960s, 1970s, and 1980s. Nor should we overlook Mikhail Gorbachev and his grandmother, who managed to teach the beliefs of her Christian faith to the last general secretary of the CPSU when he was a little boy in communist youth groups.

It is also encouraging to remember the history of the United States. American culture survived the crisis of the Civil War and was stronger after the evil of slavery had been purged from the land than it had been before in living with that contradiction of the American cultural principle of equal freedom. The president who led the United States through the ordeal of the Civil War, the greatest crisis yet in American history, spoke the truth in saying that the soldiers who died in it gave their lives so that "this nation, under God, shall have a new birth of freedom." That new birth of freedom under God did come. The willing sacrifices of life and limb in the Civil War were not in vain. What Abraham Lincoln called "government of the people, by the people, for the people" did *not* perish from the Earth, as he and many other Americans thought it might during the darkest days of the Civil War, before Union victories at Vicksburg and Gettysburg in July 1863 turned the tide of battle.

Furthermore, the practicality of the American people—one of the strongest features of American culture—gives much cause for hope that the culture war of the last forty years will not end in the replacement of American culture, but in its triumph. The American people will not indefinitely tolerate something that does not work. And the ideology of the counter-culture movement is increasingly proving to be impractical and dysfunctional.

Another heartening trend, this one going back to the first decade after World War II and only becoming manifest in recent years, is a shift in the thinking of the scientific community in regard to the Big Bang theory and the creation of life. When strict materialism was being established a century and a half ago during the lifetime of Charles Darwin, it was common to think of Christianity and science as antagonists. Later it was proposed in the writings of Stephen Jay Gould and others that science and religion are mutually exclusive in their interests. Now a third tendency is developing, the view that scientific truth corroborates religious truth. For instance, Stephen C. Meyer, who holds master's degrees in physics, geology, and the history of science, and a PhD in biology from Cambridge University, has identified six areas of scientific interest and inquiry across a range of sciences in which scientifically derived evidence supports belief in God. Meyer summarizes this evidence in his interview with Lee Strobel published in *The Case for a Creator* (2004).[8]

Besides these reasons for concluding that the threat of cultural dissolution in America will soon be overcome, there is also the nature of culture to be considered. Cultural beliefs are positive. They affirm something. They are not negative. They do not oppose anything. This characteristic of culture is contradicted by the self-conferred mission of the counter-culture movement to destroy American culture. It is essentially a rejection, a negative, a subver-

218 218 Chapter Ten

sion. The movement's unity derives from its hostility toward American culture; its appeal lies in a promise of change, which can mean whatever a person wants it to mean. The counter-culture promises perfection, someday, after American culture is destroyed. But it offers no set of positive beliefs to live by. The counter-culture requires perpetual strife and endless revolt.

Perhaps the greatest source of hope for the future, however, lies in the truth that there is more to life than political power. There is also the goodness in the nurturing tenderness of a woman cradling her baby in her arms and a husband's delight in hearing his wife's pleased laughter over something he has done for her. Then, too, there is the beauty of the coming of dawn in a lonesome mountain canyon as two owls call back and forth in the lifting twilight in their soft, solemn tones and a delicious morning breeze stirs the pine boughs, making a sound in unison with the steady flow of the creek through the canyon. Such things are enduring. They mirror the everlasting beauty, truth, and goodness of the being who created the universe, man, and the light that marks the beginning of each new day.

The counter-culture movement in the United States has proved to be a lie and a fraud: the lie that morality is a matter of who wields political power; the fraud that in making a revolution you have to break eggs but don't have to produce an omelet; the lie that more government will solve every problem; the fraud that fixing things that aren't broken can go on and on without people ever wanting to put a stop to it.

The Cold War with the Soviet Union lasted four decades. Then suddenly it was over. None of America's pundits and experts foresaw the collapse of the CPSU and the dissolution of the USSR. But no one who was privileged to be in Poland in 1981, as I was, and witnessed the unafraid, truth-telling, Christian solidarity of the Polish people in that year of grace and extraordinary spiritual power was surprised by the collapse of that Soviet imperium eight years later.

Activists in the counter-culture movement consider those who oppose them to be wickedly opposed to truth.[9] The British socialist George Orwell, who refused to let politics become a substitute for truth, said that he witnessed during the Spanish Civil War in the 1930s, "[H]istory being written not in terms of what happened but of what ought to have happened according to various 'party lines'": reports from the Nationalists of a Russian army in Spain that did not exist; reports from the Republicans of victories won in battles that never took place. "This kind of thing," Orwell wrote, "is frightening to me, because it often gives me the feeling that the very concept of objective truth is fading out of the world."[10] There has been an inordinate amount of falsehood in the United States in the last forty years. And today in America there are still academics and other sympathizers with the counter-culture movement who cling to the idea that Marxism is a humane rather than a vicious politics. They continue to lie to themselves, to believe that the illusions of their youth are attainable if only what they call the "myth" of America can be discredited and a politically correct culture put in its place.[11]

There are still communist governments in the world. But the ideology of class struggle is a spent wave. America and her allies won the Cold War. The so-called global village is unlikely to ever have a communist mayor. The future belongs to multiparty, democratic societies with republican governments and constitutions written and approved by elected representatives of the people. The United States of America led the world in being the first country to produce that kind of free government.

Like the history of every people, American history is not immaculate. But it is more than good enough to justify a love for America and a faithfulness to the beliefs of its culture. The United States of America was not "founded as a nation that practiced slavery" (as President Clinton said), but as a nation "conceived in liberty and dedicated to the proposition that all men are created equal" (as President Lincoln said).[12] It is a country that believes all men are God's creations and are endowed by God with unalienable human birthrights to life, liberty, and the pursuit of happiness.

Americans have historically lived and prevailed by acting on the principles of responsible individualism, practical improvement, and equal freedom under God. The majority of Americans have never put their faith and hopes for a better future for themselves and the rest of mankind in the expedient of making society responsible for individuals and of giving the state unchecked power.

In the forty years since the mid-1960s, the counter-culture movement has succeeded in captivating the thinking and changing the behavior of many American opinion makers, dominating some of the most important institutions and professions of American society, and using those institutions, professions, and opinion makers to advance its project of replacing American culture. These successes are especially evident in the arts, law, public school education, universities and colleges, publishing, entertainment, and journalism. Even seminaries, churches, and institutions of government have succumbed to the counter-culture's ideology of political correctness. As a consequence, many beliefs of American culture have been distorted and weakened. The damage is most apparent in regard to these American cultural beliefs:

> Everyone must work.
> Every person is responsible for his own well-being.
> A majority decides.
> God created nature and human beings.
> The least government possible is best.
> Opportunities must be imagined (rather than provided by the government).
> Society is a collection of individuals (rather than a collection of classes).
> Every person's success improves society.
> America is a chosen country.
> Doing what is right is necessary for happiness.
> Almost all human beings want to do what is right.
> God gave men the same birthrights (rather than differentiated, group rights).

The success of the counter-culture movement in eroding these cultural beliefs and in getting many Americans to behave in new ways has provoked rancorous divisions in American society. But the overwhelming majority of Americans in the last forty years has continued to act upon the historical beliefs of their cultural heritage.

In concluding a discussion like this of the present condition of American culture and its prospects, it is a matter of some interest to make some estimate of the division that forty years of persistent efforts by the counter-culture movement has effected in American society. One reads and hears a great deal in the media these days about America being "a deeply divided nation." And it is true that deep divisions have been created. But what are the approximate dimensions of the divide?

A possible answer to this question is suggested by an opinion poll conducted by CBS News and the *New York Times* the second week after the November 2004 presidential election. According to this poll, 82 percent of "adult Americans" thought George W. Bush "legitimately won on Nov. 2."[13] That left 18 percent of adult Americans who had some other opinion on the matter, or no opinion. The poll did not give that breakdown. But considering the fundamental importance of electoral legitimacy, especially in the election of a president, it would be fair to suppose that few adult Americans would honestly have no opinion if asked whether the result of the 2004 election was legitimate. Let's say no more than 2 or 3 percent might respond in that way. That would leave approximately 15 percent of adult Americans who would deny the legitimacy of President Bush's election, even though he had 3.5 million more votes than his opponent. In terms of percentages, there was nothing out of the ordinary about the 2004 presidential vote: 48 percent for the loser and 51 percent for the winner, making for a spread of 3 percent that is fairly consistent with the average spread of 4.7 percent between each winner and loser in the last five presidential elections. So those proportions may approximate how we stand divided today in America: 82 percent of adult Americans apparently accept the legitimacy of the will of the majority, and perhaps 15 percent think their judgment alone is legitimate. This is nowhere near a 50-50 division. (Remember that the winner in the 2004 election had a majority of 51 percent, but the CBS–*New York Times* poll found that 31 percent more than that thought the election was legitimate.) Who makes up this minority of perhaps 15 percent that apparently rejects the will of the majority as illegitimate when it differs from their own political judgment? Among them would be, we may suppose, Americans who came of age in the 1960s and who fully embrace the proposition that the United States is an imperialist nation striving to rule the world, that American capitalism is founded on and serves only greed, and that American history is one long, unrelieved tale of oppressive sexism and racism. It would also almost surely include Americans of earlier and later generations who believe in those propositions.

My final assessment is that a shift of momentum in the culture war in the past few years suggests that a rediscovery and rededication to America's bedrock cultural beliefs is underway.

APPENDIX A

Beliefs of American Culture

God created nature and human beings. God created a law of right and wrong. Doing what is right is necessary to happiness. Almost all human beings want to do what is right. Worship is a matter of conscience.

Improvement is possible. Opportunities must be imagined. Manual work is respectable. Persons must benefit from their work. Freedom of movement is needed for success.

Every person is responsible for his own well-being. What has to be done will teach you how to do it. Progress requires organization. The least government possible is best. The people are sovereign. A majority decides.

Human beings will abuse power when they have it. A written constitution is essential to government. God gave men the same birthrights.

Society is a collection of individuals. Every person's success improves society. Achievement determines social rank. Helping others helps yourself. Everyone must work.

America is a chosen country.

[For a discussion of these beliefs, see the author's *American Beliefs: What Keeps a Big Country and a Diverse People United* (Chicago: Ivan R. Dee, 1999).]

APPENDIX B

A Brief Homily on Needs

Cultural renewal is an urgent need in the United States today if the damage that has been done to American culture by the combined effects of the counter-culture movement, instrumental government, and the doctrine of strict materialism is to be repaired. This cannot be accomplished through coercion, especially not by more governmental regulation or more federal spending. Some problems, like substance abuse and cultural decline, are spiritual in nature and require for correction an alteration of will, belief, attitude, and feelings to correct, rather than political or financial solutions.

Tolerance of the counter-culture idea that all truth is relative to political power, for instance, harms American culture by preventing discrimination between political truth and objective truth. It is imperative therefore that this kind of moral relativism be denounced and resisted. To revive American culture, we must learn again as a people that wrong and right are not a matter of who wields political power but should be judged in light of the objective harm or benefit to persons that various choices entail. Tolerance should be a virtue that is combined with prudence; it should not be an attitude of making no moral judgments. Tolerance of the present epidemic of marital infidelity, promiscuity, abortions, substance abuse, and pornography and the constant clamor for more and more rights is not virtuous. It is condoning the conduct that is week by week, month by month, year by year, destroying American culture. It is acquiescing in cultural suicide. The absoluteness of the tolerance that the counter-culture insists on is devastating the lives of millions of Americans and dismantling American society. The bogus virtue of indiscriminate tolerance is destroying belief in virtue. Tolerance alone, by itself, means the end of right and wrong. There are behaviors that should not be tolerated because they destroy civilized society.

Freedom is another virtue that has been bent into an instrument of social destruction. Freedom is not an endless round of instantaneous gratification. Nor is freedom the sort of self-centeredness that goes by the name of self-esteem and excludes respect for the equal freedom of other people. There must be a renewal of democratic virtues. In a society like the United States, the virtues that are most needed, besides civility and respect for truth, are self-restraint and personal responsibility. If American culture is to survive, these four virtues—civility, truthfulness, self-restraint, and individual responsibility—must be practiced by the rising generation of young Americans; and older generations of Americans must restore them to a place of primary honor in their behavior as well.

Tolerating disrespect for the American flag, the symbol of the men and women who have sacrificed their lives for America, is not a virtue. Nor is it a virtue to accept the lie that corruption and immorality are the way things have always been in America. Nor is it a virtue to think of marriage as anything except a sacramental bond between a woman and a man in which the fidelity of each is as pleasing to God as it is to their spouse.

Furthermore, we must discriminate between scientism (worshipping science and giving it authority over every human concern) and the pursuit of truths about nature that is science. The claim of scientism that human beings are only animals must be dismissed as the anthropomorphism of atheism that it is. Those who make a religion of strict materialism are hostile to the Judeo-Christian beliefs about man on which America's culture has been constructed, and their strict materialism cannot be accepted in silence when put forward as a basis for public policy.

Federal courts must be forced to break their acquired habit of nullifying the will of the majority as expressed in legislative acts, especially acts of the state legislatures. Congress ought to curb the judicial activism of the Supreme Court by using the authority granted to it in Article III, Section 2, Paragraph 2 of the Constitution to restrict the Court's appellate jurisdiction "under such Regulations as the Congress shall make." Likewise the states, using the reserved powers provision of the Tenth Amendment, ought to insist on the return of some of the powers that the federal government usurped from them during the twentieth century. And although amending the Constitution is difficult to accomplish, several amendments to the Constitution ought to be attempted to reverse the gains of the counter-culture in the culture war. First of all, there should be an amendment clarifying and updating the free exercise and establishment clauses of the First Amendment regarding freedom of religion (see p. 129 above); and an amendment should be adopted to define marriage, the foundation of Western civilization, as the union of one man and one woman. To address the unconstitutionality of instrumental government, an amendment similar to the Twenty-second Amendment, which in 1951 limited the term of the president, should be added to the Constitution to limit the terms of U.S. senators, representatives, and federal judges. This would go a long way toward preventing the long-term incumbency in office that unduly concentrates power in persons and political parties rather than in the law. (Perhaps twenty-five years on the bench or age eighty, whichever comes first, would be appropriate for a federal judge and eighteen years in Congress or age seventy-five would be prudent for senators and representatives.) If two-thirds of both houses of Congress refuse to initiate this needed amendment, which is likely, then two-thirds of the legislatures of the states should take the necessary steps, without Congress, as provided for in Article V of the Constitution.

To curb the wastefulness of the federal government, taxpayers should relentlessly pressure Congress and the president to undertake a systematic reauthorization of every agency, bureau, council, department, office, committee, and subcommittee that has been added to the federal government since 1950, starting with those that were added in that year and moving forward chronologically. Every federal program and service that is *nonessential to the national interest* should be eliminated, no matter how tiny a portion of the astronomical federal budget it may consume. Even one unessential unit in the federal government is one too many; even one dollar that does not have to be spent by the federal government should not be spent. Above all, what accountants call "generally accepted accounting practices" (see John Steele Gordon's *Hamilton's Blessing: The Extraordinary Life and Times of Our National Debt*, [New York: Walker, 1997], 186ff.) must become mandatory throughout the federal government, so that the expenditure of hundreds of billions of dollars annually for unspecified "other services" is curbed.

Because it is unacceptable in today's world that millions of American citizens should come of age without basic knowledge and skills, the teaching of such knowledge and skills, instead of teaching an ineffective secular doctrine of self-esteem, must once again become the paramount goal of public schooling. And teacher-certification laws in the states should make knowledge of the academic subjects and skills that teachers teach more relevant to their training, hiring, retention, remuneration, and promotion than academic courses in education as a process. In correlation with these realignments, the politically correct concepts of diversity, bilingual education, and multiculturalism that have had the effect of dividing Americans and weakening the culture of America should be eliminated from the curriculum of public schools, district by district.

Legal immigrants who want to become citizens of the United States should be not only encouraged to do that, and welcomed as new Americans in the great tradition of American citizenship, but they should also be informed that America has one culture, not many. They and every public school student should be taught to understand and respect the national motto E Pluribus Unum (One from Many). The meaning of this motto should be made so clear that no candidate for high public office could ever confuse it with the counter-culture's motto Many from One, as happened to the Democratic Party's candidate for president during the 2000 presidential election.

American culture will be restored to its full vigor when enough Americans speak for objective truth rather than political correctness, when there is again intolerance of shameful behavior, and when traditional Judeo-Christian morality and the will of the majority once again are the twin pillars of law and policy in America.

APPENDIX C

Some Recommended Further Reading

David Horowitz's autobiography, *Radical Son: A Journey Through Our Times* (New York: Free Press, 1997), demonstrates the connection between American Marxism and the counter-culture movement. Ronald Radosh's *Commies: A Journey Through the Old Left, the New Left and the Leftover Left* (San Francisco: Encounter Books, 2001) and *Second Thoughts: Former Radicals Look Back at the Sixties*, edited by Peter Collier and David Horowitz (Lanham, Md.: Madison Books, 1989) provide instructive commentaries on the 1960s by former activists in the counter-culture movement. For a laudatory study of the 1960s, see Terry H. Anderson, *The Movement and the Sixties* (New York: Oxford University Press, 1995). Ann Charters in *The Portable Sixties Reader* (New York: Penguin, 2003) has collected documents, nostalgic memoirs, and essays on the decade that launched the counter-culture movement (this collection includes a chronology). For a raw example of the counter-culture's ideology and the intensity of its hostility toward American culture at the outset of the movement, one should read Jerry Rubin's illustrated paperback *We Are Everywhere* (New York: Harper and Row, 1971). Saul D. Alinsky's *Rules for Radicals: A Programmatic Primer for Realistic Radicals* (New York: Vintage, 1989), first published in 1971, told middle-class Americans who were active in the counter-culture movement of the 1960s how to create and sustain a "revolution" "within the system" (Alinsky's terms).

For an introduction to the fundamental importance of culture in human affairs, one could do no better than the foreword and introduction to *Culture Matters: How Values Shape Human Progress*, edited by Lawrence E. Harrison and Samuel P. Huntington (New York: Basic Books, 2000), and the twenty-two essays in this collection, particularly those by Harrison, David Landes, Carlos Alberto Montaner, and Orlando Patterson. On the fallaciousness of multiculturalism's claim that all cultures are equally meritorious and beneficial, see Harrison's *Underdevelopment Is a State of Mind—The Latin American Case* (Lanham, Md.: University Press of America, 1985); and Landes's *The Wealth and Poverty of Nations: Why Some Are So Rich and Some So Poor* (New York: Norton, 1998). Huntington's *Who Are We? The Challenges to America's National Identity* (New York: Simon & Schuster, 2004) is a comprehensive analysis of contemporary American society. Thomas Sowell's summary of his three books on the role of culture in the history of nations in *Conquests and Cultures: An International History* (New York: Basic Books, 1998), 328–79, offers an exceptionally wise perspective on the subject.

Why the Left Hates America: Exposing the Lies That Have Obscured Our Nation's Greatness (Roseville, Calif.: Prima Publishing, 2002) by Daniel J. Flynn, and *Anti-Americanism* (San Francisco: Encounter Books, 2003) by Jean-François Revel (translated from the French by Diarmid Cammell) are recent analyses of the phenomenon of anti-Americanism inside the United States and abroad. David Horowitz's *Unholy Alliance: Radical Islam and the American Left* (Washington, D.C.: Regnery, 2004) explains the connection between the counter-culture movement in America, the Cold War and the war with Islamic terrorists. *In Denial: Historians, Communism, & Espionage* (San Francisco: Encounter Books, 2003) by John Earl Haynes and Harvey Klehr analyzes communist subversion in the United States and the refusal of the American Left even today, after the archives of the Communist Party of the Soviet Union have become available, to admit that anything of that sort ever happened.

"Interviews from the Front" in Paul Copperman's *The Literacy Hoax* (New York: Morrow, 1978) contains vivid statements by administrators, teachers, and students on the grave deterioration of American public schools in the 1970s; and Diane Ravitch and Chester E. Finn, Jr., in *What Do Our 17-Year-Olds Know? A Report on the First National Assessment of History and Literature* (New York: Harper and Row, 1987) survey the same subject in regard to the 1980s. Jeffrey Hart's *Smiling Through the Cultural Catastrophe: Toward the Revival of Higher Education* (New Haven, Conn.: Yale University Press, 2001) describes the liberal education that was once prevalent at American universities, and which the counter-culture movement has all but obliterated.

With regard to the culturally important matter of religion and science, see physicist Stephen M. Barr's *Modern Physics and Ancient Faith* (Notre Dame, Ind.: University of Notre Dame Press, 2003), which examines data, first noticed in the 1970s by physicist Brandon Carter, suggesting the possibility that life and the universe are not chance effects of material causes but rather the result of foreordination. *Darwin on Trial*, 2nd ed., by Phillip E. Johnson (Downers Grove, Ill.: InterVarsity Press, 1993) sets forth the nature of the scientific controversy surrounding Darwinism as the foremost example of strict materialism in today's world. Lee Strobel's *The Case for a Creator* (Grand Rapids, Mich.: Zondervan, 2004) is a series of interviews with scientists about developments in scientific research in the last fifty years that point toward the validity of belief in God.

Robert P. George's *The Clash of Orthodoxies: Law, Religion, and Morality in Crisis* (Wilmington, Del.: ISI Books, 2001) is a clearly-reasoned critique from a Christian perspective of such matters as abortion, bioethics, justice, pornography, and same-sex marriage by a distinguished scholar of constitutional law; see also George's *In Defense of Natural Law* (New York: Oxford University Press, 1999). Daniel A. Faber and Suzanna Sherry in *Beyond All Reason: The Radical Assault on Truth in American Law* (New York: Oxford University Press, 1997) critique "the radical multiculturalism" taught in law schools today and its corrosive effect on the concept of law. *The Tragedy of American Compassion* (Washington, D.C.: Regnery, 1992) by Marvin Olasky analyzes the nature and results of counter-culture social programs of the late twentieth century.

Human Cloning and Human Dignity: The Report of the President's Council on Bioethics (New York: Public Affairs, 2002) addresses the most momentous cultural issue of today. The resolution of this dispute will have immense human consequences. Every American having any sense of responsibility for the future of America ought to read, think about, and discuss with others the opposing arguments in *Human Cloning and Human Dignity*.

Notes

Chapter One

1. "Constitution (Fundamental Law) of the Union of Soviet Socialist Republics, adopted by the 7th Extraordinary Session of the Supreme Soviet of the USSR (9th Convocation), October 7, 1977" (Moscow: Progress Publishers, 1977), pars. 6, 12.

2. Stéphane Courtois et al., *The Black Book of Communism: Crimes, Terror, Repression*, trans. Jonathan Murphy and Mark Kramer (Cambridge, Mass.: Harvard University Press, 1999), x–xi. This study is the first to undertake an estimate of the tens of millions of deaths occasioned by the attempt to impose communism on the world in the twentieth century.

3. *Rand McNally Cosmopolitan World Atlas*, rev. ed. (1996), 257, 260.

Chapter Two

1. "Constitution (Fundamental Law) of the Union of Soviet Socialist Republics, adopted by the 7th Extraordinary Session of the Supreme Soviet of the USSR (9th Convocation), October 7, 1977" (Moscow: Progress Publishers, 1977), conclusion to preface.

2. Quoted in Paul Johnson, *Modern Times: The World from the Twenties to the Eighties* (New York: Harper and Row, 1983), 13–14.

3. President Truman's presidential proclamation of August 16, 1945, called upon Americans to observe a national day of prayer and thanksgiving in remembrance of "the help of God, Who was with us in the early days of adversity and disaster [in the war], and Who has now brought us to this glorious day of triumph." Harry S. Truman, *Memoirs* (Garden City, N.Y.: Doubleday, 1955), 1:452.

4. *Princeton Alumni Weekly*, November 19, 2003, 26.

5. Richard Pipes, *Communism: A History* (New York: Modern Library, 2001), 151–52.

6. Jim Hougan, "Madison's Trashers: What Makes Them Do It?" *Capital Times* (Madison, Wisconsin), May 7, 1970, 1, 6.

7. Hilton Kramer's untitled remarks on the 1960s collected in *Second Thoughts: For-*

mer Radicals Look Back at the Sixties, ed. Peter Collier and David Horowitz (Lanham, Md.: Madison Books, 1989), 176.

8. Kramer, *Second Thoughts*.

9. Kramer, *Second Thoughts*, 177.

10. Saul D. Alinsky, *Rules for Radicals: A Practical Primer for Realistic Radicals* (New York: Vintage, 1989), xviii, 10.

11. Alinsky, *Rules for Radicals*, xxvi, 120, 130.

12. Alinsky, *Rules for Radicals*, xix–xx.

13. Alinsky, *Rules for Radicals*, 63–64.

14. Alinsky, *Rules for Radicals*, 184.

15. Alinsky, *Rules for Radicals*, 194–95.

16. Alinsky, *Rules for Radicals*, 128.

17. Alinsky, *Rules for Radicals*, 136.

18. Alinsky, *Rules for Radicals*, 151–52.

19. Arthur M. Schlesinger, Jr., *The Disuniting of America: Reflections on a Multicultural Society* (New York: Norton, 1992); William L. O'Neill, *Coming Apart: An Informal History of America in the 1960s* (New York, Quadrangle Books, 1979); William J. Bennett, *The De-Valuing of America: The Fight for Our Culture and Our Children* (New York: Summit Books, 1992); Patrick J. Buchanan, *The Death of the West: How Dying Populations and Immigrant Invasions Imperil Our Country and Civilization* (New York: St. Martin's, 2002); Bob Rosio, *The Culture War in America: A Society in Chaos* (Lafayette, La.: Huntington House, 1995); Robert H. Bork, *The Tempting of America: The Political Seduction of the Law* (New York: Free Press, 1990); Allen J. Matusow, *The Unraveling of America: A History of Liberalism in the 1960s* (New York: Harper and Row, 1984); Robert Hughes, *The Culture of Complaint: The Fraying of America* (New York: Oxford University Press, 1993); Martin L. Gross, *The End of Sanity: Social and Cultural Madness in America* (New York: Avon, 1997); Philip K. Howard, *The Death of Common Sense: How Law Is Suffocating America* (New York: Random House, 1994); Allan Bloom, *The Closing of the American Mind: How Higher Education Has Failed Democracy and Impoverished the Souls of Today's Students* (New York: Simon & Schuster, 1987); Philip K. Howard, *The Collapse of the Common Good: How America's Lawsuit Culture Undermines Our Freedom* (New York: Ballantine, 2001); Katharine Washburn and John Thornton, eds., *Dumbing Down: Essays on the Strip-Mining of American Culture* (New York: Norton, 1996).

20. Julián Marías, *America in the Fifties and Sixties*, ed. Michael Aaron Rockland, trans. Blanch de Puy and Harold C. Raley (University Park: Pennsylvania State University Press, 1972), 437–39.

21. Hougan, "Madison's Trashers," 6.

22. Matusow, *The Unraveling of America*, 307; Kenneth J. Heineman, *Put Your Bodies Upon the Wheels: Student Revolt in the 1960s* (Chicago: Ivan R. Dee, 2001), 226; Gross, *The End of Sanity*, 306.

23. Bennett, *The De-Valuing of America*, 13.

24. Bork, *The Tempting of America*, 1–2.

25. Washburn and Thornton, *Dumbing Down*, 11, 13.

Chapter Three

1. Ray Raphael, *The First American Revolution, Before Lexington and Concord* (New York: New Press, 2002), suggests that such fully formed American cultural beliefs existed among ordinary American farmers on the eve of the American Revolution and determined their behavior.

2. Benjamin Franklin, *Writings* (New York: Library of America, 1987), 1339.

3. *American Enterprise* (July/August 2003), 10.

4. Philip K. Howard, *The Death of Common Sense: How Law Is Suffocating America* (New York: Random House, 1994), 50–51. See also Howard's more recent study *The Collapse of the Common Good: How America's Lawsuit Culture Undermines Our Freedom* (New York: Ballantine, 2001).

5. The two episodes involving University of Pennsylvania students are cited in Lynne V. Cheney, *Telling the Truth: Why Our Culture and Our Country Have Stopped Making Sense—and What We Can Do About It* (New York: Simon & Schuster, 1995), 63. The late Charles Polzer was a friend and colleague of mine at the University of Arizona. I was in the audience that showed up for Linda Chavez's canceled talk and also in the audience that witnessed William Buckley getting hit in the face with the cream pie. (The same despicable intimidating action was perpetrated recently against conservative Ann Coulter as she spoke at the University of Arizona, but she was nimble enough to avoid getting hit in the face.) The professors in the Creative Writing program at the University of Arizona were colleagues of mine in the Department of English. The draconian punishment of the Duke University administrator happened while I was on a sabbatical leave from 1990 to 1991.

6. Larry Elder, *The Ten Things You Can't Say in America* (New York: St. Martin's, 2000).

7. The inexpensive, effective rehabilitation program known as Alcoholics Anonymous, run by volunteers who are themselves recovering alcoholics, starts with the addict taking responsibility for his addiction. *As Bill Sees It: The A. A. Way of Life* (New York: Alcoholics Anonymous World Services, 1967) gives a brief overview of the person-to-person spiritual rehabilitation of alcohol addicts that this nongovernmental organization has delivered for many years.

8. Sylvia E. Bowman et al., *Edward Bellamy Abroad: An American Prophet's Influence*, (New York: Twayne, 1962), intro., chronology, chap. 1; Sylvia E. Bowman, *Edward Bellamy* (Boston: Twayne, 1986), 111–13.

9. Seymour Martin Lipset and Gary Marks, *It Didn't Happen Here* (New York: Norton, 2000).

Chapter Four

1. "Free Blacks in the Antebellum South" in *Blacks in America: Bibliographical Essays* (New York: Doubleday, 1971); Eugene D. Genovese, *Roll, Jordan, Roll: The World the*

Slaves Made (New York: Vintage, 1976), 406–9; and John Hope Franklin, *From Slavery to Freedom: A History of Negro Americans*, 5th ed. (New York: Knopf, 1980), 165–66.

2. U.S. Department of Commerce, Bureau of the Census, *Historical Statistics of the United States: Colonial Times to 1970* (White Plains, N.Y.: Kraus International, 1989), 1:9; *The World Almanac and Book of Facts 2003* (New York: World Almanac Books, 2003), 400.

3. U.S. Department of Commerce, *Historical Statistics of the United States*, 1:14.

4. Phyllis Schlafly, *The Power of the Positive Woman* (New Rochelle, N.Y.: Arlington House, 1977).

5. Mark Twain may have been the first American to use the phrase *new deal* in print to mean a revolutionary change in a society's culture. He did so in chapter 13 of his novel *A Connecticut Yankee in King Arthur's Court* published in 1889. This fantasy about a time-traveler who tries to impose his nineteenth-century American culture on sixth-century England through "peaceful revolution" climaxes in a mass slaughter of the knights of the old regime. In other words, "Sir Boss"—the title Twain's protagonist chooses for himself when he becomes King Arthur's chief adviser—starts off trying to create his new deal the way Edward Bellamy in his 1888 novel *Looking Backward* claimed it could be done, through peaceful change. But he ends up the way Jack London in his 1908 novel about the future, *The Iron Heel*, thought the new age would have to be ushered in, that is, through violence. The phrase *a new deal* is used in poker in reference to a player's hope of being dealt a winning hand, and the counter-culture movement promised every player except white males a winning hand all the time. It also promised an increasingly bigger pot of federal money to divvy up each time the cards are dealt.

6. Robert Rector and William F. Lauber, *America's Failed $5.4 Trillion War on Poverty* (Washington: Heritage Foundation, 1995), 1–2.

7. Rector and Lauber, *America's Failed War on Poverty*, 5, 11.

8. National Organization of Women, "Revolution: Tomorrow Is NOW," part 2, sec. M, 1.

9. *World Almanac and Book of Facts 2003*, 74.

10. Charles J. Sykes, *A Nation of Victims: The Decay of the American Character* (New York: St. Martin's, 1992), 118–19.

11. Shelby Steele, "Group Entitlements behind U.S. Social Evils," *Arizona Daily Star*, March 21, 1994, A9, originally published in the *New York Times*. Shelby Steele is the author of *The Content of Our Character: A New Vision of Race in America* (New York: St. Martin's, 1990).

12. Bernardine M. Haag, *SHAM: Social Change Through Contrived Crisis* (Sahuarita, Ariz.: Sahuarita Press, 1993), 195–96. The quotation within the passage is from an article in *Off Our Backs* by Beverly Leman, July 31, 1970, 7.

13. Schlafly, *Power of the Positive Woman*, 17.

14. *Daily Sentinel* (Nacogdoches, Texas), editorial, September 26, 1983. This editorial was based on U.S. Bureau of the Census and Office of Management and Budget statistics.

15. *The World Almanac and Book of Facts 2003* (New York: World Almanac Books, 2003), 15.

16. Marvin Olasky, *The Tragedy of American Compassion* (Washington: Regnery, 1992), 222, 227, 231.

17. Charles Murray, *Losing Ground: American Social Policy, 1950–1980* (New York: Basic Books, 1984), 211–18.

Chapter Five

1. Benjamin Franklin, *Franklin: Writings* (New York: Library of America), 367–74.

2. See Arthur F. McGovern, *Marxism: An American Christian Perspective* (Maryknoll, N.Y.: Orbis Books, 1989), 178–203; and Philip Berryman, *Liberation Theology: The Essential Facts About the Revolutionary Movement in Latin America and Beyond* (New York: Pantheon, 1987).

3. Julián Marías, *America in the Fifties and Sixties*, ed. Michael Aaron Rockland, trans. Blanch de Puy and Harold C. Raley (University Park: Pennsylvania State University Press, 1972), 440–42.

4. Marías, *America in the Fifties and Sixties*, 444.

5. Marías, *America in the Fifties and Sixties*, 440.

6. Henry David Thoreau, *Walden*, ed. Stephen Fender (New York: Oxford University Press, 1997), 67.

7. James Burnham, *The Suicide of the West: An Essay on the Meaning and Destiny of Liberalism* (New Rochelle, N.Y.: Arlington House, 1964), 100.

8. Fidel Castro has been in power at the time of this writing ten years longer than the previous record holder for a military dictatorship in Spanish America, General Alfredo Stroessnor, the fascist dictator of Paraguay from 1954 to 1989.

9. Thomas Omestad, "So, What's Castro Smoking?" *U.S. News & World Report*, April 29, 2002, 30.

10. Burnham, *Suicide of the West*, 99–124.

11. Burnham, *Suicide of the West*, 118–19.

12. Thoreau, *Walden*, 75–76.

Chapter Six

1. Jacques Soustelle, *Daily Life of the Aztecs on the Eve of the Spanish Conquest*, trans. Patrick O'Brian (Stanford, Calif.: Stanford University Press, 1962), 9.

2. K. L. Billington, "Afterword: A New Left Balance Sheet," in *Second Thoughts: Former Radicals Look Back at the Sixties*, ed. Peter Collier and David Horowitz (Lanham, Md.: Madison Books, 1989), 254.

3. Associated Press, *Arizona Daily Star*, February 25, 2003, A4.

4. Diane Ravitch, *The Language Police: How Pressure Groups Restrict What Students Learn* (New York: Knopf, 2003), app. 1, 171–83. Another recent book on this subject is by Tammy Bruce, *The New Thought Police: Inside the Left's Assault on Free Speech and Free*

Minds (Roseville, Calif.: Prima, 2001). See also Henry Beard and Christopher Cerf, *The Official Politically Correct Dictionary and Handbook* (New York: Villard Books, 1992).

5. Beard and Cerf, *Official Politically Correct Dictionary*, 67.

6. Ravitch, *The Language Police*, 201–2.

7. Ravitch, *The Language Police*, 176, 177, 180.

8. Tom Wolfe, *The Painted Word* (New York: Bantam, 1976), 14–15.

9. Lynne V. Cheney, *Telling the Truth: Why Our Culture and Our Country Have Stopped Making Sense, and What We Can Do about It* (New York: Simon & Schuster, 1995), 143–46.

10. Ericka Doss, *Twentieth-Century American Art* (Oxford: Oxford University Press, 2002), 119–21.

11. Quoted in Wolfe, *The Painted Word*, 63.

12. Cheney, *Telling the Truth*, 114–15, 149.

13. Jerry Rubin, *We Are Everywhere* (New York: Harper and Row, 1971), 38, 41, 254.

14. Robert H. Bork, *Coercing Virtue: The Worldwide Rule of Judges* (Washington, D.C.: AEI Press, 2003), 64–65.

15. Bork, *Coercing Virtue*, 68.

16. Bork, *Coercing Virtue*, 68.

17. *Index of International Public Opinion Survey, 1993–1994*, 441; and *Wilson Quarterly* (Winter 1996): 128.

18. Thomas Jefferson, "Second Inaugural Address," in *Thomas Jefferson* (New York: Library of America, 1984), 519–20.

19. Thomas Jefferson, "Second Inaugural Address," 510.

20. Quoted in George Weigel, *The Final Revolution: The Resistance Church and the Collapse of Communism* (New York: Oxford University Press, 1992), 61.

Chapter Seven

1. Neil Postman, *Amusing Ourselves to Death: Public Discourse in the Age of Show Business* (New York: Penguin, 1996), 150–51, 154.

2. Richard Bernstein, *Dictatorship of Virtue: How the Battle Over Multiculturalism Is Reshaping Our Schools, Our Country, Our Lives* (New York: Vintage Books, 1995).

3. Heather McDonald, "Writing Down Together," in *Dumbing Down: Essays on the Strip-Mining of American Culture*, ed. Katharine Washburn and John Thornton (New York: Norton, 1996), 80.

4. Tom Bethell, "Why Teachers Can't Be Trusted," *American Spectator*, March–April 2003, 19.

5. Daniel R. Levine, "Cheating in Schools: A National Scandal," *Reader's Digest*, October 1995, 66–67.

6. *Arizona Daily Star*, February 7, 2002, A4.

7. "A Nation Still At Risk," conference report, *Policy Review* (July–August 1998): 24. This conference was sponsored by the Heritage Foundation, Empower America, the Center for Education Reform, and the Thomas B. Fordham Foundation.

8. *Wall Street Journal*, February 4, 2003, B1, B4.

9. *New York Times*, July 6, 2004, D2.

10. *Princeton Alumni Weekly*, July 7, 2004, 64.

11. "Our Brown v. Board," *Wall Street Journal*, February 19, 2002, A26.

12. *Arizona Daily Star*, August 15, 1999, E5.

13. Christopher Jencks and Meredith Phillips, eds., *The Black-White Test Score Gap* (Washington, D.C.: Brookings Institution, 1998).

14. Laurence Steinberg, "Symposium," *Insight on the News*, October 7–14, 1996, 27, 29.

15. *New York Times*, March 20, 2003, A18.

16. *Tucson Citizen*, May 20, 2003, A5.

17. *Historical Statistics of the United States Colonial Times to 1970*, Series H 506, 1:373; and *The World Almanac and Book of Facts 2003* (New York: World Almanac Books, 2003), 235. A factor of .224 was used to deflate the national average in 2000 of $7,392 per student to 1970 dollars.

18. Bethell, "Why the Teachers Can't Be Trusted," 19.

19. Paul Copperman, *The Literacy Hoax: The Decline of Reading, Writing, and Learning in the Public Schools and What We Can Do About It* (New York: Morrow, 1978), 35, 43; tables 2 and 3.

20. *World Almanac 2003*, 238.

21. "A Nation Still at Risk," *Policy Review*, 23.

22. Anthony DeCurtis, "I'll Take My Stand: A Defense of Popular Culture," in Washburn and Thornton, *Dumbing Down: Essays on American Culture*, 161, 162–63.

23. Quoted by Heather MacDonald, "Writing Down Together," in Washburn and Thornton, *Dumbing Down: Essays on American Culture*, 91.

24. University of Arizona Department of English, graduate catalog, 1985.

25. *The Manufactured Crisis: Myths, Fraud, and the Attack on America's Public Schools* (Cambridge, Mass.: Perseus Books, 1995), 14–17.

26. Charles Murray and R. J. Herrnstein, "What's Really Behind the SAT-Score Decline?" *Public Interest* (Winter 1992): 32–56.

27. David C. Berliner, "Symposium," *Insight on the News*, October 7–14, 1996, 26.

28. Berliner, "Symposium," 29.

29. Etta Kralovec and John Buell, *The End of Homework: How Homework Disrupts Families, Overburdens Children, and Limits Learning* (Boston: Beacon, 2000), 52, 98–99, 97.

30. Steinberg, "Symposium," 27, 29.

31. *World Almanac 2003*, 235, 241.

32. U.S. Department of Education, *A Nation at Risk: The Imperative of Educational Reform* (Washington, D.C.: U.S. Department of Education, 1983), 5.

Chapter Eight

1. Alfred H. Kelly, Winfred A. Harbison, and Herman Belz, *The American Constitution: Its Origins and Development*, 6th ed. (New York: Norton, 1983), 739.

2. John Dewey, *Liberalism and Social Action* (Amherst, N.Y.: Prometheus Books, 2000), 16.

3. Dewey, *Liberalism and Social Action*, 34.

4. Dewey, *Liberalism and Social Action*, 54.

5. Dewey, *Liberalism and Social Action*, 56.

6. Dewey, *Liberalism and Social Action*, 39–40.

7. Dewey, *Liberalism and Social Action*, 57.

8. Richard Bernstein, *Dictatorship of Virtue: How the Battle Over Multiculturalism Is Reshaping Our Schools, Our Country, Our Lives* (New York: Vintage, 1995), 231.

9. John Harmon McElroy, ed., *The Sacrificial Years: A Chronicle of Walt Whitman's Experiences in the Civil War* (Boston: David R. Godine, 1999), 147, a reproduction of the U.S. Attorney General's Office payroll sheet.

10. Clarence B. Carson, *The Welfare State 1929–1985*, vol. 5, *A Basic History of the United States* (Wadley, Ala.: American Textbook Committee, 1986), 32.

11. Kelly, Harbison, and Belz, *The American Constitution: Its Origins*, 728–30.

12. Harold W. Dodds, *Out of This Nettle, Danger* (Princeton, N.J.: Princeton University Press, 1943), 34.

13. Dodds, *Out of This Nettle, Danger*, 39.

14. Neil R. McMillen, with Charles C. Bolton, *A Synopsis of American History*, 8th ed. (Chicago: Ivan R. Dee, 1997), 341–42.

15. Milton Friedman and Anna Jacobson Schwartz, *A Monetary History of the United States 1867–1960* (Princeton, N.J.: Princeton University Press, 1963).

16. David Kennedy, *Freedom from Fear: The American People in Depression and War, 1929–1945* (Oxford: Oxford University Press, 1999).

17. Martin L. Gross, *A Call for Revolution: How Government Is Strangling America—and How to Stop It* (New York: Ballantine, 1993), 265.

18. Peter G. Peterson, *Facing Up* (New York: Simon & Schuster, 1993), 30.

19. Calculations based on information in Martin L. Gross, *The Government Racket: Washington Waste from A to Z* (New York: Ballantine, 1992), 9.

20. See Gross, *The Government Racket*, 173; and Gross, *A Call for Revolution*, 33–34.

21. Gross, *The Government Racket*, 178–82.

22. *The World Almanac and Book of Facts 2003* (New York: World Almanac Books, 2003), 144.

Chapter Nine

1. F. A. Hayek, *The Counter-Revolution of Science* (Glencoe, Ill.: Free Press, 1952), 15–16.

2. Nora Barlow, ed., *The Autobiography of Charles Darwin* (New York: Norton, 1993), 236.

3. Edward J. Larson and Larry Witham, "Scientists and Religion," *Scientific American*, September 1999, 90.

4. John Stuart Mill, *The Collected Works of John Stuart Mill* (Toronto: University of Toronto Press, 1963), 7:625–26.

5. W. E. H. Lecky, *History of the Rise and Influence of the Spirit of Rationalism* (London: Longman, Green, Longman, Roberts, and Green, 1865).

6. Steven Pinker, *The Blank Slate: The Modern Denial of Human Nature* (New York: Viking, 2002).

7. Edward O. Wilson, *On Human Nature* (Cambridge, Mass.: Harvard University Press, 1978), 159–60.

8. Paul Johnson, *Intellectuals* (New York: Harper and Row, 1988), 52.

9. C. S. Lewis, *The Abolition of Man*, (New York: Macmillan, 1955), 53.

10. Arthur C. Clarke, *Profiles of the Future: An Inquiry into the Limits of the Possible*, (New York: Harper and Row, 1963), 213.

11. Clarke, *Profiles of the Future*, 220.

12. Lewis, *The Abolition of Man*, 72.

13. Charles Darwin, *The Origin of Species By Means of Natural Selection, or The Preservation of Favored Races in the Struggle for Life* (New York: Modern Library, 1998), 247.

14. David P. Barash, *Human Nature Review* 2 (2002): 283–92.

15. Michael Behe, *Darwin's Black Box: The Biochemical Challenge to Evolution* (New York: Simon & Schuster, 1996), 193; see also 39–45.

16. Charles Darwin, *The Descent of Man and Selection in Relation to Sex*, 2nd ed., 1874, facsimile with an introduction by H. James Birx (Amherst, N.Y.: Prometheus Books, 1998), 152.

17. Peter Singer, "Unsanctifying Human Life," in *Unsanctifying Human Life: Essays on Ethics*, ed. Helga Kuhse (Malden, Mass.: Blackwell, 2002), 216–17.

18. Peter Singer, ed., *In Defence of Animals* (New York: Basil Blackwell, 1985), 4–6, 210–11.

19. Peter Singer, *Writings on an Ethical Life* (New York: Ecco, 2001), xvii.

20. Peter Singer, "Darwin for the Left," in *Unsanctifying Human Life*, 358. This essay may also be found in Singer's *Writings on an Ethical Life*.

Chapter Ten

1. *Arizona Daily Star*, August 15, 1995, B1.

2. Mona Charen, *Useful Idiots: How Liberals Got It Wrong in the Cold War and Still Blame America First* (Washington, D.C.: Regnery, 2003), 245, 247, 250.

3. Anemona Hartocollis, "Campus Culture Wars Flare Anew over Tenor of Debate after Attacks," *New York Times*, September 30, 2001, A24.

4. Charen, *Useful Idiots*, 245–56, the quotations and descriptions in this paragraph condense material taken from these pages.

5. See Peter Collier and David Horowitz, *Destructive Generation: Second Thoughts About the Sixties* (New York: Summit Books, 1990), 16.

6. Charen, *Useful Idiots*, 256.

7. Onyria Herrera McElroy, in conversation with me one day when I was disheartened by my perception of the grip the counter-culture seems to have on some Americans.

8. Lee Strobel, *The Case for a Creator* (Grand Rapids, Mich.: Zondervan, 2004), 69–91.

9. See Andrzej Paczkowski, "The Storm over *The Black Book*," *Wilson Quarterly* (Spring 2001): 31.

10. George Orwell, "Looking Back on the Spanish War," *A Collection of Essays by George Orwell* (San Diego, Calif.: Harcourt Brace Jovanovich, 1953), 197–98.

11. See John Earl Haynes and Harvey Klehr, *In Denial: Historians, Communism, and Espionage* (New York: Encounter Books, 2003).

12. Abraham Lincoln, "Gettysburg Address," November 19, 1863.

13. *New York Times*, November 21, 2004, A18.

Index

About the Author

John Harmon McElroy, a professor emeritus, taught American literature at Clemson University, the University of Wisconsin–Madison, and the University of Arizona and has been a Fulbright Professor of American Studies at universities in Spain and Brazil. His two previous books on American culture are *Finding Freedom: America's Distinctive Cultural Formation* (1989) and *American Beliefs: What Keeps a Big Country and a Diverse People United* (1999). He is the editor of *The Sacrificial Years: A Chronicle of Walt Whitman's Experiences in the Civil War* and Washington Irving's *History of the Life and Voyages of Christopher Columbus*. He and his wife, Dr. Onyria Herrera McElroy, a writer of bilingual dictionaries, live in Tucson, Arizona.